UN BACIO AL CIORNO TOCLIE IL DENTISTA DI TORNO

A kiss a day keeps the dentist away

To my father, Stevan Larner,
who died as this book was being written
and who loved my mother in the
most profound way I have ever seen.

M.L.

Dear Cindy,
Enjoy your time in Italy — You
deserve it!! Happy 50th. Love Patti

12009

IN LOVE IN ITALY

A TRAVELER'S GUIDE

to the Most Romantic Destinations in the Country of Amore

MONICA LARNER

RIZZOLI
NEW YORK

First published in the United States of America in 2006 by
Rizzoli International Publications, Inc.
300 Park Avenue South, New York, NY 10010
www.rizzoliusa.com

© 2006 Monica Larner

2006 2007 2008 2009 / 10 9 8 7 6 5 4 3 2 1

Design by Susi Oberhelman

ISBN-13: 978-0-8478-2935-4
ISBN-10: 0-8478-2935-9

Library of Congress Control Number: 2006929627

Printed in China

CONTENTS

PREFACE

A re you in love with me or with my country?" asked my first love, an Italian, as our relationship was well into its final descent. With the clarity of thought and self-evaluation that comes after a breakup, I recognized that whatever line separates the personality from the nationality had in fact become hopelessly blurred at some point during our affair. He was an embodiment of Italy. Italy was a characterization of him. After all, I had been introduced to them contemporarily, grew with them simultaneously, and made a commitment to both at the same time. As it turned out: Only one kept my heart.

This book is my love letter to Italy. Although I stopped counting the years I have lived here (about 15 – or roughly half my life), I grew closer to my adopted home during this project than at any other time. Yet for many reasons this was a difficult book to write, and throughout it all I struggled with a frustrating inability to render the magic of a country that has shaped me so intimately. I suppose the same thing could be said about falling in love.

In Love in Italy is not a standard guidebook. You will not find historical chronologies, cataloguing of monuments, timetables, or price lists. Little emphasis is placed on travel logistics or transportation. I leave those details to the dozens of excellent country guides available today. Instead, this book is a literary companion meant to arouse your amorous appetite with love lore, historical anecdotes, and romantic places to see, eat, and sleep. It is designed for lovers, couples, honeymooners, spouses celebrating an anniversary, and all travelers who want to unleash their inner Eros for a day, a week, or a lifetime in Italy.

A few notes about the book. In Love in Italy starts in Sicily and moves up the peninsula in ten distinct chapters. The South-to-North structure is a nod to my affections for southern Italy and a tribute to Stromboli, the book's muse. The chapters represent the ten most romantic destinations according to my criteria, and in many cases personal preference. Not all of Italy is covered.

Photographs were shot on Kodak 100ASA slide film with a Nikon FE2 and two lenses (24mm and 105mm). A handful of pictures were taken with the Ricoh GR1 I always keep inside my purse.

I would like to stress that, with very few exceptions, I have personally visited the hotels and restaurants recommended within these pages. Great care was taken in selecting them, and only those with a romantic edge (whether it be a special honeymoon suite or an aphrodisiac dish) made the final cut. Opening times and prices were omitted or left intentionally vague because this is not an annually updated guide and because in many instances (as with wedding receptions) they are negotiable.

I have also included a chapter that outlines the bureaucratic procedures for getting married in Italy. Regulations may have changed since the book went to print, so please check them before committing money to your destination wedding. At the end is an encyclopedia of Italy's sexiest foods and select recipes.

Research and photography were complied over several years with the bulk completed during a truly exceptional road trip that started in Palermo and ended in Bolzano three months later. You might expect a young woman, traveling alone, on a quest for romantic places to raise many eyebrows in Italy. I certainly did. But love is a compelling cause, and my unusual pilgrimage sparked a generous outpouring – from the many strangers I met along the way—of enthusiasm, stories, and romantic recommendations that are the backbone of this book.

I know you will receive the same warm welcome in the country of *amore*. And I hope In Love in Italy will help set the mood for many kisses in your own voyage of the heart.

Buon *viaggio*, MONICA LARNER

For more information, please visit www.inloveinitaly.com. If you have questions, comments, corrections, or would like to share your own love-in-Italy story, please write me at monica@inloveinitaly.com.

LOVE
AND
LAVA

CULL'ACQUA STISSA TU NON T'HÀ LAVARI,
TA PURAMENTI MI NNI GILUSIU
QUANNU SSA BEDDA FACCI T'HÀ LAVARI
TI L'HÀ LAVARI CU LU SANGU MIU

not even with water should you wash your face
because I am jealous even of it
when you want to wash your beautiful face
you had better do so with my blood

excerpt from a letter written by a sulfur miner,
found in an archive in Palermo

There is something about Sicily, something raw, carnal, exciting, epic, unpredictable, tragic, a tad violent, and totally magnetic. That something is linked to its two temperamental volcanoes, Mount Etna and Stromboli, with whom the islanders submissively share their living space. If a place can have sex appeal, Sicily has it in spades.

This triangle of enchantment, excess, and contrasts sits on the crossroads of Europe and Africa. Because of its desirable geography, history has seen it both enriched and plundered by a barrage of foreign occupants: The Greeks, Carthaginians, Arabs, Normans, Swabians, the fanatically Catholic House of Aragon, the opulent French, and the Bourbons have all left their mark. The Middle Ages marked a golden age for the island. Under Arab occupation starting in the late eighth century, architecture, engineering, and science flourished at such a rapid pace that the rest of Italy seemed like backwater overrun with bloodthirsty thugs in comparison.

Despite the eternal presence of outsiders, the Siculi—the indigenous inhabitants after whom the island is named—maintained a unique personality and keen craftsmanship, borrowing only what they required from their foreign overlords. Sicilians are a stoic, intelligent, and intensely proud people often described as the "most Italian" of the Italians. "To have seen Italy without having seen Sicily is not to have seen Italy at all, for Sicily is the clue to everything," remarked the German poet Goethe. Sicilians, on the other hand, may tell you they are the least Italian of the Italians. Perennial delays in plans to build a suspension bridge over the Strait of Messina, connecting Sicily to the boot of Italy—ever poised to kick the island into oblivion—is another telling clue.

What truly sets Sicily apart from the rest of the country is its mixed spirituality. Pagan, Catholic, and Muslim rites are all celebrated, and at times are even combined in one festival. Every town puts on a lavish party for its patron saint, and inevitably he or she is the personification of a pagan god. Lovers still flock to the temple of Venus on St. Valentine's day in Erice, and fertility rites are practiced near the ancient temple of Demeter in Agrigento. In fact, this is an island obsessed with fertility. Numerous gifts of earth and sea on the island—from grapes to eggplant, from tuna to gelato to goat cheese—are celebrated with their own annual *sagra*, or feast, of abundance that invariably ends with dinner, dancing, and fireworks. In some rural communities, the celebrations are truly bizarre. In June, for example, in the small town of San Giovanni, not far

from the island's capital Palermo, young women build phallic statues called u *muzzuni*, which they decorate with gold string and flowers and place in their windowsills. The town's bachelors respond to the signal by inviting the women to sing love songs in the main square. In the town of Terrasini, at Easter bachelors attempt to win women's attention by competing in a contest of strength and will called La Festa dei Schietti: 150-pound (seventy-kilogram) orange trees are decorated with ribbons, and each man must hold the tree with one arm in front of a bachelorette's house for as long as he can endure.

Stories of passion have been part of the island's history from the beginning. According to legend, a king and queen had a beautiful daughter with almond eyes and mahogany skin named Sicilia. One day a man in a black cape came knocking at their door. He introduced himself as Destiny and said he was the bearer of bad news: They must sacrifice Sicilia on the day she turns fifteen to save their entire people from imminent death. After the distraught king and queen begged him to save their daughter, Destiny replied: "Her life will be spared and she will live a happy life with many children, but you will never see her again." On the day Sicilia turned fifteen, dressed in a white gown and crown of jasmine, she was placed in a small boat and floated out to sea, as Destiny had instructed. The courageous girl accepted her fate and lived with only the sea, sun, moon, and stars as her companions for many long days. Finally, one morning she awoke to find that her boat had landed on a brilliant white beach covered in flowers, and beyond lay a forest of trees with a dazzling array of colorful fruits. No sooner had she stepped from the boat than a handsome man appeared, and by the clothes he wore, Sicilia could tell he was a prince. "Who are you?" asked Sicilia, to which the prince responded: "My parents and my people have all been killed by a horrible plague. I am the only survivor. Destiny said I would soon be joined by a beautiful young woman." The two fell madly in love. Sicilia gave birth to many children, and the mysterious land was quickly repopulated.

As you travel through this fiery land, you will undoubtedly encounter countless more such romantic stories. This chapter highlights the very best of what the island has to offer for lovers, and at the top of that list is the Aeolian Archipelago.

STROMBOLI AND THE AEOLIAN ARCHIPELAGO

The Aeolian Archipelago is the birthplace of romantic Italy. Located some twenty miles (thirty kilometers) off the northeastern tip of Sicily facing Milazzo, these seven stunningly beautiful islands, sculpted by the forces of wind, water, and fire, provide the model for the rest of this heavenly country. On clear days a little white cloud hangs above each island like a halo; but up close, the landscape can be downright devilish, with black beaches, contorted lava formations, indigo water, hissing steam, and sometimes fierce winds.

The happy male of the Aeolian group is Stromboli, whose satisfaction is expressed with the burps and belches of smoke that rise from its active volcano. It is located ever so slightly beyond the other inhabited islands, almost in its own little world, but still close enough to visit the "six wives," as the other islands are known: Panarea, Lipari, Vulcano, Salina, Filicudi, and Alicudi.

According to Greek mythology Aeolus, god of wind, lived on Stromboli. In Homer's *Odyssey*, when the hero Odysseus stopped by the island following his tangle with the Cyclops, Aeolus gave him an oxhide bag to help him on his voyage back to Ithaca, and to his love, Penelope. Disobeying Aeolus's instructions, Odysseus's curious crew opened the bag and unleashed the winds hidden inside. The raging storm pushed Odysseus back to Stromboli.

Stromboli is a black, smoke-spewing cone that rises from the Mediterranean, with whitewashed homes clustered at its base. Its ancient name was Strongyle, for "round island." But you shouldn't think of Stromboli as an island: It is, in fact, the most active volcano on the planet, and underwater it is twenty-five times larger in mass. Its flaming cone, affectionately named Iddu, or "him" in the local dialect, explodes every ten minutes or so, as it has for 160,000 years, spewing molten rock and spitting lava. Minor tremors are a reminder of its presence and power.

You can ascend a poorly marked trail to the peak of the volcano with a guide. The hike, which takes about three hours up and two down, isn't for the faint of heart: At times you scale near-vertical slopes and balance on ridges left by lava. At the summit, some 3,000 feet (900 meters) above sea level, you are rewarded with spectacular views that extend to Sicily's Mount Etna, Stromboli's volcanic big brother. Peer into the craters for a display of nature's best fireworks, smell the sulfur, and listen to the hissing and hiccupping. Visitors have described chunks of smoldering volcanic debris landing at their feet or whizzing past their ears. Most people start the climb at about 5 p.m. in order to watch the sunset and Iddu's fountain of fire against a star-studded sky. But be very careful, and bring a flashlight; each year there are a few fatalities because of Stromboli's antics. Lovers searching for a dangerously erotic setting can arrange for an overnight stay in a tent by the crater's rim.

For those who don't wish to make the ascent, watching the climbers and their string of flashlights trickle down the side of the volcano at night like a string of Christmas lights is an unforgettable sight. A great vantage point for this is at the San Vicenzo Ferreri church. Walk past the other parish, the pink San Bartolo, to the Osservatorio di Punta Labronzo for a view of the volcano's red sparks with binoculars.

At daybreak on Stromboli, you can count on being roused from your sleep by cries of "pesce fresco" bellowed out by a fishmonger, Nino Basile, an island institution. (After so many years, it's a wonder he has any voice left.) Spend the day by hiring a boat from the port, Scari, to circle the majestic island. You'll pass the islet of Strombolicchio, which looks like a fortified village floating at sea, and the cube-shaped homes of Piscità that typify Aeolian architecture. The twisted rocks of Stromboli's shores speak of the enormous power of nature, frozen in their form. Stop at the Ficogrande beach, an expanse of black sand that will burn your bare feet like hot coals. On the opposite side of the island at the Sciara del Fuoco, you can admire an apocalyptic carbonized lava runway that extends from the crater to the sea below. Boat trips can also be made at night.

Stromboli's other town, Ginostra, is home to Italy's smallest port; just two fishing boats can squeeze in at a time. Its twenty full-time residents must rely on solar panels and cellular phones for power and telecommunications. Food, medicine, and even water are brought in by boat. Yet this seemingly idyllic village has been torn by the great Ginostra War: Half of the town's residents want to expand the port to accommodate more visitors, and the other ten vehemently oppose plans to modernize. The feud has grown to ghastly proportions, and neighborly love has been replaced with the satirical posters and accusatory graffiti.

Among the other inhabited islands, Panarea would be considered Stromboli's "high maintenance" spouse. Panarea is the smallest and, according to many, the prettiest of the seven inhabited islands. To the ancients, her name was Euonymos, or island "of good omen." Today it is the smartest and most sophisticated of the Aeolian Islands, thanks to the vacationing fashion-istas from Milan, who sport power tans and mirrored sunglasses. By 1988 electricity had been brought in for their nightclubs, and restaurants and a 24-karat social scene soon followed.

A single road links the island's three towns—San Pietro, Ditella, and Drauto. Near Ditella a path with hairpin turns leads to the Spiagga della Caldara, where steam fumaroles make patches of sand hot to the touch; in other places, the sea appears to boil as steam bubbles to the surface. On the south side, past Punto Milazzese, is the breathtaking Cala Junco, a natural pool enclosed by volcanic walls.

Smaller islets surround Panarea like ladies-in-waiting. The most interesting is Basiluzzo, with its lava columns and tubes. Thanks to strong currents, the water is exception-ally clear here, and it is not unusual to be able to see fifty feet (sixteen meters) below the surface. With luck, you can discern the outlines of an ancient settlement dating from 2600 BC that rests at the bottom on the sea floor.

As the name suggests, the island of Vulcano once was home to an active volcano, but its temper has subdued over the years. Whiffs of sulfur, steam fumaroles, mud geysers, and odd coloration—ranging from yellow to burnt amber—are a reminder of the molten unrest below.

In the Middle Ages travelers believed Vulcano was the gateway to hell; for couples on holiday today, it is paradise. Vulcano boasts some of the Aeolians' most spectacular beaches. Who can forget Piscina di Venere, "Venus's Pool," in the Cala della Grotta del Cavallo? It is best reached by boat, and you can swim in the pool's turquoise water, joined by dancing squid and rainbow-colored fish. The Scorcio della Baia di Ponente beach is made of the blackest of sands. White pumice pebbles that have washed ashore make the beach sparkle like a midnight

sky studded with stars. At the end of a small isthmus lies the crater of Vulcanello, the island's "cuter" volcano. Past the pine forest is the romantic Valley of Monsters, with unearthly rock formations designed by nature's surrealist muse. But the highlight of Vulcano is its thermal waters. The hot springs Acqua del Bagno and Acqua Bollente attract bathers who come to soak up curative minerals in what is, to put it plainly, an unattractive mud pond.

Lipari is the matriarch of the archipelago, home to administrative offices and the holy cathedral of San Bartolomeo, patron saint of the seven islands. You'll find more hotels, a greater variety of restaurants, and more frequent hydrofoil service here. This is also one of the few islands that allows cars. But don't let the hustle and bustle turn you away; this grand dame of the islands is worth exploring. One-fourth of Lipari's surface is pumice. The Capo Bianci beach is entirely made of this lightweight rock, and it lends the seawater lapping its shores the appearance of milk. When Aeolus wind blows hard, pumice is swept into the air like snow brushed off Alpine peaks, forming odd clouds that turn and twist with the air currents.

The last three of Stromboli's "wives" are Salina, Filicudi, and Alicudi. Because spring water rushes through Salina's veins instead of lava, it is the greenest of the Aeolian Islands, covered in ferns and vineyards. The widely planted Malvasia grape is pressed into a delicious sweet white nectar here. The other two islands are the most remote, which has made them hardest to tame. Rustic Filicudi, once surrounded by sponge and coral reefs, is especially popular among divers thanks to its complex marine ecosystem. Even more pastoral, Alicudi is popular with those craving true seclusion: You won't find scooters, bicycles, or even paved roads here.

There is boat service to the Aeolian Islands from Naples, or hydrofoil service from Milazzo (all year), Reggion di Calabria, Messina, Palermo, and Cefalù (summers only). Island hopping is easy, as high-speed boats offer connecting service to the islands several times a day.

❧ CASALE'S FAMOUS BIKINIS ❧

Of Sicily's archaeological sites, the Villa del Casale is the most extraordinary and should not be missed. Located three miles (five kilometers) beyond Piazza Armerina, near Enna, at the heart of Sicily, this ancient villa is fitted with the largest and best-preserved collection of Roman mosaics in the world: Its forty mosaics cover 37,000 square feet (3,500 square meters) of floor space to reveal faces, animals, and scenes from the end of the third century AD. They are rendered immaculately, with millions of tiny stone shards, or *tesserae*, that look like pixels on a low-resolution digital photograph.

Many questions about the villa's past remain unanswered. Although the ruins were uncovered in 1820, it took archaeologists a long time to understand the site's importance. In the 1950s serious excavations were launched, revealing the masterpieces on view today. The single-story building is centered around a peristyle, or inner courtyard, with a vestibule decorated with scenes of visiting guests. (How far a visitor was allowed into the house was a reflection of his or her social clout.) To the left, the Hall of the Circus shows chariot races at Rome's Circus Maximus. To the northwest are thermal baths—the defining architectonic indulgence of the Roman aristocrat—with images of sea monsters emerging menacingly from white foam.

Nearby, the Room of the Little Hunt serves as a preface to the Hall of the Great Hunt. Both depict dynamic scenes of wildlife being hunted and removed from Africa for transport to Rome's Colosseum for bloody face-offs with gladiators. These are among the world's most precious mosaics. Movement is frozen in the stone like a single frame of a film reel. Shortly after these mosaics were laid down, at least one of the beasts depicted here—the North African lion—became extinct due to the Romans' hunting zeal; no other illustration of the species exists.

The adjacent cubicle is Villa del Casale's most famous room and depicts ten women in red bikinis. Postcards and calendars of these bathing beauties are sold throughout Sicily as if they were *Sports Illustrated* swimsuit models. But what is most striking about these mosaics is how similar the bikinis are to today's fashions. The composition is divided into two halves: On the top is a woman with hand weights, another about to throw a discus, and two runners; on the bottom tier are two women playing with a ball, and one twirling an umbrella-like object, which some speculate symbolizes a chariot wheel. In the middle stands the most attractive figure, a woman with golden locks. With her right hand, she places a rose crown on her head, and in her left, she holds a palm leaf. She is the undisputed winner of a contest of athletic ability and beauty.

A corridor leads to the Elliptical Courtyard, where clichéd fertility symbols involving grape harvests, cupids, and fishing are depicted before the Banquet Hall, or *triclinium*. In the latter, a mythical storyboard includes Hercules, the cyclops, and Odysseus. Interestingly, these mosaics hold a story within a story. The cyclops, for example, is believed to be an actor playing the one-eyed monster, because he has three eyes: two human ones, and a third painted on his forehead.

In the adjacent Chamber of the Erotic Scene, theater masks are shown encased in hexagonal borders. The masks depict "ugly" and "pretty" girls. In the center, a spicy love scene shows a woman, her back bared, being embraced and kissed by a man holding a *situla*, or bucket. This room raises the question of what activities took place in the villa, yet many historians believe the masks and sexual innuendo are simply a reflection of the owner's eccentric tastes.

Villa del Casale offers a masterful example of the African mosaic tradition. North African provinces were at the artistic forefront during this era, and a specialty was polychrome mosaics, as seen in Carthage. The skilled tile layers, or *tessellarii*, came to Sicily from Africa bringing some of the *tesserae* with them to add colors not available locally. Many of the motifs are African in nature, especially the hunting scenes, and historians think parts of the mosaics were prefabricated abroad. What is almost certain is that the *tessellarii* had catalogues of motifs made to order for clients. Like today's proliferation of Ikea kitchens, the same designs, such as the popular "fishing cupids," have been discovered in Roman villas throughout the peninsula.

AGRIGENTO, ALMONDS, AND MOTHER EARTH

On the southern base of the triangle of Sicily lies the glorious city Agrigento, founded by the Greeks as Akragas in 581 BC, with its sun-bleached temples positioned proudly to greet visitors arriving by sea. Elsewhere in the ancient world, cities were carefully designed to shield their valuable assets from view at sea; with bloodthirsty fleets and pirates trawling the

COLD HEARTS

In Greek mythology, Demeter is the goddess of fertility and the patron of agriculture. Her daughter Persephone was so beautiful that the god of the underworld, Hades, decided he wanted her to himself. One day as Persephone was collecting flowers not far from Piazza Armerina, the earth opened up and swallowed her, condemning her to a life underground. Demeter searched high and low for her daughter, but unable to find her, she decided to halt fertility on the earth. Eventually it was learned that Hades held the young goddess, and the god Hermes was sent down to rescue her. Before Persephone could escape, however, Hades tricked her into eating a few seeds of a pomegranate (a symbol of marriage), and was thus forced to live with him three months a year (one month for each seed she ate). Demeter was so sad during the three months in which her daughter was absent each year that she temporarily stopped the earth's fertility—thus creating winter.

Mediterranean, port cities were considered vulnerable. Not Agrigento. In its glory years the city boldly put its wealth on display for everyone to admire. Of course, this was bound to cause problems. Ironically, it was the Carthaginians, whose peaceful trade with Agrigento made both partners rich and powerful, who triggered the city's demise. They besieged, looted, and burned the city and exiled its inhabitants. Agrigento enjoyed better times under the Romans, and later with the Arabs, but its ancient wounds never healed.

Nonetheless, neither the Carthaginians, Muslims, nor Christians have been able to weaken the feisty pagan spirit of this mystical spot. Ancient Akragas gave the world the poet and philosopher Empedocles, who was the first to name earth, fire, water, and air as the earth's four elements. He also elaborated the romantic concept that the forces that govern the world are attraction versus repulsion, love versus strife, and Eros (love) versus Thanatos (death).

This pagan spirit is tangible when you visit Agrigento's Valley of the Temples, one of the world's most important archaeological sites. Within the park, you can walk among the ruins of several temples, including the Temple of Concord (among the world's best-preserved Greek temples), the Temple of Olympian Zeus (the largest Greek temple in the world), and the Sanctuary of the Chthonic Deities, or gods of the underworld.

One last site within the Valley of the Temples was to the ancients as important to understanding Sicily as it was to understanding life on earth. According to mythology, this enchanting island shaped the personality we identify as Mother Earth—to them, she was

Demeter (known to the Romans as Ceres), goddess of fertility. Her cult is still celebrated, despite the fact that a Catholic church now stands on the remains of her temple. The church of San Biagio's northern altar has a hole called a *bothros*. Worshippers of Demeter would drop little phalluses shaped from dough inside, to guarantee fertility at home and in the fields.

The best time to come to Agrigento is at the end of winter, just as Demeter begins to smile again and ushers in spring. Thanks to special climatic conditions in Agrigento, almond trees bloom in February, and the countryside is completely transformed by the hundreds of almond trees hanging heavy with blossoms in brilliant white and shades of pink. From the first to the second Sunday of the month, Agrigento puts on the *sagra del mandorlo in fiore*, or the feast of almond blossoms, which until recently was known as *la festa di l'annata nova* (festival of the new year) because it marks the start of a new growing season. As part of the celebration, local men and women dressed in colorful costumes, some riding inside painted horse-drawn carts, sing and dance their way to the Temple of Concord. (For more about almonds, see chapter twelve.)

✤ TAORMINA ✤

Nature and humans conspired to create the perfect honeymoon destination in Taormina. Grafted to a rocky peak, the town is sandwiched between blue seas and sky and enjoys epic views that extend over a good chunk of Sicily.

In the third century BC the Greeks built a theater here, and framed perfectly between the columns that mark the stage looms Mount Etna. From this perspective, you are eye level with the volcano, and if you climb to the upper tier of the theater, you actually feel as if you are peering down at it. Sometimes Mount Etna is covered in a thin veil of snow that looks like powdered sugar, and sometimes it is wrapped romantically in the mist. Little bursts of steam and smoke constantly puff from the crater, and when Mount Etna erupts, you are treated to bursts of lava. It's hard to imagine how ancient audiences could keep their attention on the stage with such drama brewing in the background.

With its beautiful villas, outdoor cafés, and romantic beaches and coves, Taormina reached its zenith as a holiday spot in the twentieth century, thanks to a long succession of romantic pilgrims and eccentrics who vacationed here.

From 1920 to 1923 the writer D. H. Lawrence had a villa in Taormina on via Fontana Vecchia, where he penned what was at the time considered to be the most erotic novel published in English, *Lady Chatterley's Lover*. Completed in 1928 and first released in Florence to avoid censorship, it tells the story of Constance Chatterley, a British aristocratic woman with a wheelchair-bound husband, and her love affair with the Sicilian groundskeeper of their

country estate. Lawrence based his explicit romantic novel on a true story. Apparently, the real model for Lady Chatterley—who was unmarried—became somewhat of a local celebrity following a naked frolic through an olive grove in the August rain with a local farmer. To this day, too many men in Taormina claim to be the grandson or relative of Lady Chatterley's lover.

The roots of Taormina's modern tourist trade can be traced back to the Prussian painter Otto Geleng, who arrived here in 1863 and fell in love with Sicily, and a Sicilian girl. When he exhibited his paintings of Taormina in Paris, the critics scoffed at what they perceived to be an overactive imagination. How could someone paint a snow-capped volcano with fruit trees and flowers blooming in the foreground? Geleng challenged them to visit Taormina and see for themselves: If it was not like he depicted it, he would pay for their trip. But of course that didn't happen.

In the late 1890s the photographer Baron Wilhelm Von Gloeden, who specialized in photos of nude young men, opened a studio in Taormina, which was visited by the writers Oscar Wilde and Thomas Mann, among others. The town emerged as a popular resort for gay men, ladies looking for amorous adventures outside of their marriages, and anyone else determined to escape the confines of puritan values.

Among the most eccentric figures was Englishwoman Florence T. Trevelyan, who descended on Taormina in 1882 with a caravan of movers lugging all of her possessions, furniture, suitcases—and thirty dogs—to her new home. According to rumor, she had been forced into exile because of an alleged affair with Prince Edward. Exiled or not, she was determined to be noticed. She demanded to be carried around Taormina in a hoisted chair followed by bagpipers and a procession of admirers. Over the course of her time in Sicily, she made important botanical contributions, introducing the concept of English landscaping as seen at the public gardens.

During World War II Taormina was damaged by Allied bombing because it had become a German command center. However, it wasn't long before the celebrities wandered back to this irresistible spot. The authors William Faulkner, Tennessee Williams, and Truman Capote, who stayed in Lawrence's old villa, all visited. In 1955 Taormina hosted its first annual international film festival, and it has since become a world-class star magnet. From Cary Grant to Woody Allen, countless pairs of famous feet have paraded down Taormina's main drag, Corso Umberto I; Richard Burton and Elizabeth Taylor escaped to Taormina for some privacy when they fell in love during the filming of *Cleopatra* at Rome's Cinecittà Studios. Favorite hangouts are the Wunderbar on Piazza IX Aprile, where you can watch the residents stroll by, and the panoramic terrace of Hotel Timeo.

Directly below Taormina are a succession of coves and beaches with azure water and rocks for sunbathing. The coolest beach, as well as the most photographed, is the one in front of Isola Bella. "Beautiful Island" is not really an island but an isthmus connected by a thin, sandy bank. You can walk across and steal a look at the charming house built on the rock (which is only rarely open to the public).

BUONO COME IL PANE

Sicilian cuisine is generally spicier and sweeter than that found in the rest of Italy. The vineyards and citrus, almond, and olive groves that flourish in the unrelenting sunshine and fertile volcanic soil, along with the natural salt fields and a sea brimming with red tuna, swordfish, lobster, and red mullet, have inspired chefs since antiquity. The very word *gastronomy* is derived from one of the first treatises ever written about food. The epicurean Archestratus, a Greek poet born in Sicily in the fourth century BC, wrote *Gastronomia*, a cookbook in 330 verses describing the "best edibles and best drinkables" of the time.

Throughout the centuries the basis of Sicilian cooking has been simplicity. In fact, for Sicilians the highest compliment is to say *buono come il pane*, or "as good as bread."

The Greeks introduced whole grain and refined flour to the region, along with a dish called *makaria*, an ancestor of macaroni. They also were among the first to plant vines, and ancient recipes suggest they scraped snow off Mount Etna and mixed it with fruit and honey in a precursor to *granita*, a specialty of Catania flavored today with coffee, lemon, almond milk, or peach. However, the most significant culinary contributions came during the three centuries of Arab occupation. They established exotic citrus trees and, most important, the sugar cane that fed Sicily's famously insatiable sweet tooth. Eastern culinary preferences leaned toward eggplant, mint, olives, pine nuts, capers, fennel, and dates.

Among modern dishes, expect to find fresh vegetables baked with cheese or meat, or stewed and served cold as *caponata*. This eggplant-based stew with capers and vinegar typifies the pairing of sweet and sour tastes, or *agrodolce*. Eggplant is also fried and served with salted ricotta cheese, tomato, and basil in *pasta alla Norma*. New World vegetables such as tomatoes, squash, beans, and peppers (stewed as *peperonata*) came later with the Spaniards. Saracen pirates are said to have left behind semolina grain; unlike North African couscous, however, the versions found around Trapani are made with fish.

Sicilian seafood can't be beat. The dish that most represents the island is *pasta con le sarde*. According to legend, a chef charged with feeding the conquering Arab army found himself desperately shy of raw materials. He sent troops to forage for food in the surrounding countryside, and they retuned with a motley assortment of edibles: sardines, wild fennel, olive oil, dried currants, pine nuts, and saffron. The chef threw it all together, and a classic was born.

Islanders are also particularly attached to their fast food. Snack bars offer *arancine*, deep-fried rice balls filled with meat and tomato; *panelle*, fried chickpea pancakes; *sfincione*, a pizza topped with sautéed onions and anchovies; and *panini con la milza*, beef lungs cut thin and cooked in fat.

Sicily definitely takes top prize in the dessert category as well. *Cassata* is made with sweetened ricotta, almond paste, sponge cake, and candied fruit. Pastry-shop windows throughout the island are decorated with miniature oranges, bananas, figs, and cactus pears carefully shaped from almond paste, known as *frutta di Martorana*. First invented by La Martorana nuns in Palermo, legend says these little works of art were once hung from trees to fool a visiting archbishop into believing fruit grew in winter in Sicily.

The island's trademark treat is *cannoli*, or pastry tubes filled with ricotta cheese, chocolate bits, and candied fruit. At one time the city of Caltanissetta—from the Arab *Kalat an-nisa*, or "ladies' castle"—was where the sultans kept their harems. A collective of bored wives decided to turn their energies to making *cannoli* to pass the time while waiting for a late-night knock at the door.

CUPID'S CORNERS

RESTAURANTS

La Scuderia
Viale del Fante, 9
90100 Palermo
Tel: (+39) 91 520 323
www.lascuderia.it

Set at the foot of the majestic Monte Pellegrino, La Scuderia is a bastion of traditional Sicilian cuisine, using gourmet ingredients to add sparkle to homey local dishes from fresh pastas to roasted lamb and pork. The outdoor dining area is beautiful, draped in canvas sheets to shade tables from the sun, and the wine cellar is one of the best in Palermo, so order a chilled Pinot Grigio and enjoy a meal on one of the city's most romantic terraces.

Monte San Giuliano
Vicolo San Rocco, 7
91016 Erice
Tel: (+39) 09 23 869 595

There is no better way to end a day in the medieval hilltop village of Erice than by stumbling upon this romantic restaurant hidden at the heart of its labyrinth of cobbled streets. Discovering Monte San Giuliano by accident is such a pleasure that I almost kept the details to myself—but this wonderful trattoria is too good to be missed, with a beautiful, intimate garden and some of the best seafood in Sicily.

Granduca
Corso Umberto 172
98039 Taormina
Tel: (+39) 09 422 4983
www.granduca-taormina.com

The grandest restaurant in Taormina has a terrace that affords diners breathtaking views of the nearby Necropolis and the surrounding Mediterranean. The menu is full and varied, with a range of excellent prix-fixe options that are especially suited to large groups, and the tented garden can be reserved for intimate receptions and parties. Granduca is

situated within the beautifully restored medieval walls of a fifteenth-century villa, high enough above the bustle of the town that the sound of the sea crashing against the rocky shore below is your only accompaniment to a long, slow dinner.

Spizzulio
Via Panoramica del Templi, 23
92100 Agrigento
Tel: (+39) 0922 20712
www.spizzulio.it

Spizzulio is the perfect lovers' den, a cozy food and wine bar in the heart of Agrigento's historic center, with warm wooden benches, red-brick walls, and a spectacular wall of wine bottles flickering in the candlelight.

HOTELS

Collovere Park Hotel
Via Panoramica dei Templi
92100 Agrigento
Tel: (+39) 0922 29555

Colloverde Park Hotel is not only one of the most pleasant hotels in the Agrigento area but also the truest to local feeling and tradition. Inside, warm, comfortable, and homey rooms are characterized by exposed wooden beams and tiled bathrooms, while the hotel's amazing verdant garden is a lovers' paradise, with a maze, a terrace, and entire glades shaded from the afternoon sun by soft white canvas shades. It's no surprise that the Colloverde Park Hotel is one of the most popular sites for local weddings.

Hotel Baglio Santa Croce
Via del Cipresso, 1
(2km east of Erice on N187)
Tel: (+39) 0923 891 111

This small, idyllic farmhouse hotel strikes the perfect balance between open and intimate, rustic and modern. Simple interiors retain details of their original, seventeenth-century architecture, while a pretty terraced garden affords panoramic vistas of the sea nearby.

Hotel Elimo

Via Vittorio Emanuele 75
91016 Erice
Tel: (+39) 0923 86937

For centuries this aristocratic building in the heart of historic Erice was maintained as a private palazzo, and its recent renovation into a hotel retained a sense of its calm, privacy, and intimacy. Exposed beams, terracotta tiles, and high arched ceilings bring austerity to the rooms, and the hotel is perfectly located to explore the busy cobbled streets and artisanal shops of the town.

Massimo Plaza Hotel

Via Maqueda 43t
90133 Palermo
Tel: (+39) 913 25657
www.massimoplazahotel.com

Among the best—and the most expensive—hotels in Palermo, the Massimo Plaza somehow manages to provide its guests with an oasis of absolute peace and quiet, despite being at the very heart of the city's historic district. The perfect place for active, energetic honeymooners who will be happy to have such a pleasant base so close to the center of town.

Hotel Monte Tauro

Via Madonna delle Grazie, 3
98039 Taormina
Tel: (+39) 0942 24402
www.hotelmontetauro.it

Built subtly into the hillside, with spectacular views of Mount Etna, the Mediterranean, and the rolling Sicilian countryside, the Hotel Monte Tauro is something of a romantic anomaly beside the quiet town of Taormina. With a stark, bold exterior and clean, white interiors, the hotel brings a distinctly modern flavor to an area steeped in classical lore. Each room has a thoughtfully designed terrace, with fabulous views and privacy enough to feel like you're alone on the hillside, and the hotel is within walking distance of some of the region's spectacular Greek ruins.

PUGLIA'S MAGIC SPELL

CA POI LA TERRA PO ESSERE RICCA

SE ETI RICCU CINC' A NATU

E NO RICCU PI LI SOLDI A NPAUTA

MA RICCU A NPIETTU E A NCAPU DE

AMORE

just like the soil is rich
you too are born rich
not because of money in your pocket
but rich in the heart and in the mind
with love

From a Puglian poem

O n the night before her wedding, my Puglian friend Francesca tried to explain her land to me: "*La Puglia è un posto magico*"—Puglia is a magic place—she said. Everything I have seen and experienced since in the "heel" of the boot of Italy has confirmed the hyperbole.

This thin peninsula, flanked by the Adriatic Sea to the east and the Ionian Sea to the west, is a deeply superstitious land where residents believe the supernatural is always around the corner. Millions of knotted olive trees, some planted hundreds of years ago, stand in line like soldiers on the rust-colored soil, and their gnarled bark has been home to miraculous images. People travel miles, for example, to see an image of the Madonna in an overzealously pruned olive tree near Ostuni. And if you sleep in a *trullo*—a traditional stone dwelling with a conical roof found only in Puglia—you are said to be exposing yourself to a generous serving of paranormal energy. Navigating the myriad superstitions can be daunting. Not meeting the gaze of your dinner companion when you raise your wine glass is like identifying yourself as the antichrist. The only thing worse is passing the salt at dinner from hand to hand, without letting it rest on the table first: that means you are sending along bad luck. Naturally, the region's gastronomy also is rich in bewitching properties.

Located at the heart of the Mediterranean, most everyone has left their tracks on Puglia, including the Greeks, Romans, Byzantines, Arabs, Normans, and Spanish. During the crusades the region became a revolving door for strange people and ideas thanks to pilgrims on their way to and from the Holy Land. In some ways, it has been in a time warp ever since.

Today Puglia is among Italy's least explored regions. For those who make time for it, Puglia often becomes their favorite part of Italy. Its mystic pedigree makes it the perfect destination for lovers, and you may have a hard time resisting its spell. This is true in my case. It's easy to fall in love with Tuscany, Rome, or the Lakes region, but Puglia will haunt you, and you'll want to come back for more. I think I've figured out my personal fascination with this peninsula: Puglia is a frontier land. It is only a few steps away from being opened to mass tourism (the number of new hotels and restaurants is growing exponentially), and like the lull before a storm, the excitement is palpable. Even the old men loitering on benches outside the local cafés seem to sense that something big is about to happen to the region. I recommend you go while it's still relatively undiscovered.

SPIDER DANCING

Of Puglia's magic and mystic undercurrents, none is more fascinating than tarantism. The *tarantolati* are people who have been bitten by a tarantula and dance in a trancelike state until the venom has been cleansed from their bodies. In their frenzied state, it is said the dancers defy gravity to walk up walls, lose control of their bodies, and pull their hair out. A cult that shares common elements with other primitive religions in Morocco, Basil, and Cuba, it was once practiced by peasants in Italy across Molise, Puglia, Calabria, Campania, and Sicily. Today only pockets of it exist, although the rhythmic dance music associated with tarantism, the *tarantella*, is known the world over.

In the lore of tarantism, once bitten (the bite is called the *pizzica*, or "pinch") the victim enters a possessed state and must engage in a therapeutic dance until he or she collapses in exhaustion. Dances can last one night or several days. The victims (the *pizzicati*) dance with a colored ribbon or cloth that corresponds to their "inner tarantula." Four musical instruments are essential—a violin, flute, guitar, and tambourine—and musicians use a thumping beat to whip the dazed *tarantolati* into a frenzy of hysteria that borders on rapture. Bodies writhe, sway, bob, wiggle, undulate, palpitate, tremble, and quiver before falling to the ground.

There are dozens of *tarantella* dances, and the most beautiful ones come from Puglia's Salentine Peninsula. Some versions of the *tarantella* are intended as an erotic ritual dance between a man and the woman he is courting. In a poetic touch, their two bodies must never touch, no matter how loud and fast the music is played. Acrobatic gestures and fake embraces are choreographed to bring the two bodies just shy of contact—yet close enough to feel the heat.

Although the practice of tarantism has mostly died out, a new movement called neo-tarantism is quickly gaining popularity. Its supporters are Internet-savvy youth, many of whom embrace the antiglobalization cause. Music festivals are staged in the Salentine and the Gargano peninsulas throughout the summer, drawing people from all over. Recently, singer Eugenio Bennato released a fabulous CD titled *Taranta Power*, which ranks among Italy's best modern folk music. I am addicted—better yet, "pizzicata"—to the exotic sound. As for my own experience seeing the *tarantolati*: It was a bit like attending Puglia's Woodstock, and no, I never did see people walk on walls or rip their hair out. But it was a great dance party and food fest that lasted until the wee hours of the morning.

❧ The Gargano Peninsula ❧

This peninsula is the "spur" of the boot of Italy—a little knob of rocky land that juts into the sea at the northern part of Puglia. Without a doubt, the Gargano Peninsula is home to the most beautiful beaches on Italy's Adriatic side.

From Venice spanning to the tip of Puglia and continuing along the "arch" of the boot, wide sandy beaches characterize most of Italy's Adriatic flank. The Gargano, with limestone cliffs, tight bays and inlets, and a honeycomb of marine caves, is a surprising exception, and for good reason. Millions of years ago, when the contours of Europe were beginning to take shape, two geological plates parted to form the Adriatic Sea. A little chunk of what is today Croatia broke off and meandered over to Italy, where it attached itself, and thanks to this geological orphan from the Balkans, Italy gained more miles of stunning coastline.

This bit of chalk, rock, and oak and pine forests could not have selected a more curious mooring spot. The province of Foggia is Italy's wheat capital, and it is famous for its golden plains that supply the nation's pasta industry. Against the flat farmland stands the Promontorio del Gargano, rising an imposing 3,000 feet (900 meters) above the Tavoliere plains (whose name is derived from "flat as a table"). The scenic segue between plains and mountains is startling, to say the least. On the Gargano peninsula, the vegetation is different, the strange light seems crisper, and the sea appears bluer.

Approaching the Gargano Peninsula from the north, you will pass the lakes of Lesina and Varano before arriving at the fishing hamlet of Péschici, picturesquely perched over the sea. Romantics will not want to miss the sunset here. Because of the town's position on the peninsula, it is one of few places on Italy's Adriatic side where you can watch the sun dip into the sea. Pink and orange rays paint the whitewashed town during the final minutes of daylight and make for an unforgettable moment.

Past Péschici the coast becomes more gnarled and contorted by cliffs and sandy inlets. You'll see stone arches at sea and wind-shaped formations. Defensive towers dot the rocky ledges every few miles—a reminder of how vulnerable this little peninsula was when Saracen pirates would stage surprise attacks. Some twenty-five miles (forty kilometers) away lie the Tremiti Islands, which are easily reached by boat from the towns of Rodi or Péschici. Three islands make up the archipelago: San Domino is the largest, San Nicola is smaller, and Capraia (also called Caprara) has virtually nothing on it. San Domino's most famous inhabitant was Julia, the granddaughter of Augustus, who died on the island after twenty years in exile. She was being punished for adultery, in the same way her mother (also Julia) had been outcast. Once, when Augustus was asked to forgive his daughter, he became enraged and

NICKING THE BONES OF SAINT NICK

Bari is the capital of Puglia and until recently was branded by the activities of criminals and smugglers. Today, some of it has been cleaned up and "reborn" thanks to an ambitious public works campaign. Even Bari Vecchia, the old quarters with its labyrinthine streets reminiscent of a North African bazaar, are generally safe to explore. In quintessential southern style, in Bari many households are on the first floor, making pedestrian zones analogous to living rooms. At the heart of the old town is the Basilica di San Nicola, which houses the bones of the person we identify as Santa Claus. But Saint Nicholas was apparently not a potbellied, bearded man with rosy cheeks in a red suit. He was a dark-skinned Turk.

Born in Patara in 265 AD to a rich family, Nicholas was a priest by age seventeen, and was soon appointed bishop of Myre in southwestern Turkey. Legend has it that Nicholas met an impoverished aristocrat who was planning to sell his three daughters into prostitution. He crawled up to their house at night and threw three bags of gold through the windows. His gifts provided the father with dowries, and the three girls were married off within a week. And eventually Nicholas became the patron saint of unmarried women.

Toward the end of the eleventh century, with their town sliding into depression, authorities in Bari decided they needed a marketing gimmick to restore their fortunes. In 1087, a troop of sailors embarked on a voyage to Turkey and stole the saint's bones from its shrine, leaving the sarcophagus behind because it was too heavy. Pleased with the undertaking, Pope Urban II ordered the construction of the Basilica di San Nicola in Bari. For years, Turkish authorities have been demanding that the bones be returned. The Baresi scoff at the request, and each May 8 celebrate a festival in which their clever tomb robbery is reenacted.

---

roared, "May the gods curse you if you bring this up again with a daughter as lecherous as mine and with wives as adulterous!" Today the Tremiti are famous for having Italy's most fluctuating population. In winter months a mere fifty people call the islands home. That figure skyrockets to 100,000 inhabitants in the summer.

The town of Vieste sits at the easternmost extreme of the peninsula, and this is where most vacationers choose to make their base for exploring the region. Vieste basks in the brilliant white splendor of a wide sand beach to the south, dominated by the landmark Pizzomunno rock, named for a tragic love story. Pizzomunno was a young fisherman who fell in love with Cristalda, the most beautiful girl in Vieste. Each morning Pizzomunno went fishing, and each evening he returned happily to the arms of his love. But the fisherman's handsome looks caught the attention of the mermaids, who sang sweet songs to keep him company while he fished alone at sea. The sirens promised Pizzomunno immortality if he pledged his love to them, but his heart belonged to Cristalda. One evening the couple went to the beach to watch the night fall over the sea. The mermaids, enraged with jealousy, grabbed Cristalda and pulled her into the depths of the Adriatic. Pizzomunno could not save her. The next morning a huge slab of limestone stood on the beach, and townsfolk concluded that Pizzomunno had been petrified by his pain. The legend also tells that every hundred years Cristalda emerges from the sea for one night of love with Pizzomunno.

THE PUZZLE OF CASTEL DEL MONTE

For lovers who enjoy a little mystery, Puglia's magical Castel del Monte is not to be missed. A dramatic drive leads to the 1,500-feet (540-meter) mount on which the castle stands some twelve miles (twenty kilometers) from Andria, north of Bari. The enigmatic octagonal building, known to many as the powerful symbol depicted on the flip side of Italy's one-cent coins, is a monument to the unexplained.

Although the thirteenth-century castle, built by Holy Roman Emperor Frederick II, was assigned to Europe's smallest coin denomination, its symbolic value is much greater. Not only is Castel del Monte the only monument south of Rome depicted on Italian-minted euros, it is also a symbol of a unified Europe. In 1996 UNESCO put the Castel del Monte on its World Heritage list, noting that the monument "possesses an exceptional universal value because of its perfect shape, the harmony and the blending of cultural elements coming from the North of Europe, the Islamic world and classic antiquity."

Very little is known about Castel del Monte, its positioning, the logic behind its layout, or even its function. The more historians search for clues, the more the answers appear to be rooted in mystery, astrology, and complex mathematics. Constructed over ten years and completed in 1250, the year of Frederick II's death, its design uses an octagonal floor plan flanked by eight towers and eight rooms on the castle's two floors. In the center is an eight-sided courtyard once fitted with an octagonal fountain. The eight towers contain spiral staircases and bathrooms showcasing advanced plumbing for the time. In an unsettling touch, nearly all the sixteen trapezoid-shaped rooms have interconnecting doors, leaving no privacy for guests.

The castle does not seem to have been a residence, nor does it appear to have served a military function. Its single entrance led some to think it might have been a prison, but its

original interior, now lost, of green marble and mosaics was far too elaborate to be enjoyed by outlaws or heretics. The most likely explanation for the castle's purpose has to do with the emperor's favorite leisure pursuit: falconry.

Yet Castel del Monte's complex design and perfect proportions indicate it was more than a simple hunting lodge. Frederick II pursued interests not common for a king, such as astronomy, astrology, and physics. Born in Sicily in 1194, he spent his childhood in Palermo, the capital of the Norman kingdom but still strongly under the influence of Islamic culture at the time. In 1215 he was crowned king of the Romans, and in 1228 he left the port of Brindisi on the sixth crusade to the Orient, where he expanded his knowledge of science. Later he founded the University of Naples and was a friend to the great mathematician Leonardo Fibonacci, who introduced the Arabic representations for zero and ten into Western calculations. The obsessive repetition of the number eight in Castel del Monte has led some historians to believe it conceals a magical meaning. The figure "8" has been a symbol of infinity, and therefore represents the universe. It is also the Christian symbol of resurrection; the Bishop of Milan, Ambrogio, introduced the octagonal shape for baptisteries in order to underline the number's importance. Written reports also suggest Frederick II was enamored of eight-sided buildings after seeing the Mosque of Omar in Jerusalem. Others have pointed out that the emperor's first name, as spelled in the language of the day, has eight letters and is the sum of the numbers in the year of his death, 1250.

A visit to Castel del Monte will astound you. Everything about it, from its dramatic location to the mysteries of its inhabitants and the astrological and pagan symbolism in its construction, make it one of the spookiest spots in Europe. Don't go alone: Go with someone you can cling to.

❧ The Land of Trulli ❧

The romance of Puglia's countryside and its unique architecture is best experienced south of Bari. However, start your trip just north of the city, with a stop at the Romanesque cathedral of Trani, which stands majestically before the open sea.

Traveling along the coastal road, you pass Cozze, appropriately named "mussels" after the quantities of aphrodisiac mollusks consumed here, and Polignano, which claims to have more gelateria per square mile than any other place in Italy and boasts a truly unforgettable restaurant built inside a marine cave. In Monopoli, named after the Greek for "main city," the addition of Albanian, Arab, and Greek words to the local dialect create what is in effect a foreign language.

A few miles inland from the coast by Fasano, the earth rises and opens onto a wide plateau, where the earth is carpeted in wildflowers, the light is warmer, and the temperatures are cooler. This fairy-tale setting is the Itria Valley, home to Puglia's emblematic cone-shaped trullo homes. No one knows much about the origin of their name or their construction, although it appears locals borrowed building blueprints from some distant Middle Eastern land. Trulli are made by assembling cut stone and fitting the pieces tightly together. A "key," shaped like a globe and symbolizing the earth, holds the wedges together. Mimicking American Indian teepees, they are engineered to keep inhabitants cool in the summer. But astrological and religious symbols painted on the conical roofs suggest the farmers who built them centuries ago were just as concerned with warding off the evil eye.

Because everything about the trulli is shrouded in mystery, locals have simply given up on explanations and claim instead that they are magic dwellings. It's not hard to become a believer: Enter a trullo and you can almost feel the presence of unknown forces. Couples who sleep in a bed placed directly under the trullo cone are said to enjoy more tender and meaningful nights together. The symbols painted outside on some are completely open to interpretation, but the occasional heart might imply cupid is a frequent visitor.

As trulli owners grew richer, they added more cones to the existing ones, and it is common to see as many as six trulli clustered together, each cone a separate room. Italians and foreigners alike are now scrambling to buy real estate in trullo country. The trulli capital par excellence is Alberobello, where 2,000 cones form a little trulli metropolis. There you can visit the most complicated trullo (now a museum), which has two stories.

Around Alberobello, the Itria Valley offers many other surprises for traveling lovers. The nearby towns of Ostuni, Martina Franca, and Locorotondo look like they belong in Greece. Whitewashed Ostuni flaunts a sixteenth-century cathedral and a maze of cobblestone streets. Martina Franca puts on a special musical festival in August, with Dixieland bands playing from overhead balconies, brass bands crammed onto street corners, and samba dancers filling the squares. From Locorotondo you can enjoy views of the whole valley. All of these towns are popular holiday destinations among young intellectuals, artists, and filmmakers, and consequently there is always an exciting buzz in the air during the late-afternoon *aperitivo* hour. At the same time, you'll love the quiet of siesta hour.

❦ THE SALENTINE PENINSULA ❦

The southern tip of Puglia is known as the Salento, or the Salentine Peninsula, and starts in the provinces of Brindisi and Lecce. The land is flat and diligently dissected by an elaborate network of dry walls built by farmers to delineate their properties. Within the confines of these hand-assembled stone walls are prickly pears, olive groves, and vineyards firmly rooted in iron-rich topsoil. The peninsula is known as the "land of two seas," as either the Adriatic or Ionian sea is never much more than twelve miles (twenty kilometers) away. The best way to approach the peninsula is to drive around it, from Brindisi to Lecce to Otranto, around the cape at Santa Maria di Leuca, and north along the Ionian side to Gallipoli. (The stretch from Gallipoli to Taranto, however, is barren and sad.)

Make an effort to schedule your visit here when the moon is full. The thin air and flat lands of the Salento create a spectacular effect that is not repeated anywhere else. The moon rises with such speed, you can actually watch it float upward like a helium-filled balloon, and it is so big it's tempting to try to reach out and touch it. Turn around and see the sun, a fiery ball of red light, dropping down to the earth with matched speed. The moon's ascent and the sun's descent move in counterbalance, and in the Salento you are positioned to admire them both at the same time.

When the crusaders took to the sea to embark on their grueling pilgrimage to the Holy Land, they would glance back at Italy and vow to return to the port city of Brindisi. This promise soon turned into the verb brindare, and today when Italians raise their glasses in a toast, they say "brindisi." First known as Brundusium, the ancient Romans brought wealth to this natural harbor of Brindisi by making it the last stop in Italy on the via Appia trade route between Rome and Greece. A column near the harbor marks the end of the road and the "gateway to the Orient." The town's gatekeeping tradition continues, with the army of backpacking Eurorailers that descends on Brindisi each summer to catch the ferry to Athens and the Greek islands.

Further south and slightly inland lies the city of Lecce, one of the most beautiful, and fittingly romantic, places in southern Italy. Lecce is to the Baroque what Florence is to the Renaissance. Heavily influenced by Spanish rule and injected with newfound wealth during the seventeenth century, the city blossomed in Salentine Baroque splendor that was evenly and abundantly applied to the cityscape. A supply of soft limestone with a unique golden hue called pietra di Lecce is available in abundance, and local artisans have been carving it for centuries: You'll see intricately carved angels and rosettes, and in many cases man's handiwork has been elaborated upon by the dry sirocco winds from North Africa. On the facade of the Santa Croce church erosion has chiseled the cheeks and hollowed the foreheads of the cherubs, giving them a grotesque appearance.

From Lecce drive straight in almost any direction and you're bound to hit the sea. If you continue south on the sea road, you'll reach Otranto and cross the invisible line to where Italy looks and feels like North Africa, and tangible influences from the East will further confuse your inner compass. At the end of a road outside Otranto, a signpost marked "Albania" points toward some undefined place in the distance. On a clear day, you can actually see the mountains on the small country's western flank. The Norman-Arab-Byzantine city of Otranto has plenty of excellent outdoor fish restaurants and a beautiful walk along its ramparts, where couples, hand in hand, take an evening stroll.

Further south still, the coast gets rocky and is marked with marine caves, which can be explored by boat or on foot, and lone lookout towers on the waterfront spaced about six miles (ten kilometers) apart. Sometimes the lucky visitor will chance upon a religious festival, such as the one held in Santa Cesarea Terme, known for its thermal baths, in honor of its patron saint on September 11. A wooden statue of the Madonna is carried from the chapel to the port, where it is floated out to sea in a fishing boat filled with flowers and candles. The local high school band plays, while leather-faced men in dark suits and women in colorful headscarves follow the procession. As the story goes, Santa Cesarea was a local girl, and when her mother died, her father decided to marry her because she reminded him of his dead wife. The young girl devised a plan: She told her father she was going to take a bath, but instead she tied two pigeons together and let them thrash about in the tub, using the time to escape. The father ran after her but got lost in the mist, and the girl

rushed to the safety of a nearby cave, guided by a brilliant light. She is said to still live in that cave, and fishermen swear they see it light up when Santa Cesarea ventures outside.

Past the town of Tricase, with its posh Moorish summer villas, is *finibus terrae*, or "land's ends." Santa Maria Leuca marks the tip of the peninsula and represents a symbolic point of contact for people of the Mediterranean basin. It's also where the Adriatic and the Ionian seas meet, crashing into each other with a strong surf.

Head north on the Ionian side, where you'll be amazed by the color of the sea. The water is a lighter shade of blue, and the rocky bluffs of the Adriatic are replaced with sandy beaches that continue, almost uninterrupted, to Calabria. The pearl of this side of the peninsula is Gallipoli, which gets its name from the Greek *kalli polis*, or "beautiful city." It is built on an island connected by an isthmus, and thirty years of Saracen rule was enough to leave a strong Islamic imprint, evident in the circular city plan. Like a round lifesaver, the city appears to float on water. "Once you start driving around Gallipoli, you'll never stop," warn the locals.

✤ THE CAVE DWELLERS ✤

The northwestern part of Puglia that borders the Basilicata region is scarred by deep ravines that make the landscape look like bunched fabric. Nestled deep within its folds are little towns such as Gravina and Matera (in Basilicata) that have been safeguarded from pirates and invaders since antiquity. But this barren place with its lunar landscape has also suffered extreme isolation, making it one of the poorest and most forgotten corners of Europe today. Only a handful of foreigners trickle down here, but those who do leave with a profound understanding of the Italian identity. And to this pair of foreign eyes, this is Italy at its most romantic.

What sets Gravina and Matera apart from "normal" towns is that a large part of the urban fabric is underground. Nature left deep gorges that slice into the landscape like wounds, and humans carved further into the soft tufa walls to build rudimentary homes. Subterranean rooms and cavernous homes are bunched together within the gullies, making them almost invisible as you approach by car. Matera, now a UNESCO World Heritage site, is the biggest and most impressive town. Its cave houses are called *sassi*, and its two main neighborhoods are Sasso Barisano and Sasso Caveoso, each lining the two ravines that intersect here. Until recently, families lived inside the caves, sharing their living space with pigs and chickens in inconceivable squalor. Although most of the *sassi* are abandoned today, you may still see a garden hose fastened to a public fountain, bringing water to the handful of people who refuse to leave their grottoes.

Happily, government incentives have made it easy, and cheap, to buy a *sasso* and restore it. Young people who had left Basilicata to make their fortunes elsewhere are returning to invest in

Matera real estate. Within the course of one year, three very good restaurants and one new hotel had opened in the *sassi* neighborhoods. You can eat and sleep inside the same caves that were a symbol of national shame just a few decades ago. Tourists are also beginning to discover the more than 150 *chiese rupestri*, or underground churches, in the region of Basilicata alone. You'll find one just a few miles from Matera, on the road to Montescaglioso, called Cristo La Selva. It is crammed into a deep crevice in the earth and is visually stunning. In Montescaglioso, the abandoned Santa Lucia church makes for another unforgettable photo opportunity.

On the road from Matera to the port city of Taranto, you will pass the town of Castellaneta, atop another tight ravine. It is the birthplace of the greatest latin lover of all time: Rudolph Valentino. Born in 1895 as Rodolfo Alfonso Raffaello Piero Filiberto Guglielmi de Valentina d'Antonguolla, he immigrated to the United States as a dancer at the age of eighteen, and his smashing good looks soon delivered him to the silver screen. (He was also persuaded to shorten his name.) Few women could resist his colossal charm and he became the definition of male sex appeal. In his book *A Traveller in Southern Italy*, H. V. Morton notes, "I was glad to have seen Castellaneta, and went away recollecting that one of the penalties of being in love with a girl in the 1920s was the ordeal of having to see Rudolph Valentino." When the heartthrob died at age thirty-five, women everywhere started a collective mourning process, and it soon became fashionable for those who had been favored with Valentino's magic touch to claim he hadn't been such a great lover after all.

SMALL EARS AND BIG APPETITES

Nowhere is Puglia's magic more tangible than in the kitchen. Thanks to ancient forests that have long since decomposed, the region's soil is incredibly rich and fertile. Sniff a handful of it, and your nostrils will be overwhelmed by a distilled essence of earth with lingering musky overtones. Because of Puglia's idyllic growing conditions, the region is home to meaty wine grapes, centuries-old olive groves, flourishing fields of grain, and oversize fruit and vegetables that are bright in color. All of these ingredients—but especially the pungent and greenish olive oil—play a fundamental role in local cuisine. No matter how refined the meal, you will always detect that distinctive essence of the earth in what you eat here.

Puglia has two emblematic dishes. The first is the protein-packed *fave e cicoria*: a puree of broad beans served with a side of wild chicory and a few splashes of olive oil poured on top. The second is *orecchiette*, or pasta shaped by the thumb into "small ears." *Orecchiette* can be served with tomato sauce and shaved *ricotta salata*, salted sheep cheese. Sometimes it is accompanied by liquid *ricotta forte*—cheese made to go bad and celebrated for its rancid taste and smell—that is trickled over the pasta; just a few drops are enough to knock out your taste buds for hours. Other local specialties include *taralli*, or doughnutlike dried bread crackers, and *burrata* cheese. Part of the mozzarella family, no Italian cheese is more divinely decadent than Puglia's *burrata*. When you pierce the tear-shaped cheese with a knife, cream and shredded mozzarella pour out and flood your plate.

Seafood, especially shellfish, is an important building block of the local diet, making the Pugliesi among the most aphrodisiac-fed people on the planet (see chapter twelve for more information on shellfish). Raw *ricci*, or sea urchins, are cracked open like nuts, and the orange flesh is scooped out with bread. The city of Taranto, on the Ionian Sea, is famous for its oysters, which are smaller and tastier than others, as well as for its mussels. *Tartufi di mare*, or "sea truffles," are gooey creatures that look like unappetizing greenish rocks, and *cannolicchi* is a razorfish, or a mollusk protected by a pencillike gray shell. Today *datteri di mare* are illegal to sell commercially because fishing them damages the marine environment, although these "sea dates" are still considered a prized local delicacy by those who have a trusted supplier.

What is new to Puglia's epicurean scene is its wine. Known as a producer of bulk grape juice until recently, wineries are beginning to shift to quality vintages. Two native grapes, Negroamaro (meaning "bitter black") and Primitivo, are beefy and musky, and beautifully reflect Puglia's *terroir*.

CUPID'S CORNERS

RESTAURANTS

Il Poeta Contadino

Via Indipenza, 21
70011 Alberobello
Tel: (+39) 080 432 1917
www.ilpoetacontadino.it

Il Poeta Contadino is the finest restaurant in which to taste the many distinct flavors characteristic of the Puglia region. Set in a beautiful eighteenth-century stone barn in Alberobello, the dining room is both cavernous and intimate, its high arched ceilings containing the warmth of the restaurant's fireplaces and echoing every whisper from every corner. The menu is seasonal and always draws on regional delicacies: Spectacular fresh seafood and shellfish crop up in the summer, while game with truffles, herbed beef, and earthy fare such as pumpkins and artichokes return in the cooler months. The wine list at Il Poeta is legendary—the restaurant added a *Wine Spectator* award to its Michelin star almost a decade ago—and features vintages that are more than worthy of toasting to an engagement.

HOTELS

La Grotta Palazzese

Via Narciso, 59
70044 Polignano a Mare
Tel: (+39) 080 4240677
www.grottapalazzese.it

Among the most striking and beautiful hotels in the world, La Grotta is perched on the rocky coastline of Polignano a Mare, an old fishing town overlooking the sea just south of Bari. The outdoor dining rooms of the restaurant are set within dramatic caves carved out of the rock over millennia by the crashing waves of the Adriatic—legend has it that Duca Letto, an amorous local nobleman, used the natural halls to host decadent parties when he resided here in the eighteenth century. The menu is rich in aphrodisiac seafood, from fresh lobsters to herbed mussels and oysters, and the wine cellar has something to suit every mood. Many rooms at the hotel have private balconies that overlook the caves and the rocky shoreline below, and the distinctive surrounding landscape gives the place an isolated, intimate feel that is perfect for an intense romantic getaway.

Hotel Dei Trulli

Via Cadore, 32
70011 Alberobello
Tel: (+39) 080 432 3555

This remarkable hotel in the heart of the Itria Valley invites guests to stay in their own private trulli, centuries-old conical apartments characteristic of the Alberobello region. Single rooms are available, but for the full experience reserve a suite of two or three interconnected trulli. There is an air of mystery surrounding settlements of trulli, and staying here gives you a sense that you're engaging in a forgotten, more sensual, more primal way of life.

Masseria San Domenico

Strada Litoranea, 379
72015 Brindisi
Tel: (+39) 080 482 7769
www.imasseria.com

A stunning fifteenth-century watchtower on the Brindisi coast is now home to the Masseria San Domenico, one of the most exclusive and sophisticated resorts in the country. The hotel is modern and Mediterranean in style, with spacious, cool rooms, tiled floors, and dozens of gardens, terraces, bars, and lounges scattered around. While it's a prime location for cultural exploration—the Castellana grottoes and an abundance of natural caves and archaeological sites are within easy traveling distance—the hotel works best as a place for luxurious sensual indulgence, from the soft white sands of the hotel's beaches to the refreshing Mediterranean cuisine of the restaurants, the delicious wines, and the vast range of relaxing massage therapies available in the spa.

AMORE, AMALFI, AND MORE

E TU DICE: "I'PARTO, ADDIO!"
T'ALLUNTANE DA STU CORE . . .
DA STA TERRA DE L'AMMORE . . .
TIENE 'O CORE' E NUN TURNA?

You say: "I am leaving, goodbye!"
You will leave behind my heart . . .
Do you have the strength to leave . . .
this land of love?

Verse from *Torna a Sorrento*
by Gian Battista De Curtis

Some of the first "tourists" to descend on the Campania region came in the name of a rose. Roses have long been associated with love and beauty, but the *Bifera Rosaria Paestum* rose, in particular, won the praise of Virgil, Ovid, and other Latin poets, and not just for its beauty. This rose is a myth of antiquity because it bloomed twice in one growing season, something roses were not known to do before modern horticulture. The twice-blooming rose was said to only exist in the ancient city of Paestum (previously Poseidonia), a Greek city south of Naples in the seventh century BC. The romantic myth of this unique flower attracted a stream of international botanists and poets—including Goethe—who set out to examine it for themselves.

Naples, the regional capital, was Neapolis for "New City" to the Greeks, and this vibrant metropolis makes an interesting stop on the way to the Amalfi coast. Naples is not for the faint of heart; the adage "you'll either love it or hate it" does apply. Citizens of this wild city, on the other hand, proudly declare of its beauty, "See Naples and die." Naples is a city of sound: Turn the radio on and the songs you hear are epic love stories, usually involving tragic death, and the comments from your waiter are declarations of profound love at first sight, no matter how ridiculous that may sound to you. And if a love ballad is not dedicated to a woman, it is dedicated to *il sole*, the sun, the main object of worship here.

I can try to sum up Naples after meeting a boy named for the city's patron saint, Gennaro, who was selling Neapolitan folk music CDs on the sidewalk. He wore a gold chain with a lucky charm and drank warm Coca-Cola from a glass bottle. He was so fat the outline of his undergarment pressed against the fabric of his shirt. Across his chest in bold black letters was the English word *Overkill*.

✤ THE AMALFI COAST ✤

The magic of the Amalfi Coast is in its colors. No other place has a pink that rivals the neon hues of the native bougainvillea in Positano. No yellow can match the glowing brilliance of the lemons hanging heavy from groves beyond Sorrento. And no body of water reflects the same lapis lazuli tint as the sea that snuggles up to the coastline's cliffs.

The technicolor vitality of the Amalfi Coast has lured sun-seekers since the time of Odysseus. But it wasn't until the 1930s that Amalfi became cupid's playground. Scores of Hollywood starlets, international business moguls, and the literary elite began flocking to this succession of picturesque fishing villages. They came to rest their bodies and minds and give their hearts a holiday. Images of Greta Garbo gazing at the azure sea from the cliff-top Villa Cimbrone in Ravello or of Jackie Kennedy shopping for handcrafted sandals in Positano are as much a part of the local landscape as rainbow-colored church domes.

The Amalfi coastline runs approximately twenty-five miles (forty kilometers) along a thin peninsula between the Bay of Naples and the Gulf of Salerno. Rocky cliffs plunge into the water, allowing for only a few sandy coves that are wide enough for beach towels. The landscape is so precipitous, you have to wonder how ancient engineers thought they could build here. They did so by perfecting the concept of a cascading town. Like a waterfall, peach and pink stucco buildings descend to the shore, with more elaborate buildings near the bottom, and a public square and oversize church dome inevitably positioned at the convergence.

Positano and Amalfi are the most famous towns here, and they are linked by a two-lane road (Route 163) known as the "Amalfi Drive," or the *via Smeraldo*. This corniche extraordinaire is the backbone of the Amalfi Coast, snaking along hundreds of turns and hairpin curves that open onto breathtaking panoramas of the sea (by one count, the number of curves was put at a thousand). Traffic can be bad, especially when it bottlenecks at the entrances of the

towns; the design philosophy behind the tiny Fiat 500 and the three-wheeled "Ape" scooter/pickup truck will be clear when you see this road. Indeed, the best way to visit the Amalfi Coast is by Vespa, as many couples do. Mopeds (motorini) can be rented at each town and are ideal for a day of adventure in which clinging and hugging play a prominent role.

Overlooking the Gulf of Salerno and the trio of seductive islands of the Sirens (also Li Galli) that gave so much torment to Odysseus's crew, Positano is perhaps the most picturesque and popular village. Resembling a giant amphitheater, it encloses a good-size beach and a small harbor with brightly colored fishing boats. The yellow and green dome of the Santa Maria Assunta church dominates the cityscape, and flower-covered terraces, the odd palm tree, and brilliant examples of the city's dozen bougainvillea species enliven the buildings. For the best views, head up the steep stairs off via Positanesi d'America, named after the immigrants who left here in the early 1900s. Nestled in the side streets are botteghe where artisans make leather sandals to size. Ironically, they often face luxury boutiques that hawk the same item interpreted by a Milan designer.

The central Piazza del Duomo is framed by a flight of sixty-two stairs leading to an Arab-Norman-style cathedral where the headless remains of Saint Andrew are kept inside the crypt. The apostle's body is said to exude manna, which locals refer to as the saint's "sweat." The liquid is jealously guarded, and the faithful drink it for its curative properties. (Manna is a plant extract that was also a metaphor for spiritual nourishment for the Israelites). Sant'Andrea in a more composed and complete state can be seen atop the square's fountain, where the nymphs at his feet bountifully spout water from their breasts.

Mythology provides a romanticized version of the city's founding. The Greek hero Heracles fell in love with a sickly nymph named Amalphi. She died shortly thereafter, and the man of iron searched the earth for the most beautiful spot for her burial. He found it here. There are many ways to describe paradise on earth, but the words chiseled on an inscription near the harbor say it best: "For the people of Amalfi who go to heaven, judgment day will be a day like any other."

Even closer to heaven, perhaps, is the town of Ravello. Perched on a balcony of rock 1,200 feet (370 meters) above the sea, you can drink in aerial views of the Amalfi Coast here. Ravello was first settled by aristocratic Romans, who built their lavish summer places beyond the reach of invaders—and, presumably, the stench of the fishermen. Its link to the fortunate continues today, and it has cast its spell on such personalities as Greta Garbo, D. H. Lawrence, E. M. Forster, and Virginia Woolf, to name but a few.

In addition to the San Pantaleone cathedral (where the saint's blood is said to miraculously liquefy in a sacred vial), Ravello's main attractions for lovers are Villa Cimbrone and Villa Rufolo.

Every panoramic lookout point in the world should aspire to match Villa Cimbrone's *belvedere dell'infinito* or "lookout point of infinity," where poet Gabriele d'Annunzio claimed to have been "kissed by eternity." Marble busts of Roman deities stand with their backs against an azure sea. If they could turn around and admire the view, they'd marvel at the harmonious collaboration between mortals and mother nature.

Villa Rufolo is a curious mix of architectural styles, including Romanesque, Gothic, and Sicilian-Moorish. Much of the palace and cloisters was built in the eleventh century, but the main draw is the garden. Shaded by umbrella pines and palms and home to floral specimens from all over the world, these lush gardens afford a picture-perfect panorama of the twin bell towers of the Church of the Annunciation and the landscape beyond.

THE MAGIC GARDEN

In 1877 Richard Wagner started to compose the opera *Parsifal*, based on the Holy Grail tale of Amfortas and Klingsor. In the story a young aspirant to the Grail Order named Klingsor discovers he can't overcome his lust. Despite taking a rather extreme measure—self-castration—his desires remain, and he is eventually banished from the order. He decides that earthly delight and guiltless pleasure are not so bad, and he constructs a magic castle and garden inhabited by "women of fearsome beauty." When Wagner visited Villa Rufolo, he understood what Klingsor's pleasure palace would have looked like. If you are visiting from April to October, you can indulge in the delights of the Ravello Music festival, when celebrated orchestras and soloists perform with the setting sun as the only backdrop.

Vietri sul Mare is the last town in the Amalfi chain and is the coast's ceramics capital. Production began under the ancient Romans, who scoured nearby terra-cotta deposits for the raw material to make oversize urns and pots for transporting goods. By the fifteenth century craftsmen had turned ceramics into an element of design. Hand-painted tiles with lively geometric patterns and flower and animal motifs are a distinctive element of Campania's architectural style. Look down when you enter Vietri's main square for a superb hand-painted rendition of the same sea scenery that comes into view when you lift your gaze again. If you're in the market for majolica, tiles, tabletops, or kitchen crockery for your love nest back home, you'll find the cheapest prices here.

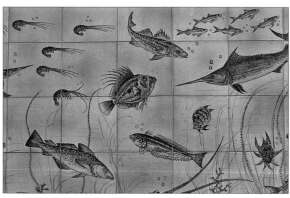

Capri, Ischia, and Procida

When Emperor Augustus saw Capri, he liked it so much he ordered the municipality of Naples to give it to Rome in exchange for the larger island Ischia. His successor, Tiberius, was so enamored of it he decided to rule the Roman Empire from his cliff-top palace here. You can visit the remains of his Villa Jovis and see where the emperor's critics were hurled over a balustrade into the abyss from a precipitous cliff. It was stunts like these that helped give rise to the word *capricious*. Everybody likes Capri—and that is its biggest problem. Crowding is an issue in the high season, but the island can be a delight in the early spring and late fall (hydrofoils, boats, and helicopters arrive regularly from Naples, Sorrento, and Positano). A trip here takes some planning and reserving ahead, especially if you're on a honeymoon.

Capri offers the best of the Mediterranean on a plot of land that takes only a few hours to circle with a small motorboat. The island's main attraction is the Grotta Azzurra, where the sun's rays are reflected back into the dark pool of a marine cave, creating a spectacular underwater lighting effect. Legend says a ship with a cargo of purple dye—the exclusive color of the emperors—sank here and permanently tinted the water. Wooden boats loaded with tourists wait for the lull in the waves before slipping into the tiny mouth of the cave. In the late afternoon, when the boats have gone, romantics can swim to the cave and rest on a tiny beach at the back wall. Even Tiberius is said to have come here for moments of quiet reflection. Another geological wonder are the Faraglioni, three stone towers that jut out of the sea. The via Krupp, a thin walkway that zigzags down the face of a cliff to the Marina Piccola, is also a treat, albeit a manmade one.

In the town of Anacapri you can see the love story of Adam and Eve depicted in hundreds of hand-painted tiles on the floor of the San Michele church. There's a touch of southern irony there—so much attention paid to recreate the Garden of Eden on an island that is often described as paradise; it's as if the artists intentionally left all those nasty scenes of purgatory and hell for their northern colleagues to mull over. Make time to stop at the celebrated *piazzetta*, the main square, where you can sip chilled *aperitivi* or shop for designer keepsakes. As the English writer and island resident Norman Douglas remarked, this is the place to "watch the world go by."

Despite the island's generous offerings, many couples choose Ischia or Procida over Capri as a romantic hideaway. Located on the other side of the Bay of Naples, the beaches are better, the crowds are less concentrated, and as an added bonus Ischia has thermal springs.

Both islands are part of the immense underwater volcanic network that extends to Stromboli. They face the mainland's fiery Phlegrean fields, a landscape that helped shape the Greeks' idea of hell, where sulfur fumes and mud exude from openings in the hollow ground, and the earth emits sounds like a sleeping giant. This is one of the earth's most complex geological structures, with some thirty volcanoes, and it is under the watchful eye of volcanologists.

This underground fire, however, has shaped Ischia's above-ground fairy-tale appeal. Filled with nooks and crannies occupied by ideal Italian fishing villages, this island (and the smaller Procida) is where scenes from the fictitious town Mongibello were filmed in the movie The Talented Mr. Ripley. Ischia was cast as the idyllic setting for the start of a complicated love affair.

The island scores high on the romance meter for many other reasons. With more than a hundred hot springs (the highest concentration in Europe), it is possible to swim year-round. Even the Greek love goddess Aphrodite is said to have bathed here, at the Giardini di Aphrodite, and the major springs are named after her. The island's mythological appeal was boosted by the discovery of the fabled Cup of Nestor, dating from the eighth century BC. Found inside the grave of a ten-year-old boy, the cup displays one of the oldest examples of written Greek, reading: "I am the Cup of Nestor from which one can drink with pleasure, but whoever drinks from this cup will immediately be seized by desire for Aphrodite of the beautiful diadem." (The cup is on display at Ischia's Museo Archeologico di Pithecusae.)

Whatever magic potion poured from the Cup of Nestor, it presumably did more than act as an aphrodisiac. Curative mineral water from Ischia has been identified as a veritable fountain of youth, and the island's many luxury spa hotels have used it as a marketing tool to ensure a steady flow of faithful clients. Bask in *fumarole*, or plumes of steam, with your special someone, or take a nap on thermally heated beaches: In short, you can both bask in your love and stay young on this magical island.

Ischia has two musts. First, visit (or preferably book a stay in) the fishing hamlet of Sant'Angelo. This appealing little town with its pastel-colored buildings perches on one side of a thin isthmus to the Punta Sant'Angelo, where there is a second cluster of adorable buildings. You can sunbathe on the rocks and enjoy clear water brimming with colorful fish.

The second "must-see" item is the fireworks display held each year on July 26 over the Castello Aragonese at Ischia Ponte, in celebration of the town's patron, Sant'Anna. Pyrotechnic experts produce what I think is the most beautiful show of fireworks anywhere. (Fourth of July event organizers could surely pick up new tricks here.) You can opt to view them by boat and watch the glowing embers sprinkle down from directly overhead. People come from far and wide for the show and link their boats together to form floating islands, passing food and drink from one vessel to the next. If you are part of this floating audience, you also get better views of the "burning of the castle," when red fireworks engulf the towering Castello Aragonese (built in 1438 and home to Michelangelo's friend and poetess Vittoria Colonna) in a reenactment of a famous attack by pirates.

Other places worth a visit include the town of Forio, home to the whitewashed Santuario del Soccorso church that is filled with wooden models of fishing boats, created in thanks for the many times local men have returned from their sea expeditions unharmed. In nearby Lacco Ameno you can see the wind-carved *fungo*, or tufa "mushroom," at the top of the port—Ischia's most photographed natural monument.

The smaller island of Procida has often played the role of matchmaker and is referred to as *Isola delle Fanciulle* (Island of Girls, literally) or *Isola Felice*. This is a more rugged and rustic alternative, where volcanic rocks define an otherworldly terrain. In 1849 the poet Alphonse De Lamartine wrote about his passionate affair with an island native named Graziella. In one beautiful passage he describes her almond-shaped eyes as colored by the sun, sky, and sea. The novelist Elsa Morante dedicated her 1957 book, *L'isola di Arturo*, to this island. With Freudian overtones that are about as subtle as a clove of raw garlic, the story tells of a young boy, Arturo, who falls for his father's new young bride. Procida has also been featured on the silver screen,

in the Oscar-winning *Il Postino*, which starred Naples's beloved comedian Massimo Troisi, as a mailman who uses romantic verse to seduce the island bombshell, Maria Grazia Cucinotta.

Procida is home to secluded beaches where lovers can enjoy each other's company in complete privacy. The coves around the Scoglio del Cannone are hidden from indiscreet eyes, as is the Spiaggetta degli Innamorati (the little beach of lovers), beyond Pozzo Vecchio.

⚜ POMPEII PROIBITO ⚜

Slightly after noon on August 24 in 79 AD, nature expressed herself in a moment of extreme violence. A huge mass of pumice stone, molten rock, and ash representing the top third Mount Vesuvius suddenly shot up 65,000 feet (20,000 meters) into the air in what one witness, the Roman author Pliny the Younger, described as an "enormous umbrella pine." Within minutes that debris, with poisonous gas in tow, crashed down onto the volcano's slopes. Gaining momentum as it slid down the sides, it slammed into the seaside city of Pompeii at speeds of more than sixty miles (100 kilometers) per hour. Ash and debris turned day into night, and when the light returned two days later, this model Roman city had been wiped out of existence. Ash from the explosion settled beyond the furthest reaches of the empire.

Vesuvius locked a moment in Roman life into a vault that remained sealed for fifteen centuries, preserving it from being picked clean by vandals. Modern archaeologists entered Pompeii as if they were walking into the house of a suddenly deceased relative: Bread had just been popped into the ovens, pots had been set out for scrubbing, and gold jewelry was left sitting on a mantle.

They also found a city caught with its pants down, so to speak, and a visit here can set the blood racing. Pompeii exposed the brazen sexuality and Vegas-style raunchiness of the Romans. As recently as the 1970s women and children were not allowed to visit Pompeii's most "public" rooms. Today the sexiest artwork is secured in the *Gabinetto Segreto*, in room 65 of the National Archaeological Museum of Naples.

A tour of Pompeii *proibito*, Italy's "forbidden" city, starts at the Casa dei Vettii, which houses the notorious fresco of Priapus, in which the god of male fertility is weighing what my Italian guidebook calls his "hypertrophic phallus symbol of happy luck." The English travel writer H. V. Morton tartly describes it as an "impossible deformity." Once you train your eyes, you will see phalluses everywhere in Pompeii—over doors, embedded in walls, and carved into the pavement. Historians believe the obsessive depiction of the phallic symbol has more to do with luck than libido: The phalluses are charms, derivatives of the red *corna*, or "ox-horns," that still dangle around the neck of any self-respecting virile man south of Rome today. Phalluses are placed near entrances and doorways, like the Priapus at the Casa dei Vettii, to ward off the evil eye. Off the via dell'Abbondanza is the "fertility garden," where barren women would rub one of these symbols in the hope of being able to conceive.

Whatever their intention, these phalluses were like road signs that point in the direction of Pompeii's red light district. Although the coastline has changed, Pompeii was still a port town, and a seedy one at that, home to some thirty *lupanare*, or brothels, to service merchants and travelers. The name comes from the word *lupo*, or "wolf," because women were said to howl from second-story balconies to attract clients. If their cries successfully seduced a client, he would wait in a room where he could select from a "menu" of Kama Sutra–like positions painted on the wall.

Several villas in Pompeii are decorated with scenes of acrobatic lovers, hermaphrodites, lustful satyrs, and other mythological misfits, but none compares to the palatial Villa dei Misteri (Villa of Mysteries), located a short walk outside the city walls. It contains twenty-nine life-size figures painted against a brilliant red background, portrayed celebrating what is believed to be the forbidden Bacchic (or Dionysiac) initiation rite. There are scenes of flagellation and sacrificial ceremonies that were said to be at the center of this cult.

Nearby is the Casa di Venere, Venus's House, with a spectacular depiction of the goddess of love rising from the sea on a shell, using her scarf as a sail. Given Pompeii's fascination with sex, it should come as no surprise that Venus was the divine protectress of the city. She proved disastrously inadequate at the task: Soon after city officials had given the green light to rebuild her temple, damaged during the 62 AD earthquake, the other, more deadly, natural disaster struck. The gods are said to have awakened Vesuvius and ordered it to erupt as a way of erasing Pompeii's hedonistic excesses.

The "Anti-Amalfis"

Mother nature clearly outdid herself when she whipped up the scenic masterpiece that is the Amalfi Coast. So it's hard to believe she would bestow many of those same magic ingredients on an area just a few hours south. Only this time, fate—and a *superstrada* that veers too far inland—has kept her creation a secret.

Few foreigners have heard of Acquafredda, Maratea, and the romantically named Punta Santavenere, in the Basilicata region, and even fewer have visited this rocky resort area that lies beyond the Cilento Coast. Yet this stretch of sea bluffs, beach coves, and meandering roads will delight your senses just like its northern neighbor.

The Lucana part of the coast, which belongs to the region of Basilicata, spans twenty miles (thirty-two kilometers) facing the Tyrrhenian Sea from the Gulf of Policastro. One highlight is the village of Acquafredda, amply endowed with villas and lavish summer homes from the decadent 1920s and before, when a handful of well-to-do families bought the most beautiful properties. Continue on Strada Nazionale 18 to Maratea. Along the way, you pass a succession of marine caves (Grotta di San Pietro, Grotta dei Palombi, and Grotta di Fiumicello) that can be explored by boat for a delightful excursion. Along the road, the mountainsides are dotted with oaks and wind-bent pine trees (*Pino Loricato*) that resemble the type found in Monterey, California. Maratea, the biggest town here, nestled under Mount San Biagio, is becoming a smart and sophisticated summer destination, where you can lose yourself in a maze of narrow streets. You won't find the crowding that plagues the Amalfi Coast, but you will find those special sunsets that set the summer sky ablaze.

A few more turns of the steering wheel takes you into Calabria, stronghold of the mighty Magna Graecia, the biggest colony of the ancient Greeks. This "toe" of the boot of Italy saw the rise and fall of crucial Greek trading posts, such as Rhegium (today Reggio di Calabria), Croton, Locris, and Sybaris. Of these ancient cities, perhaps none catches our imagination like Sybaris. Its inhabitants were so rich and opulent that the city became known throughout Greece; this reputation gave rise to the English word *sybarite*, for someone devoted to luxurious decadence. Gold abounded, and every house was furnished with expensive awnings.

The most romantic part of Calabria is the province of Vibo Valentia, where the volcanic island of Stromboli looms on the horizon, sometimes appearing close enough to touch. The setting sun silhouettes the cone-shaped island, making for an unforgettable image. The seaside town of Pizzo is where cavalry commander Joachim Murat (Napoleon's brother-in-law) made his final appearance. Decked out in French lace and a flamboyant uniform he designed himself, the so-called "King of Feathers" pranced from his boat in an unlikely attempt at sparking a revolution to regain his throne as King of Naples after

Waterloo. A furious crowd nearly turned him into fish food, and shortly after the Bourbons executed him. His last words reportedly were: "Aim at the heart but spare my face." Today, Pizzo is famous for its *tartufo*, or black "truffle" ice cream—a luscious, sugary seduction that oozes fudge and creamy chocolate at its core. Down the coast, near the tip of Capo Vaticano, is the lovely resort town of Tropea, another haunt of Venus. You can climb to the Santa Maria dell'Isola monastery ruins for more spectacular views, stargazing, and a kiss or two.

If you are drawn to this side of Italy, do not miss the Festa del Maggio held in Accettura, southeast of Potenza, and tied to the Pentecost (the feast lasts several days). What makes Accettura's Festa del Maggio truly unique is that it is overtly dedicated to libido and lust, despite being practiced in a corner of Italy often identified with sexual repression. At the center of the festival is the belief that all of nature's creations can be united in the act of lovemaking. The townsmen scour the nearby Montepiano forests for the tallest and straightest tree and chop it down. The tree symbolizes *Maggio*, or "May." On the other side of town, in the Gallipoli forest, they search for its mate, *la Cima*, the top part of a holly tree with an abundance of branches that looks like—you guessed it—a "bush." The two are carried into town and ceremoniously "married" on the Sunday of Pentecost. On Monday the *Maggio* is stripped smooth and cleaned, and on Tuesday it is united with *la Cima*, amid feverish dancing and chanting, in a procedure that reflects the act of sex.

NATURAL VIAGRA
IN EVERY BITE

Hands down, no other Italian regions can claim as many reportedly aphrodisiac foods as Campania, Basilicata, and Calabria. These regions have always been fertile grounds for heavy hitters such as hot pepper, pungent basil, wild mushrooms, pomegranates, and fish (see more about each in chapter twelve).

Campania's tastiest traditions start off with simple ingredients. Mozzarella di bufala, as large as a grapefruit, paired with sweet cherry tomatoes (pomodorini Vesuvio) and broad basil leaves is the culinary perfection known as the insalata caprese (Capri salad). Coffee is stronger in Campania, and the thick-crust pizza cooked in wood-burning ovens is considered among the best in the world. The island of Capri also inspired the most unexpected of pizzas: the capriciosa, topped with artichoke, boiled egg, mushrooms, and ham.

Although these are not prominent wine regions, a Campania white called Greco di Tufo is on its way to becoming Italy's trendiest beverage. Another culinary delight is limoncello, a sweet and sour after-dinner drink made from the fermented rinds of Amalfi lemons; the syrupy nectar is a powerful love potion. A specialty of Sorrento is Rosolio, a liqueur made from walnuts.

Food in Calabria is spicy. Hot peppers are added to most dishes, both for taste and superstition (they are said to ensure male prowess). A spicy sausage called 'nduja is so soft it can be spread with a butter knife. Swordfish, shellfish, and almond pastries are among the other prominent foods in local culinary tradition. Calabria's most famous export is bergamot, a peculiar greenish orange that is squeezed for its extract and used as the base for perfumes and in Earl Grey tea.

CUPID'S CORNERS

O f Italy's resort areas, none offers a greater concentration of luxury hotels than the Amalfi Coast and Capri. These are immensely popular areas for couples looking to arrange a destination wedding, those on honeymoon, or those celebrating an anniversary. As a result, accommodation options are pricey, and you should reserve well in advance. The plus side is that virtually all the hotels listed below have long experience dealing with the needs of foreigners in love, especially those needing assistance in planning and logistics. Many have in-house photographers, caterers, florists, drivers, and even wedding planners.

Another popular option, especially for honeymooners, is to visit the coast and islands by boat. Charter yachts can be rented for two people or a group of up to ten, and most include an English-speaking skipper and a chef. Prices vary according to season, number of days at sea, and itinerary (with many companies set to take you all the way to Sicily's Aeolian Islands). To learn more about charting a romantic Mediterranean sailing trip, see: www.sail-italy.com, www.sailingcharters.com/Italy.htm, or www.napolicharter.net.

THE AMALFI COAST AND SORRENTO

RESTAURANTS

Don Alfonso 1890
Corso Sant'Agata, 11
80064 Sant'Agata sui due Golfi (Sorrento)
Tel: (+39) 081 878 0026
Fax: (+39) 081 533 0226

Known as the best restaurant in the south, Don Alfonso 1890 is one of a handful in Italy to have earned three Michelin stars. Alfonso Iaccarino attends to every detail, from china to crystal wine glasses, and is the fourth generation of Alfonsos to do so. Only six miles (ten kilometers) from Sorrento, on the peninsula separating the Gulf of Naples from the Amalfi Coast, the restaurant uses its own organically grown vegetables and olives for oil. Even the butter is freshly churned, and the gelato is homemade. You can feast on paper-light potato gnocchi with tomato and smoked scamorza cheese or ravioli con alici e caciotta, containing anchovies and a cheese that must be consumed within twelve hours. Wife

Livia oversees the vast collection of Italian wines stored in the underground cave. If you are looking for a lovely spot to celebrate a special date, such as an anniversary, this is the place.

Ristorante and Pizzeria da Gigino
Via Nicotera, 15
80069 Vico Equense (Napoli)
Tel: (+39) 081 879 8309
Fax: (+39) 081 801 6447
www.pizzametro.it

The motto at da Gigino is "size does matter." This self-defined University of Pizza outside of Sorrento serves sumptuous pizza pies by the meter with a dizzying array of toppings. This is not the place for a cozy dinner for two but rather a family restaurant with décor that relentlessly explores the design depths of the 1970s. Waiters scoot antipasti carts laden with eggplant prepared in every which way, cheese, green peppers, and stuffed mushrooms; the dessert tray is just as impressive.

Da Adolfo

Via Laurito, 26
84017 Positano
Tel: (+39) 089 875 022

From Positano port, look for fishing boats marked "da Adolfo" or "Laurito." They provide a free ferry service to the trattoria located on the next bay. Don't miss the *polpo con le patate* (squid and potatoes), to be enjoyed in a casual setting under Adolfo's straw canopy next to the sea.

Caravella

Via Matteo Camera, 12
84011 Amalfi
Tel: (+39) 089 871 029
www.ristorantelacaravella.it

People in the know will tell you Caravella, opened in 1959, is the place to go for fish. Start with the house appetizer, *stuzzichino della Caravella*, and continue with *tagliata di pasta allo zafferano con zucca e crostacei*—pasta with shellfish, saffron, and a surprising touch of pumpkin. The menu includes a heavenly swordfish grilled inside lemon leaves, too.

HOTELS

Grand Hotel Excelsior Vittoria

Piazza Tasso, 34
80067 Sorrento
Tel: (+39) 081 807 1044
Fax: (+39) 081 877 1206
www.exvitt.it

This 1834 Grand Hotel is a Sorrento landmark. In the midst of the action of the city center, the hotel has ninety-eight museum-quality rooms and five acres of private gardens. The views, which extend to the Bay of Naples and Vesuvius, are so achingly beautiful that the tenor Enrico Caruso found his muse for his rendition of *Torna a Sorrento*, or "Come Back to Sorrento," here. He kept one of the frescoed rooms until his death in 1921. The hotel staff will organize special trips and activities for newlyweds. Sorrento, located on the other side of the peninsula closer to Naples, is not part of the Amalfi Coast, but it is its own little enclave of paradise.

Le Sirenuse

Via Cristoforo Colombo, 30
84017 Positano
Tel: (+39) 089 875 066
Fax: (+39) 089 811 798
www.sirenuse.it

Facing the Li Galli islands, where the sweet song of the sirens almost lured Odysseus off course, the Sirenuse will also keep you from going home. Located in Positano and filled with precious antiques and hand-painted tiles, this burgundy hotel has been named among the best in Europe and is a first choice for honeymooners or those celebrating an anniversary. It opened in 1951, when the Sergale family decided to convert a summer residence into an eight-room hotel. Today there are sixty-two rooms, but that distinctive family touch is still evident—even the garden is attended to by them. A pool lined with potted citrus trees and a world-class restaurant complete the amenities. Gorgeous wedding gifts are available at the Emporio, which also sells pottery, glassware, and other handicrafts over the Internet. As John Steinbeck remarked: "A first class hotel, spotless and cool."

Hotel Il San Pietro

Via Laurito, 2
84017 Positano
Tel: (+39) 089 875 455
Fax: (+39) 089 811 449
www.ilsanpietro.com

The only thing better than staying in Positano is having a place with a view of it. The exceptional San Pietro enjoys the best views of this village. In 1962 local entrepreneur Carlo Cinque bought land around the small San Pietro chapel, about a mile from Positano, to build a house and a hotel. When he finished, he had created a new level of luxury accommodation. The highlight is the terrace, with its trademark yellow-tile benches and panoramic views. Below it is a downward spiral of rooms, each with a balcony and many with a Jacuzzi, restaurants, gardens, and a pool that comes to an abrupt end at a private beach.

Hotel Santa Caterina
S.S. Amalfitana, 9
84011 Amalfi
Tel: (+39) 089 871 012
Fax: (+39) 089 871 351
www.hotelsantacaterina.it

With a guest roster that reads like a who's who of the political and entertainment worlds, the Santa Caterina (just west of Amalfi) is one of Italy's most celebrated love nests. Its terrace, restaurant, and sea views also make it a popular spot for wedding receptions (you can even plan seating arrangements on its website). Walk through the bright lobby and peer over the balcony at the far end. Directly below a perfectly perpendicular drop are the blue and white umbrellas of the hotel's seaside tanning deck. You'll feel as if you are floating on air.

Palazzo Sasso
Via San Giovanni del Toro, 28
84010 Ravello
Tel: (+39) 089 818 181
Fax: (+39) 089 858 900
www.palazzosasso.com

This is my favorite hotel along this heavenly stretch of coast. A twelfth-century Moorish villa, it was restored and reopened as a luxury hotel in 1997. There are thirty-six rooms and eight suites, the delectable Rossellini restaurant, and a sun deck and pool set a thousand feet above sea level. Pampering is a house specialty. One example: The next day's weather forecast is left on your pillow the evening before. When you wake, you will be greeted with a sumptuous breakfast spread including smoked salmon, mozzarella, and fresh cinnamon cakes on the outdoor patio. The restaurant will accommodate wedding receptions with a maximum of seventy people.

Hotel Villa Cimbrone
Via Santa Chiara, 26
84010 Ravello
Tel: (+39) 089 857 459
Fax: (+39) 089 857 777
www.villacimbrone.it

When visiting hours end at sunset and the tourists are asked to leave, guests of Hotel Villa Cimbrone are left with the *belvedere dell'infinito* to themselves. Amorous pairs could not ask for a more idyllic place. The guest registry reads like a book of lovers, and it was here that Greta Garbo conducted a steamy secret affair with maestro Leopold Stokowski. Built on the remains of a Roman villa, the building did not take its present form until the early 1900s, thanks to Englishman Ernest William Beckett, who sold it to its current owner. But the English lord never forgot his house. At the end of World War II he landed off the coast of Salerno with Allied troops. He managed to get his hands on a jeep, drove to Amalfi, and climbed up the rocks to get one last glimpse of his beloved villa. After a thorough renovation, the hotel reopened in 2004. Because demand is so high, Villa Cimbrone has organizing weddings down to a science.

NIGHTLIFE

Africana Night Club
Via Torre a Mare, 2
84010 Praiano
Tel: (+39) 089 874 042

Snug in its own bay, with a dynamite-blasted dancing nook, the Africana was once frequented by Frank Sinatra and Jackie Kennedy. The theme here is Mondo Bongo meets the fishing industry: There is an aquarium under the dance floor, and a Blue Grotta that becomes a summertime sanctuary for merrymakers. During the day, Luca and his buddy, Luca, lower a gigantic fishing net to catch new pets for the aquarium. The nets are painted with glow-in-the-dark colors, so he can repeat the exercise at

night for the benefit of his audience as a topless woman in a boat serves spaghetti to the guests. The whole thing is wonderfully absurd.

THE ISLANDS

RESTAURANTS

Le Grottelle
Via Arco Naturale, 5
80073 Capri
Tel: (+39) 081 837 5719

You can't beat the romantic impact of this characteristic *ristorante* carved inside a grotto. Inside, the dark ambiance is peppered with an array of colors that come from the tomatoes, thick-skinned lemons, and braids of garlic that dangle from the ceiling. For those who prefer a bit more light, there's a sunny outdoor terrace, too. The restaurant is located near the natural arch on Punta Tragara and is reached by climbing 120 steps.

Da Paolino
Via Palazzo a Mare, 11
80073 Capri
Tel: (+39) 081 837 6102
Fax: (+39) 081 837 5611

"Under that sky of lemons as big as stars, I'd like to go with you my love," promises the restaurant brochure—and it's impossible to envision this, until you come to this legendary Capri love nest. The entire outdoor patio nestles under a canopy of citrus trees with plump, sun-infused

lemons directly overhead. The menu offers such delights as cherry tomatoes with creamy mozzarella, spaghetti with *rucola* and clams, and rigatoni with zucchini flowers.

La Capannina
Via le Botteghe, 12/14
80073 Capri
Tel: (+39) 081 837 0732
Fax: (+39) 081 837 6990
www.capannina-capri.com

La Capannina is a restaurant and gourmet shop that ranks at the top of Capri's list of best eateries. The pale pink tablecloth will soon be crowded with goodies such as eggplant stuffed with ricotta, linguine with redfish, and stuffed squid. Save room for the *torta Caprese* and mulberry crêpes.

Lo Scoglio
Via Cava Ruffano, 58
80070 Sant'Angelo, Ischia
Tel: (+39) 081 999 529
Fax: (+39) 081 999 419

Fabulously fresh fish and a view to die for distinguish this restaurant and bar carved into the rock on a sea bluff, the most romantic place in

Sant'Angelo. The menu offers local specialties such as spaghetti with mussels "stained" with fresh tomato and *fritto misto*, a plate of delicately fried shrimp and squid. You can also sample some of Ischia's famous white wines.

HOTELS

Capri Palace Hotel and Spa
Via Capodimonte, 2b
80071 Anacapri, Capri
Tel: (+39) 081 978 0111
Fax: (+39) 081 837 3191
www.capri-palace.com

Because the town of Capri is inundated with camera-toting day trippers from the mainland, many of the island's VIP guests have migrated to higher elevations in Anacapri, and the Capri Palace is their hotel of choice. The hotel was previously known as the Europa Palace until the owner's son took over and gave it a facelift. The new look includes a floor-to-ceiling coat of white patina and carefully chosen classics: a Louis XVI gilded chandelier here, a Roman column there. Six of the eighty-two rooms include a private garden and pool, and hotel amenities include a "Beauty Farm" and the *vinissimo* health plan that involves large quantities of wine. The swank La Terrazza restaurant is one of the best on the island. The Palace is a mecca for

weddings large and small—there's a full-time wedding coordinator on staff, and newlyweds are treated to a tour around the island by sailboat.

Grand Albergo Mezzatorre
Via Mezzatorre, 23
80075 Florio d'Ischia (Ischia)
Tel: (+39) 081 986 111
Fax: (+39) 081 986 015
www.mezzatorre.it

The Mezzatorre is definitely the most eye-catching hotel on Ischia, built inside a sixteenth-century fortification majestically situated in a grove at the end of a rocky promontory. The hotel is painted pink, complete with towers and white turrets, and has fifty-nine rooms and seven suites (of which three have a private garden and Jacuzzi). Thick tapestries surround the canopy beds. Both the pool and beach afford plenty of privacy.

Casa sul Mare
Via Salita Castello, 13
80079 Procida
Tel/Fax: (+39) 081 896 8799
www.lacasasulmare.it

Procida has only a handful of hotels, and Casa sul Mare (located near Marina Corricella) is the best alternative for couples seeking a clean, private room. The building dates back to the 1700s. Hotel staff will happily ferry you to the romantic La Chiaia beach by boat.

HOTELS

Romantik Hotel Villa Cheta Elite
Via Timpone, 46
85041 Acquafredda, Maratea
Tel: (+39) 0973 878 134
Fax: (+39) 0973 878 135
www.villacheta.it

I have stayed at Villa Cheta (its name means "quiet" or "tranquil") and can attest to the powerful romantic allure of this pink Art Nouveau–style building on the Lucanian coastline. The building was a former summer residence until the Aquadro family, headed now by the young and dynamic Stefania Aquadro, took it over in 1982 and lovingly converted it into a hotel. More than charming, Villa Cheta prides itself on being a "five-sense" hotel, meaning your taste buds will join you on a holiday spree. The restaurant is excellent and so is the selection of local wines—Stefania is both a chef and sommelier. Its greatest attributes, however, are that a room costs much less here than on the Amalfi Coast, and you can't beat the privacy of this undiscovered paradise.

ICE CREAM

Antica Gelateria Belvedere
Piazza della Repubblica, 43/44
89812 Pizzo (Vibo Valentia)
Tel: (+39) 0963 531 423

Plan a pit stop in the picturesque town of Pizzo, in Calabria, for what is considered by many to be the best tartufo ice cream in Italy. A meal in itself, fudge, syrup, and decadence appear to be its prime ingredients.

NAPLES

HOTELS

L'Albergo del Purgatorio
Palazzo Marigliano
Via San Biagio dei Librai, 39
80138 Naples
Tel: (+39) 081 551 6625
Fax: (+39) 081 299 579

If you are looking to spend time in Naples, forget the luxury waterfront hotels and try a room in "purgatory" instead. This place is not for everyone —as the owner Nathalie de Saint Phalle (wife of the nephew of artist Niki de Saint Phalle) says, "it is romantic but in a particular way." With only three rooms, the hotel is part art exhibit, part North African bazaar, and part intellectual quandary. The hotel is a club, and members get first pick; only when rooms are empty are they rented out to others. "Young and curious" guests are preferred, as is anyone who appreciates contemporary art. Guests are asked to contribute a book to the library before leaving. A word of caution: It is not located in the best part of town—but then again, that's the whole point.

ROMAN
HOLIDAY

ROMA NUN FA' LA STUPIDA STASERA
DAMME 'NA MANO A FAJE DI' DDE SÌ.
SCEGLI TUTTE LE STELLE
PIÙ BRILLARELLE CHE PUOI
E 'N FRICCICO DE LUNA TUTTA PE' NNOI.
FAJE SENTÌ CH'È QUASI PRIMAVERA
MANNA LI MEJO GRILLI PE' FFÀ CRÌ-CRÌ
PRESTAME ER PONENTINO
PIÙ MALANDRINO CHE C'HAI
ROMA, RÈGEME ER MOCOLO STASERA

Rome don't be silly tonight
give me a hand to make her say "yes"
choose your brightest stars
and a sliver of moon just for us
make her feel spring is near
send the best crickets to sing "crick-crick"
lend me your most seductive breeze
Rome, please play matchmaker tonight

Verse from the song
"Roma non fa la stupida stastera," by Armando Trovajoli

**P**lotting a romantic itinerary in Rome is like looking for color in India, or energy in New York. Love and romance are everywhere in the city whose name spelled backward is "amor." Consider, for example, the skyline at Rome's northern gateway, Piazza del Popolo: Urban planning does not get any sexier than this. A 3,200-year-old obelisk (older even than Rome) imported from Egypt stands proud, thrusting toward the blue sky. Perfectly positioned behind it are two domed churches, their curves yielding and soft. The message to the first-time visitor to Rome is clear: "Welcome to the city of Mars and Venus!"

Once inside the city, you'll feel as if you have entered a forbidden, illicit, and uncharted land. Parts of the city are damp and dark, and the visitor can get lost in a maze of *vicoletti* (little streets) such as the ones that wind through the bohemian Trastevere neighborhood or the Jewish ghetto. Turn a corner, and you'll find something completely unexpected, like a gushing fountain, an oversized church facade, or an open *piazza* bathed in sunlight. The transition is sometimes so dramatic, your eyes need time to adjust. But your heart is always one beat ahead.

A significant component of the city's seductive allure is water. Rome drips, splashes, bubbles, trickles, ripples, splatters, and gurgles. After Venice, it has the best plumbing in Italy, and it's important to remember it has been so since its conception. Of the great engineering feats of the Romans—including the Pantheon and the Colosseum—none has been more overlooked than the system of aqueducts. You can only really appreciate them today where they stand above ground on the city's periphery. Tall arches support a trough that is slanted the tiniest fraction of a degree in Rome's favor to guarantee a continuous supply of water. The train tracks to the city from the south run parallel to what's left of the aqueducts. It is an awe-inspiring sight: Sunlight flickers from between the arches like from a movie projector. Near the city walls the aqueducts descend underground and plug into a complex web of tunnels, pipes, and underground exchanges that no person in two millennia has completely understood. Barbarians and warlords used the tunnels for surprise attacks on Rome, and during World War II rumors of an "underground" city caught the imagination of resistance fighters. Whatever is down there deep under your feet, it miraculously still works. The Acqua Virgo aqueduct that supplies water to about a dozen fountains in Rome and terminates at the Trevi fountain has been functional since the age of the Caesars.

Given all that, it should come as no surprise to find that Romans are a libidinous lot. There is a funny reference to this in Jim Jarmusch's film *Night on Earth*. As taxi driver Roberto Benigni makes his rounds of Rome, with a priest in the back seat of his cab no less, he drives by couples making love against ancient walls, lampposts, and on park benches. Walk through Villa Borghese or by the lookout point at the Gianicolo hill and you will see similar scenes. It's a wonder the population figures don't skyrocket. That's part of what makes this city an aphrodisiac for foreigners: No matter how hard we fight it, our driving instinct when in Rome, is to do as the Romans do.

❧ THE TEN HILLS OF ROME ❧

Because Rome generously offers so much for lovers to see, and because there are so many excellent guidebooks that detail the city's monuments, I propose a tour of Rome's legendary seven hills (three were added later as the city limits expanded) with special attention to the love stories associated with them. Although the hills have been worn down and run together, and thus may be hard to identify, they are: the Palatine, Capitoline, Quirinal, Viminal, Esquiline, Caelian, and Aventine hills, loosely reflecting the names of the seven planets that the Romans could identify—the Sun, Moon, Mars, Mercury, Jupiter, Venus, and Saturn.

PALATINE HILL (PALATINO)

Located between the Colosseum, Circus Maximus, and the Roman Forum, the Palatine hill is where Rome came into being. According to the well-known legend, one day an old shepherd came across a she-wolf suckling two human infants. The man took the boys home and named them Romulus and Remus. As young adults, they founded a new city, but conflict arose when the two tried to agree on a name for their town. They decided that whoever could count the most birds overhead would have the final word. Romulus won and called it Roma, marking its perimeter at the Palatine hill. But he took his victory a step further and announced that no one could enter his town without first obtaining permission. Astonished by his brother's arrogance, Remus defied the ban and crossed the border. Romulus pulled out a sword, killed his twin, and pledged to destroy anyone who would insult the name of Rome.

Romulus and Remus had a distant relative named Venus, who was also a "relative" of the Caesars. And, of course, that kind of genealogy makes the goddess of love an important figure in Eternal Rome. The largest and most beautiful temple—the only one with ten columns—was built to honor her and her divine sister, the goddess Roma, a personification of the city. From this curiously "two-sided" temple, a statue of Venus looked east toward the Colosseum, and a statue of Roma faced west toward the Forum. Emperor Hadrian designed the building himself, and during its construction the "colossus Nero" (a gigantic bronze statue of Nero) had to be moved aside by twenty-four elephants. Hadrian was so pleased with his double-facing temple that he invited the most celebrated architect of the time, Apollodorus, to admire his work. It is said the Greek remarked that the ceilings were too low and if "the goddesses wanted to stand up, they'd bump their heads." Hadrian didn't think much of the criticism, of course, and ordered Apollodorus's execution. Today the church of Santa Francesca Romana is built into the temple's ruins.

CAPITOLINE HILL (CAPITOLINO)

This hill marks the heart of Rome and is home to the town hall where many civil wedding ceremonies are held. It sits snugly behind the Vittoriano, or the Altar of the Nation—an immense white building with no practical purpose to speak of. Modern Romans dismiss it as variously the "typewriter" or the "wedding cake."

According to legend, a human head was discovered on this hill, and the finding was interpreted to mean that Rome would one day become *Caput Mundi*, or "head" of the world. The hill was baptized "Capitolium" and is a root of our English word *capitol*. On this sacred site Romans built a monumental temple to their favorite god, Jupiter, ruler of the universe; he is god of light and sky and protector of the state, and his temple was the center of Roman political life. Jupiter was brother and husband of Juno Moneta, the guardian of female spirits. A temple was built for her on an adjacent site, and women would go there to mull over personal problems.

The site of her temple is now occupied by the church of Santa Maria in Aracoeli. This stern brick building seems to stare down at the visitor from the top of 124 steps. It's worth climbing up these ancient stairs (they were taken from a Roman temple to the sun elsewhere in the city) for two reasons. The first is to see the Santo Bambino, a little wooden statue that has been attributed with miraculous healing powers. He is covered in jewelry and letters from people, especially children, who write with personal issues the same way women once communicated with Juno Moneta. Some letters are simply addressed: "Il Bambino, Roma."

A second reason to visit is for the della Valle family chapel, which houses the remains of one of the world's strangest love stories. In the seventeenth century Pietro della Valle had his heart crushed by a young woman. As a distraction, his family sent him on a tour of Egypt, where the young man climbed to the pinnacle of the Great Pyramid to carve his lover's name into the stone. As soon as he did this, he was free to love again, and that's when he met a young Syrian beauty named Gioreda Manni. Pietro fell madly in love for the second time and married her in Baghdad. She died just a few years later in the Persian city Persepolis. Heartbroken, Pietro placed her body in a coffin and vowed never to part with it. He traveled across Iran, in the heat and sun, from Shiraz to India. He was on the road for five years before he brought Gioreda to Rome for burial in this chapel. Thankfully, this story has a happy ending. Gioreda's best friend had accompanied him throughout his travels to grieve at his side. As soon as Gioreda was buried, he fell in love with her.

Capitoline hill overlooks a flat area known as Campus Martius, or "Field of Mars." It extends from the Vatican to Piazza del Popolo and the Spanish Steps, and it is Rome's Renaissance and Baroque headquarters.

Close to Piazza del Campidoglio are the Jewish ghetto and the delicate Fontana delle Tartarughe (or "turtle fountain"), on Piazza Mattei. The fountain depicts four young boys gently nudging four tortoises up to a basin of water. Legend tells it was built in a single night, when the Duke of Mattei lost a good portion of his family fortune to bad investments and nearly lost his fiancée as a result. He commissioned two artists to install the fountain as a way of showing the girl's father he was still capable of great things; the move worked, and he was quickly married.

Beyond the ghetto is Santa Maria in Cosmedin and the infamous Bocca della Verità (Mouth of Truth). Located in the portico of the church, this grotesque face is said to have the power to sniff out liars. In the Middle Ages businessmen, politicians, and, of course, lovers would swear oaths here with one hand inside the Mouth of Truth. If they told the truth, they kept their hand; if they didn't, presumably it would be "bitten" off. If you have doubts about your partner, you might consider taking advantage of this service.

Past Largo Argentina is the delightful neighborhood that surrounds Campo de' Fiori (Field of Flowers). This is everybody's favorite Roman *piazza*, and the city's liveliest. Each morning it is home to a bustling fruit and vegetable market, and at night the cluster of wine bars located on its perimeter attracts a merry crowd. Thanks to the sociable nature of this

square, Rome never has had much need for dating services or clubs for singles; even its name—Campo de' Fiori—alludes to this.

On the opposite side of corso Vittorio Emanuele II are Rome's most beautiful squares: Piazza Navona, and the square in front of the Pantheon. The elliptical Navona is reason enough to visit Rome. The sensuous curves of this Baroque square and the omnipresent sound of gushing water make this the greatest of Italian *piazze*. Like an outdoor theater, it has been the stage of Rome's comedies and tragedies. The rival architects Gianlorenzo Bernini and Francesco Borromini, and the feuds between them, shaped it.

In 1651 Pope Innocent X held a contest for a central monument to be built in Piazza Navona. Borromini assumed he would clinch the contract, but Bernini stole it by dangling, literally, his proposition before the pope. Flamboyant and carefree Bernini coerced the pope's favorite sister-in-law, Olimpia Maidalchini, to wear a silver model of the fountain he envisaged around her neck. The chain was carefully calculated to allow the shiny medallion to fall squarely between her breasts. Presumably, the pope studied the necklace over the course of a night, and the next morning Bernini was commissioned to build the Fountain of the Four Rivers. Poor Olimpia, however, ended with her name forever distorted as Olim Pia, or Latin for "she *was* virtuous."

On the north side of Piazza Navona, at the foot of via dei Coronari (one of the ancient main arteries used by pilgrims on their way to the Vatican) is the enchanting Piazza Fiammetta. Its name means "little flame"—and here stands a small house where another pope kept his lover, a redhead reportedly with a fiery libido.

Not far is the Pantheon, perhaps the city's most romantic monument. Ironically, the dome-shaped building, which looks like a spaceship hovering over the city, could be mistaken for a modern building. It is, in fact, the best-preserved edifice of ancient Rome, built by Emperor Hadrian in the second century AD. It is also an architectural puzzle, with a rotunda

A ROMAN VALENTINE

The ancient Romans are associated with humanities, language, and the arts. When it comes to their concept of love, you may envisage toga-clad poets by reflecting pools, plucking verses from their sentimental repertoire to exult the cult of Venus. Nothing could be further from the truth. To the Romans, the dance between yearning hearts was as tender as gladiators wielding spiked balls at each other in the Colosseum. Roman lovers described themselves as "wounded," "wretched," and "enslaved by their lovers." Loving was described as "having your bone marrow on fire," or "suffering from double vision." Unconditional love, as a concept, is hardly mentioned; instead, a romantic valentine usually amounted to crude and vulgar phrases related to sexual organs.

of perfect proportions. The dome's 142-foot span (even greater than that of Saint Peter's Basilica) matches the 142 feet between the floor and the ceiling. Experts today are still puzzled by the complicated mathematics used to build it.

The Pantheon's most stunning feature is its *oculus*, or "eye," in its roof. Representing the sun, or the source of life, it allows a brilliant beam of light to descend to the floor and illuminate its sides. If you are in Rome during a thunderstorm, head to the Pantheon. Watching rain pour through the *oculus*, and seeing the sudden flashes of light as if you were inside a planetarium, is an unforgettable experience. A lucky few have been invited inside when there is a full moon, when the moon rests perfectly within the "eye" and moonbeams flood the massive room.

Of course, a romantic itinerary of Renaissance Rome must include the perspective-perfect Spanish Steps. A cascade of marble steps leads the eye to the Trinità dei Monti church where, as at the nearby Piazza del Popolo, a juxtaposition between obelisk and twin church domes proves to be Eros-inspired architecture.

Piazza di Spagna has a long history as a place where lovers met. In the eighteenth century English Romantics on the obligatory "Grand Tour" of Italy invaded the neighborhood, and the *ciociare*, or young women from the countryside, loitered around the square, dressed in their folk costumes and casually exposing a glimpse of leg or a little cleavage in the hopes of attracting a foreign husband. The strategy proved too easy for some, while others became models for paintings or inspiration for poetry.

That tradition continues to this day, although the roles have changed. A young foreign woman on the Spanish Steps today has about ten seconds of breathing time before she is

rimorchiata, or "picked up," by a young Latin lover. Young Italian men sometimes travel from distant provinces to make the pilgrimage to the Spanish Steps to flirt with foreign—and preferably blond—women. During the 1950s and 1960s this trend was so rampant that there is now a sizeable population of forty-something Romans with bicultural parents.

Of the many English Romantics who colonized the area, the Spanish Steps is most associated with John Keats and Percy Bysshe Shelley. Keats arrived in 1820 hoping the dry air and soothing breezes of Rome would cure his tuberculosis. He died one year later at age twenty-seven, admiring the Spanish Steps from his window until the end. His buddy Shelley wrote a poem about his death, but he too perished shortly after in a boating accident in Liguria (see chapter seven). He left behind a widow, Mary Wollstonecraft, the author of *Frankenstein*. Other Romantics followed—Lord Byron, Alfred Tennyson, and Robert Browning—in their own quest for Rome's "sweet life." You can raise a cup in their honor at the two Victorian-inspired tearooms nearby: the Antico Caffè Greco (the oldest bar in Rome, founded in 1760) and Babington's Tea Rooms.

QUIRINAL HILL (QUIRINALE)

Once home to a magnificent Roman temple, today Quirinal hill is the seat of the Italian presidential palace, the Palazzo del Quirinale. Directly under the palace's shadow is a tiny square improbably fitted with a large fountain. The Fontana di Trevi, which boldly defies all sense of proportion, is sure to bring big pleasure to lovers.

You'll hear Trevi before you see it—not the sound of gentle splashing associated with urban waterworks but a violent torrent steamrolling down a mountain pass. The water (although today it is largely recycled) is the celebrated "virgin water," or *Aqua Virgo*, that is piped into the center and feeds other central fountains, including Pietro Bernini's *La Barcaccia* (the boat fountain) at the foot of the Spanish Steps. Trevi fountain marks the aqueduct's terminus, and was designed by Nicola Salvi, who ruined his health and died in 1751 because of the extended time spent working underground in the damp aqueduct. He never saw the fountain completed.

Myths connected with this "soft and pure" water abound. Drinking the "virgin water" is associated with all kinds of benefits—from better physical health to happiness. It was once said that if you sipped from the fountain's rim, you would return to Rome, and over the years that tradition somehow morphed into: "Throw a coin in the fountain, and you will return to Rome." Today Trevi is inundated by tourists pouring pocket change into its basin. I have deposited one coin in the watery chest each time I was preparing to leave Rome, and I can assure you it works.

Despite its age, Trevi fountain came into its own only recently thanks to the director Federico Fellini, who selected the Baroque background to enhance the voluptuous beauty of the actress Anita Ekberg in the 1960 movie *La Dolce Vita*. The ironically titled film chronicles the decadence of Italy's economic boom years. Ekberg, in this fountain, symbolizes the clarity and innocence Italy was losing. She wets her body in the "virgin water" and begs the character of Marcello Mastroianni to join her, but he only watches. Ekberg is Venus, and her image flashes before the eyes of most of the people who have visited Trevi fountain since the movie's release.

In 1991 the Trevi fountain was reopened after an intense cleaning. To mark the occasion, the Italian state broadcasting agency organized a primetime television event and invited Ekberg to be a guest. Late that night, when the lights and cameras were turned off and the crowds had left, I happened to be walking by the fountain on my way home. The tiny square was empty and quiet until a black car pulled up front: From it, the aged actress herself emerged. She walked to the fountain's basin, stopped to admire it, and to my delight stepped knee-deep inside its water. I am sure she thought no one was watching her.

VIMINAL HILL (VIMINALE)

Viminal is a smaller ridge between the Quirinal and Esquiline hills, and is home to one of Rome's most picturesque neighborhoods and one of the best places for wandering. Wedged between the Colosseum and the Forum is the *suburra*, or great slum, as it was known to its ancient residents. Home to prostitutes, gypsies, and thieves, it was the place where Julius Caesar sent his troops to unwind after battle. More than 2,000 years later police still occasionally raid illegal brothels tucked away there. Now called Rione Monti, Rome's oldest working-class quarter is regarded by many as the most authentic—and tourist-free—in the city. Modern romantics intent on venturing off the beaten path will find the real Rome here.

In the square-mile neighborhood, you're likely to encounter snippets of Italian life from a bygone era. Residents of top-floor apartments, reluctant to climb three or four flights in the heat, let down wicker baskets from their windows by rope and yell down their orders to nearby shopkeepers, who fill them. Once a month, a man circles the streets with a tiny motorized cart to sharpen dull cutlery and fix broken umbrellas. If you look closely at the houses, they are a cross-section of architectural history. You might see remnants of ancient Roman columns at the foundations, with taller stories from the Renaissance, and a 1950s concrete roof terrace.

ESQUILINE HILL (ESQUILINO)

Esquiline is one of the largest hills, between the Viminal and Caelian hills. In the neighborhood are the remains of Nero's *Domus Aurea*, or "Golden House," perhaps the most extravagant monument to self-indulgence ever erected. The original estate covered one-third of Rome, with 250 rooms, vineyards, an artificial lake, a zoo, and even a revolving octagonal hall meant to represent the planetary system, in which Nero's chair was positioned as the "sun." Nero confiscated the land after the great fire of 64 AD destroyed much of the city. This infamous ruler—whom many suspect of having ordered the destructive blaze—is one of history's most conniving, chemically imbalanced, megalomaniacal, and sexually devious personalities. Nevertheless, the Venus, Cupid, and Mars frescoes and floral motifs in his golden palace later inspired Renaissance masters such as Raphael, and you can reserve a visit to admire them for yourself.

Nero rose to power thanks to his mother, Agrippina, who killed her second husband Claudius so that she could put Nero on the throne at age sixteen. Some historians believe Nero and Agrippina were also lovers: It is said that evidence of his affection was found on her clothing after the couple emerged from a chariot together, much like the "blue dress" that was evidence against President Bill Clinton. Nero's affections for his mother were short-lived. He eventually murdered her, as he did two of his three wives (one of whom is said to have been pregnant). His rampage included anyone who would not satisfy his debauched and depraved desires.

ROMANTIC ROME

Most romantic **FOUNTAIN**: Fontana delle Tartarughe, Piazza Mattei
Most romantic **BRIDGE:** Ponte Sisto
Most romantic **PIAZZA:** Piazza Navona
Most romantic **PLACE TO BE IN THE RAIN:** the Pantheon
Most romantic **NEIGHBORHOOD:** Rione Monti
Most romantic **PARK:** Villa Sciarra
Most romantic **LOOKOUT POINT:** Gianicolo
Most romantic **WALK:** Via Appia

Those who had the good fortune to be spared were kept as sex slaves to add spice to his frequent frolicsome banquets at the Golden House. Condemned to death by the Senate, Nero killed himself in 68 AD by cutting his throat. His last words were, "What an artist I destroy."

CAELIAN HILL (CELIO)

The Caelian is the southernmost of the hills and spans from the church of San Giovanni in Laterano to the Colosseum. It is also roughly where the via Appia Antica—or the *Regina Viarum*, the "queen" of all Roman trade roads—starts its long journey south to Brindisi and the gateway to the East. This stone-paved road, measured to allow five soldiers to march abreast or two carriages to pass each other, is today a popular weekend destination for cycling and walking. On Sunday it is closed to vehicular traffic, becoming for pedestrians an oasis of antiquity that has been surprisingly well preserved over two millennia.

The via Appia is one of those extraordinary places that remains etched in your mind, like a painting or photograph, or the memory of the face of someone dear to you. Majestic umbrella pines and fields of red poppies flank segments of the road, and in regular intervals you encounter Roman ruins: a headless statue, a column, a tomb (the Romans buried their dead outside the city along trade routes). This is a corridor of archaeology that walks you back in time. And, in some inexplicable way, it also overwhelms you with a profound sense of nostalgia.

Among many tombs on the via Appia, the most impressive is one of a young woman named Cecilia Metella. Little is known about her, other than that she was the daughter-in-law of Crassus, one of the richest men in Rome. No one seems to know why she was given such a large and important mausoleum. The mystery surrounding her roused the imagination of the British traveler and poet Lord Byron, who mused:

> But who was she, the lady of the dead,
> Tomb'd in a palace? Was she chaste and fair?
> Worthy a king's—or more—a Roman's bed?

If a place can be an aphrodisiac, the via Appia is the most potent arrow in cupid's quiver. If you come late in the day when the afternoon sun paints the ruins in a golden light, you will see couples amiably chatting and holding hands. If you remain after sunset, you will find dozens of cars with steamed windows parked along the way. Via Appia is the city's most frequented outdoor bedroom, and it has been reserved by lovers throughout the centuries.

AVENTINE HILL (AVENTINO)

The Aventine Hill, the last of the seven hills, is separated from the Palatine by the valley of the Circus Maximus. It is a residential area today, with a public rose garden and a very famous keyhole. Ask for the Priorato di Malta, or the residence of the Grand Master of the Order of the Knights of Malta, and peek through the tiny opening in the outer wooden door. Your eye will be trained on a perfect view of the dome of Saint Peter's Basilica framed in the keyhole.

Near the Aventino are the Pyramid of Cestius and the Protestant Cemetery. The latter is the final resting place for the remains of some 4,000 people, including Romantics John Keats, Percy Bysshe Shelley, and his son William, and Goethe's son.

THE LAST THREE HILLS

The three most recent hills to be annexed by Rome are the Pincian hill (Pincio), the Janiculum hill (Gianicolo), and the Vatican hill (Vaticano). The panoramic views of the cityscape from both Pincio and Gianicolo make them favorite spots for amorous couples.

The Pincio, which is part of the enormous Villa Borghese park, overlooks Piazza del Popolo and the Campus Martius. In antiquity it was referred to as the Collis Hortolorum, or "hill of gardens." Luckily, it has remained green and today includes lakes, moss-covered statues, and paths for running and cycling. In the summer its open fields are dotted with young couples locked in affectionate embraces, finding here the privacy they lack at home.

The Gianicolo rises on the northwestern side of Rome, on the opposite side of the mud-tinged Tiber River and beyond the magnificent Castel Sant'Angelo and the angel-lined bridge of the same name. It once marked the edge of the city, and in times of war a flag was planted here to signify to the enemy waiting on the other side that Rome was ready to take them on.

Lovers can climb to its panoramic platform for spectacular views of the city at sunset, or stroll through the nearby Villa Sciarra park, an enchanting little maze of rose-covered pergolas, fin de siècle nymph and cherub statues, and isolated park benches. Sadly, the gates close at dusk.

The Vatican state and Saint Peter's Basilica occupy the last of Rome's "hills." Saint Peter, patron of Rome, was crucified on the Vatican hill in 64 AD, and since that year this spot has marked the very core of the Christian world. Despite its various transformations, the church has never missed a service in more than a millennium, and has performed countless marriage ceremonies (if you are interested in getting married here, see chapter eleven). The artistic treasures stored within the Vatican's walls are so numerous, no one has tallied them. Despite its spiritual and artistic importance, the Vatican is not often associated with women, many of whom have been relegated throughout history to the roles of nun or nurse. This may be a temple to love, but it is also a fortress against Venus.

WE OTHERS

There is one quarter of Rome where the pagan appreciation for good food, plenty of wine, beautiful women, and easy living is still going strong. Trastevere means "the other side of the Tiber," and its inhabitants distance themselves from the rest of Rome by referring to themselves as *noialtri*, or "we others."

You can cross the lusciously romantic Ponte Sisto—the only bridge in the city not open to cars—to the Trastevere banks at Piazza Trilussa. From there, a labyrinth of tight streets and poorly illuminated taverns lure you into the heart of this bohemian quarter. Trastevere once took pride in being a colony of former thieves and misfits, but today it is home to a large English-speaking component of artists, intellectuals, and wannabes.

Within its damp and dark streets, you will find at least one love story worth telling. Inside the church of Santa Maria in Trastevere, with its unique mosaic-covered facade, is a small chapel to the Madonna della Clemenza ("clemency"). It was built by Cardinal Altemps for his son, who was beheaded. Roberto Altemps was married to the daughter of the noble Orsini family, but he fell in love with a poor local girl. Unfortunately, he was the chain linking two politically significant families, and such adulterous behavior could not be tolerated. At twenty, he was imprisoned for three years, tortured, and eventually decapitated by an order of Pope Sixtus V. His parents built the chapel to clemency and to beg the pope's forgiveness— but that never came. The ghost of Roberto's restless soul is said to lurk in the heart of Trastevere.

'NAMO A MANGIÀ

Rome's culinary specialties are not for the faint-hearted; they come from a poor people's tradition in which fresh meat was not always available. In its place are macabre meals consisting of usually discarded parts of animals, deep-fried or served in a sauce. Among the favorite such dishes are *cervello fritto* (golf ball–sized fried patties of sheep brains), *trippa alla romana* (slices of calf intestines smothered in tomato sauce), *lingua di vitella in salsa piccante* (pickled lamb's tongue), and stewed ox tail. Some of the city's most refined cuisine comes from Rome's Jewish ghetto. The *carciofo alla giudia*, or crispy artichoke fried with its leaves opened like a sunflower, is perhaps the single most delightful vegetable dish in Italy.

CUPID'S CORNERS

RESTAURANTS

La Pergola
Rome Cavalieri Hilton
Via Cadlolo, 101
00136 Rome
Tel: (+39) 06 3509 2211 or 06 3509 2055
www.cavalieri-hilton.it

La Pergola guards its reputation as one of Rome's best restaurants, and it is the place to go if you are looking to impress. Perched on Mount Mario, it enjoys unparalleled views of the capital and Saint Peter's dome. Be awed by the details: Even the cocktail almonds are warm. La Pergola has earned two Michelin stars and helped put Rome—a city never associated with *haute cuisine*—on the epicurean's map. Go for the seven-course gourmet menu: It changes daily, but an example of one lineup included *ricotta tortellini* with fava beans and *pecorino* cheese, an *intermezzo* of white asparagus, and lamb cooked in an olive crust. Book in advance—and bring back-up credit cards.

Ristorante Camponeschi
Piazza Farnese, 50
00186 Rome
Tel: (+39) 06 687 4927
www.ristorantecamponeschi.it

Positioned regally on Piazza Farnese, Camponeschi occupies a top slot among Rome's restaurant elite. Gilded mirrors, crystal chandeliers, and an affable maître d' set a romantic tone. The menu is flashy (and expensive), including risotto with champagne and belon oysters, and lobster with black truffles and raspberry vinegar. Those thinking of popping the question would be hard-pressed to find a more suitable setting.

L'Archeologia
Via Appia Antica, 139
00179 Rome
Tel: (+39) 06 788 0494
www.larcheologia.it

Those linked in love should plan a meal at this 400-year-old farmhouse beyond the catacombs and before the tomb of Cecilia Metella on via Appia.

Once a rest station for horse-drawn carriages bringing wine to the city, l'Archeologia is an informal eating experience in an intimately romantic setting. In cold weather eat near the open hearth, and in the summer grapevines shade a lovely space outdoors. The menu delights with traditional homemade cuisine. Follow a long and leisurely lunch here with an afternoon nap in the grass among the ruins.

Il Convivio

Vicolo dei Soldati, 31
00186 Rome
Tel: (+39) 06 686 9432
www.ilconviviotroiani.com

The three Troiani brothers have carved out intimate eating nooks spanning a succession of elegant vaulted rooms, providing you with the best place to whisper sweet nothings in your lover's ear. Conveniently located north of Piazza Navona, the cuisine is refined and meticulously prepared.

Magna Roma

Via Capo d'Africa, 26
00184 Rome
Tel: (+39) 06 700 9800
www.magnaroma.com

When in Rome, eat as the ancient Romans did. The archaeologist-owner of this recently opened restaurant found 1,100 ancient recipes and decided to see what the emperors and gladiators ate. Although half of the recipes were impossible to re-create because key ingredients have vanished over time, tasty survivors include conchiclam pulli, chicken with peas on a shell, and amulatum, a rice soup with sausage and sesame seeds. One popular appetizer is polypus, or sliced octopus with garum—the oily fish-based sauce that was a staple of the ancients' cuisine. Long tables are laid with terracotta bowls, ligulae spoons, and low-hanging tablemats to be used as napkins. Toast is served with mulsum, a honey-sweetened must that the ancient Romans knocked back in frenzied Bacchanalian rites.

BARS

L'Antico Caffè della Pace

Via della Pace, 3–7
00186 Rome
Tel: (+39) 06 686 1216

This famously chic café draped in ivy sits on one of Rome's most photogenic squares, behind Piazza Navona. Wood paneling, chrome coffee machines, and wrought-iron tables give it a Grand Époque feel. It's a great place in the morning for frothy coffee drinks and cornetti (breakfast brioche), or come in the afternoon to sip colorful cocktails.

Sciam
Via del Pellegrino, 56
00186 Rome
Tel: (+39) 06 6830 8957

An irresistible hideaway for those with exotic tastes, Sciam is part tearoom, part glassware showcase, and part carpet laboratory in one. You can smoke a water pipe as if you were a traveler in Constantinople, while nibbling on hummus and tabouleh. The highlight is the labyrinth of subterranean rooms crammed with colored glass from Syria, ceiling lamps that look like clusters of grapes, and wooden boxes jammed with all sorts of treasures.

HOTELS

Hotel de Russie
Via del Babuino, 9
00187 Rome
Tel: (+39) 06 328 881
www.hotelderussie.it

This landmark hotel was recently refurbished with cupid in mind. Of Rome's romantic hotels, Russie is best prepared to welcome newlyweds: It organizes "honeymoon packages" with custom shopping or sightseeing excursions and romantic dinners for two. During warm months its fairy-tale Terrazza della Zarina with panoramic views can be reserved by one couple for a candlelight dinner among potted citrus trees. The hotel also has an excellent courtyard restaurant in which the sound of trickling water is never far.

Hotel d'Inghilterra
Via Bocca di Leone, 14
00187 Rome
Tel: (+39) 06 699 811
www.hoteldinghilterraroma.it

I spent my first night in Italy at the Hotel d'Inghilterra as a young girl, and in many ways I have not left the country since. This elegant hideaway is located at the heart of the so-called shopping "golden triangle," and I highly recommend it for lovers on a first visit to Rome. The ninety-eight rooms are tastefully decorated with antiques, and common areas include Persian

carpets, wood paneling, cloud-painted ceilings, and polychrome marble flooring. Don't miss the rooftop terrace.

Hotel Art
Via Margutta, 56
00187 Rome
Tel: (+39) 06 328 711
www.hotelart.it

Opened in February 2003, Hotel Art adds dashes of blue, orange, yellow, and green to the Roman palette while featuring works by contemporary artists. Each floor of this stylish hotel with forty-six rooms near the Spanish Steps is represented by a color. Illuminations on the "blue" floor give life to snippets of poetry, one of which reads: *la sera passeggeremo su strade parallele* ("at night we walk on parallel streets"). The lobby, a former chapel, has vaulted ceilings and is fitted with "space pods." Two white, lacquered "eggs" serve as reception desks.

Perched on a rock to the left of the port of Ponza is this impressive fifteenth-century fortress hotel. If you have not already arranged to rent a private room or apartment, this is a powerfully romantic alternative (and a great spot for a wedding, too). The hotel's top terrace is the best place in town to see the San Silverio fireworks (the manager lets nonguests up, too, if they ask). You are so close to them, you will feel the heat from each blast.

ICE CREAM AND OTHER SWEETS

Giolitti
Via Ufficio del Vicario, 40
00186 Rome
Tel: (+39) 06 699 1243
www.giolitti.it

Many gelaterie claim to be the best in Rome, and while newer places may periodically earn the title, Giolitti is always in the running. This family-run business has more than a century of history behind it. The store first sold milk, but Grandma Bernardina wanted to diversify and offer ice cream. She launched a unique advertising campaign: She sat her eight children outside, and when she was complimented on her beautiful family, she replied that their rosy cheeks and smiles came thanks to ice cream. Business boomed, and today there are hundreds of flavors to choose from—including watermelon gelato with chocolate chip "seeds."

Moriondo and Gariglio
Via Piè di Marmo, 21–22
00186 Rome
Tel: (+39) 06 699 0856

It's like stepping inside a chocolate box when you enter this 100-year-old specialty boutique. Cacao comes in all shapes and sizes and with a variety of colorful fillings, including chocolate Colosseums and marzipan candies made to look like the mimosa flowers traditionally given as gifts on March 8—Woman's Day. Why try to impress your lover with jewelry or lingerie, when you could delight him or her with a box of these indulgent chocolates?

es.hotel
Via Filippo Turati, 171
00185 Rome
Tel: (+39) 06 444 8411
Fax: (+39) 06 443 41396
www.eshotel.it

A newcomer to Rome, this hotel is artfully set against the industrial backdrop of the Termini train station. Its colors are clean and cool, and its lines are sleek and silky, and—surprise—there's an archaeological site in the foyer. Es.hotel's 235 rooms are state-of-the–art, with plasma screens, DVD players, and high-speed Internet access. The Presidential Suite is fitted with an outdoor Jacuzzi and a grass lawn.

Hotel Torre dei Borboni
04027 Ponza Isola (Latina)
Tel: (+39) 0771 80135, or 0771 809 763
Fax: (+39) 0771 809 884
www.torredeiborboni.com

❧ Beyond the Walls ❧

Part of a true Roman holiday is getting out of the city, and this is where those ancient trading roads that shoot off the city like the spokes of a bicycle wheel come in handy. Head north on the via Cassia and soon you'll see the cypress-lined hills of Tuscany. Take the via Aurelia for a few hours, and you'll end up drinking pastis on the French Riviera. The via Appia terminates in Brindisi, the port city for Greece-bound ships, and cuts through some of Italy's most beautiful scenery along the way. The Pontina veers south to the Pontine marshes and the ferry for Ponza. If the ancient Romans built all their roads to lead to Rome, they also built them to leave Rome.

The following are six suggestions for romantic day- or weekend trips within easy distance from the capital:

SATURNIA (NORTHWEST)

In ancient mythology the god Saturn was so angered by the violent nature of humans that he launched a lightening bolt to earth in a fit of fury. Where it punctured the surface, it released an explosive eruption of hot water that helped quell humanity's violent tendencies. Today, near the town of Saturnia mineral water still gushes from the earth's crust at a rate of 160 gallons per second and a temperature of 98.6 degrees Fahrenheit. Soaking in these natural thermal spas will surely soothe your stresses, too.

The ancient Romans were the first to recognize the healing powers of thermal water, and some of history's illustrious personalities become devotees. Many Italians still drink from hot springs, or sit in them and breathe in their vapors to stimulate the metabolism and relieve everything from asthma to backaches—and some say sexual prowess is increased.

What makes this natural cocktail so good for mind and soul? Thermal waters are chemically very similar to the body's own water. They're laden with natural salts, sulfur, and sodium bicarbonate and filtered through strata of flint, limestone, and clay, where they acquire traces of rare minerals. Italian doctors will tell you thermal water acts as an antitoxin for the liver, kidneys, and digestive tract. Many hot springs in Italy also offer inhalation therapy for bronchial and lung ailments and hydro massage for rheumatoid diseases. Regardless of the water's therapeutic properties, a soak in warm water in beautiful surroundings is bound to relax you.

You can enjoy Saturnia's thermal baths at two spots. A beautiful hotel resort (see details below) was built at the spring's source for those who want round-the-clock pampering, or you can soak in the bubbling water for free about one mile downstream at the Cascatelle del Mulino. Centuries of sulfuric and mineral buildup have produced natural pools that serve as natural Jacuzzis that are perfect for two.

Terme di Saturnia Spa Resort

58050 Saturnia (Grosseto)

Tel: (+39) 0564 600 111 | Fax: (+39) 0564 601 266 | www.termedisaturnia.com

This luxury "regeneration resort" offers all the wellness services of a traditional spa, plus horseback riding, tennis, and golf. Beauty treatments include plankton body wraps, hydro massage for tired feet, and mud masks for the face, as well as pore-opening steam sessions. The hotel has four thermal pools, a solarium, gym, hair salon, and even an art gallery. The excellent restaurant (with a non-smoking dining hall) has a menu for dieters. But don't worry, you'll also find plenty of hearty Tuscan fare and robust red wines if your appetite was piqued by the thermal water. This is an ideal place for lovers and honeymooners.

La Posta Vecchia

00055 Palo Laziale, Ladispoli

Tel: (+39) 06 994 9501 | Fax: (139) 06 994 9507 | www.lapostavecchia.com

Someone wrote of La Posta Vecchia, "If it's not the most beautiful house in the world, it certainly is a contender." The art enthusiast J. Paul Getty seemed to think so, and much of what you see here today is thanks to him. He dedicated five years of his life to the loving restoration of the palace, which he purchased from Prince Odescalchi in 1960. But he abandoned it—and Italy—in the 1970s with a broken heart when Red Brigade terrorists kidnapped his grandson and sent the boy's severed ear by post as part of their ransom demands. Getty made three attempts to build a swimming pool here despite the fact that the building practically sits on the sea. Each time he broke the earth, however, he discovered Roman ruins—including a villa attributed to Julius Caesar himself. Left with few options, he created an underground museum and placed his newfound treasures inside; the pool went into a living room.

BOMARZO (NORTH)

Midway between Orte and Viterbo (and easily reached from the A1 Rome-Florence *superstrada*, exit Attigliano) lies the only piece of Italy that was designed to be, well, ugly. Grotesque, really. In 1552, Count Pier Francesco (aka Vicino) Orsini, at a loss as to how to spend his money, built a nightmarish garden filled with ogres, dragons, devils, and a three-headed dog. Historians are still trying to sort out why he did this or what purpose it served. One theory is Orsini wanted to pay homage to his wife, Giulia Farnese, who died at a young age; the park, which he called his *sarco bosco* (sacred woods), may have been intended as some confused allegorical "poem" to his lost love.

My personal take is that it was intentionally designed with a healthy dose of Renaissance adrenaline to provide the world's most fantastic make-out corner. Moss-covered monsters

carved in tufa decorate the inside of the labyrinth, shaded by dense vegetation and trees. Enter a dark little room through the gaping mouth of a devil's face (the *bocca dell'inferno*, or "mouth of hell") with the words "all thoughts fly" engraved above. Nearby is a "crooked house" that, like an amusement-park ride, makes you lose all sense of balance. It's the perfect setting for a stolen kiss.

As you exit the park, you will see a provocative inscription by Orsini himself: "Consider what you have seen here and tell me if these wonders are deception or art." That afterthought makes the whole thing sound like one big joke. Perhaps it is. If this is your kind of humor, the private owners of the park do accommodate wedding receptions.

Solo Per Due

Via Villa di Orazio, 2 | 02040 Vacone (Rieti)
Tel/Fax: (+39) 0746 676 873 | Tel: (+39) 0746 676 951 (to speak in English, evenings only)
www.soloperdue.com

If I were to choose one restaurant in Italy to bring to the attention of lovers, it would be Solo Per Due. Impossible to find, and definitely not a hotbed of culinary innovation, it claims to be the world's smallest restaurant: As its name implies, it is "only for two." Open for dinner and lunch, the restaurant consists of a single, candle-lit table with two settings. Privacy is assured, and a silver bell is provided for summoning the staff. If you reserve for lunch, you can enjoy the garden and peek inside adjacent Roman ruins. At night, you can order a personalized fireworks display.

Only these walls know for sure how many marriage proposals have been pronounced here; the setting surely stirs emotions.

HADRIAN'S VILLA (EAST)

Emperor Hadrian's villa, just twenty miles (thirty-five kilometers) from Rome, may well have been the grandest construction that Italy has seen. Its grounds measured 180 acres—roughly as large as the urban center of the capital—and were filled with reproductions of the emperor's favorite monuments from abroad. In 2002, after much searching, archaeologists finally discovered a small part of the palace complex that had gone unnoticed for so many centuries. Appropriately located ten minutes' from the emperor's private headquarters is the temple to Antinous, Hadrian's lover.

For political reasons, at the age of twenty-four Hadrian married thirteen-year-old Sabina, the great-niece of Emperor Trajan. However, he met the real love of his life years later, during a tour of the Roman provinces in Asia Minor. When Antinous tragically drowned in the Nile River, the emperor's affections became clear. Hadrian declared him a god and founded the city of Antinopolis in Egypt on the very spot where his body washed ashore, and statues of the boy were erected throughout the Roman Empire.

Just a few miles away, the fountains of Tivoli at Villa d'Este spurt and splash. This Renaissance wonderland is a spectacular example of humankind's ability to channel and tame water, and it makes for a memorable romantic daytrip.

CASTELLI ROMANI (SOUTHEAST)

In Rome's backyard are a cluster of *castelli*, or "castles"—the towns of the Albano Hills, which offer all the laidback charm of the country within twenty miles (thirty kilometers) of Rome. More important, they provide the capital with its wine. Closest is Frascati, famous for its sociable but decidedly unsophisticated white wine. Nearby is Grottaferrata, and past that is Marino, the latter firmly embedded in the collective imagination of Roman wine aficionados for its harvest festival. On the first Sunday of each October, Marino celebrates its harvest, and wine instead of water pours from the municipal fountains. This celebration of abundance and fertility has inspired the liveliest Roman folksong— undoubtedly written by a down-and-out songwriter who came here and couldn't believe his good luck. The via dei Laghi leads to the lip of a huge volcanic lake that is character- ized by its dark blue water, and perched near the hills' highest point is Rocca di Papa. After Marino you'll pass by Castel Gandolfo, where the pope has his summer residence; next comes Albano, and furthest to the south is Velletri. On the first Sunday of June, Nemi cel- ebrates a feast dedicated to the tiny wild strawberries, *fragoline di bosco*, that grow in this microclimate. On the third Sunday of June, Genzano holds the lovely *l'infiorata*, in which a carpet of flowers is laid down on the main road through town, via Belardi.

Antica Locanda lo Specchio di Diana

Via Corso Vittorio Emanuele, 13 | 00040 Nemi (Rome)

Tel: (+39) 06 936 8805 | Fax: (+39) 06 936 8016 | www.specchiodidiana.it

Records show that a *locanda*, or restaurant, has existed on this enchanting site since antiquity. If you're one of the lucky few to catch a glimpse of Nemi's "three moons" from its panoramic outdoor terrace, you'll understand why couples love to eat here: It's difficult to top the romantic impact of seeing the moon in the sky above, its image in the mirrorlike surface of Lake Nemi, and the moonlight reflected in the distance off the shimmering Mediterranean, all at the same time. If that isn't enough, the Antica Locanda also serves aphrodisiac *fragoline* on cream desserts, as ice cream, and pickled in *grappa*. Luckily, the owners were smart enough to fix up a handful of charming rooms for rent, in the likely event you decide to spend the night (the nicest is the Specchio di Diana suite). The restaurant is a popular choice for wedding receptions in the area.

SPERLONGA (SOUTH)

The sloping whitewashed village of Sperlonga is a world apart, only three hours' drive south of Rome. Along the road here, you cross over that invisible line that marks the start of southern Italy.

This is not a five-star resort town but instead an opportunity to indulge in the natural decadences of Italy in their most distilled form. It's about eating a ripe fig directly from the tree and snacking on sweet tomatoes as if they were cherries, or examining individual grains of crystalline sand under the shade of a beach umbrella and peering down at toes while chest-deep in clear water. It's for those who already have the romance of Italy inside them.

Special offshore currents give Sperlonga some of the clearest water in the Mediterranean. You can rent umbrellas on the beaches below the town, but for more dramatic scenery head six miles (ten kilometers) south on Highway 213 (or via Flacca), past the two tunnels and the flat beach with campers. Look for the wooden *spiaggia libera* sign, or ask for the beach everyone affectionately refers to as the *trecento scalini* (three hundred stairs). At the bottom, either turn right for the family beach, or turn left for the nudist beach (definitely more entertaining).

Aperitivo hour is best spent on Sperlonga's main square, where bathing beauties mingle with old women shrouded in black. Make sure to take a walk through the narrow lanes of Sperlonga'a oldest quarter. Throughout history, the town's biggest threat came in the form of Saracen pirates. On August 8, 1534, legendary warlord Khayr ad-Din Barbarossa (Red Beard) attacked Sperlonga in a failed attempt to kidnap a beautiful countess for his harem. The bloody battle is memorialized in a fresco about 300 feet (100 meters) past the town square, and to the right it is explained how the countess outsmarted the pirate: *sola scampassi, furba la sciantosa* (female intuition saves her).

Ristoro Arenanta

Strada Statale via Flacca, kilometer 23,900 | 04029 Gaeta (Latina)

Tel: (+39) 0771 740 327

The best mozzarella on earth is served at this roadside shack about six miles (ten kilometers) south of Sperlonga (you'll recognize it on the right by the "*mozzarella di bufala*" sign). The bigger the mozzarella is, the tastier it is thought to be (see chapter twelve). Here they are so huge, each person is served only half a ball on a plastic plate smothered with tomatoes, basil, and a *filo* (thread) of golden olive oil. Press down on your cheese and watch the heavenly cream ooze out, ready to be sponged up with your bread. The experience is made more divine by Ristoro Arenanta's location. From the elongated wooden tables under a leafy canopy, you can peer down at sparkling beaches hundreds of feet below.

Ristorante Gli Archi

Via Ottaviano, 17 | 04029 Sperlonga (Latina)

Tel: (+39) 0771 548 300 | Fax: (+39) 0771 557 035 | www.gliarchi.com

Inside a former animal stall to the right of the main square is what many consider to be Sperlonga's best restaurant. In an outdoor patio, framed by bougainvillea, you can feast on *salmone marinato* (marinated salmon), stuffed mussels, *risotto alla crema di scampi* (risotto with a delectably creamy prawn sauce), or *tagliolini Gli Archi*—the house pasta topped with an abundance of fresh seafood. Order an appetizer plate, and within minutes the entire surface of your table will be covered with the sea's best.

THE PONTINE ISLANDS (SOUTH)

Multiply the magic of Sperlonga by ten, and you get Ponza. This is the largest of the five volcanic islands that make up the Pontine Archipelago and is a favorite vacation spot for fashionable Romans. The ideal time to come is around June 20, when the entire island gears up for the feast of their patron saint, San Silverio—half the population of this island is named either Silverio or Silveria in his honor. To celebrate, Ponza employs the services of Naples's best pyrotechnics to choreograph a complicated fireworks display directly above the tiny harbor. The show is unforgettable, with glowing embers that rain down on the black sea and an explosive grand finale in which gigantic red hearts are burned into the sky.

The best way to see Ponza is by boat. A rusty old school bus will trek out to the distant, more coveted beaches, but nothing replaces the experience of hugging the shoreline in a small watercraft. You can rent a fishing boat with a "captain" to take you on the grand tour, or chart your own course in a motorized vessel if you're feeling adventurous. Dive off the boat and explore marine caves or sunken ships with a pair of swimming goggles and fins. My most memorable moment was being shown how to detach sea urchins from the rocks and eat them raw. You can circle the whole island in a day and see the Piscine, a stunning chain of "pools" formed in the volcanic rock, visit Frontone beach with the remains of ancient swimming holes carved by the Romans, and admire the Chiaia di Luna Bay (a "moonlit" crescent-shaped beach).

At Ponza's port you can also hire a boat to go to Isola di Palmarola. The island is uninhabited, except for the curious O'Francese restaurant, which also rents spartan rooms for overnight stays (tel: +39 0771 808 417, or +39 081 866 1006). It is just one tiny step removed from being completely alone on a deserted Mediterranean island.

To the south is another uninhabited island: Ventotene, the island that Emperor Augustus's daughter, Julia, selected for her amorous rendezvous with her army of many lovers. Once the secret was out, however, she was punished and sent to exile here; today you can visit the remains of her love nest–turned-prison.

Boats to Ponza leave from Anzio or Formia (an eighty-minute train ride from Rome). From Anzio, the hydrofoil takes about eighty minutes, and the slow boat is two and a half hours. From Formia, a fast boat takes about an hour.

SARDINIA: SUN, SEA, AND PINK SAND

AMORE E TÙSSI NON
SI PODIRI CUAI

Love and coughing are
two things you can't hide.

Sardinian proverb

As if Italy weren't perfect enough, it has Sardinia, too. Hands down, Sardinia has the most amazing beaches in Italy—if not in Europe—and many swear it beats the Caribbean, too. Ironically, Sardinians only recently learned to love their coastline. As a result, resort areas were carefully developed within the past few decades with the modern service industry in mind. What does that mean for today's visitor? Three words: pampering, pampering, and pampering. That's what makes Sardinia perfect for romance.

Beyond the bright lights of Porto Cervo's yacht parties, the island is home to what has been called a "silent civilization." History has doled out repeated hardship in the form of foreign invaders: the Phoenicians, Carthaginians, Romans, Byzantines, Saracens, Pisans, and Genovese, the Aragons of Spain, and the Austrians all marched through before the island went to the House of Savoy. Arab pirates terrorized locals with surprise raids and ruthless violence for so long that Sardinians got into the habit of building their cities inland for protection. They developed an insular approach, and what filtered in from abroad was immediately embraced as part of the local identity. Popular rites and festivals are draped in mystery and borrow elements from distant cultures and religions. Wooden masks (*Mamuthones*) used around Nuoro are unmistakably African, and the western coast is home to religious processions first practiced in Spain. Many popular celebrations focus on equestrian exhibitions, suggesting they originated when locals were most concerned with outrunning invaders. Many more are dedicated to fertility and reproduction. Generations of shepherds developed strong links to the earth and mountains, but little interest in the sea. In fact, they never fully embraced fishing, and this is reflected on local restaurant menus.

This chapter focuses on the northern half of Sardinia, spanning from Alghero, arcing around the northern tip, the La Maddalena Archipelago, and the Costa Smeralda to the Gulf of Orosei on the eastern side. Within this territory are important ports of call, such as Alghero for those coming by air from London, and Olbia for those coming by ferry from the Italian mainland. You can rent a motorcycle or car and drive around the 9,000-square-mile (24,000-square-kilometer) island comfortably in two weeks, or charter a boat and search for your personal paradise in a smaller area. Sardinia is packed with exciting offerings, making it the ideal destination for couples who want to disappear on a Mediterranean island and be indulged.

Alghero and
✣ la Riviera del Corallo ✣

On the west side of the island, the fortified city of Alghero protectively overlooks the Sea of Sardinia. It has two aspects that make it irresistible: It is one of Italy's few historic cities built on the water's edge, and it is unlike anything you will see in Sardinia. Alghero, whose name is derived from the word *alghe* (seaweed), was under Spanish rule for so long that a Catalan personality supplanted its Italian one. Yellow and red flags fly where you'd expect to see Italy's *tricolore*, and the local language has the fiery sassiness of the Iberian Peninsula. Algherese, an archaic form of Catalan, is the voice of traditional love poems and ballads called *romanços* that spawned a cultural movement know as the *Renaixença Algueresa*.

First and foremost a fishing village, Alghero has thick protective walls that were installed by the Genovese, who understood its strategic importance. In 1353 Alghero was conquered by the Catalans and the Aragonese, and it remained in Spanish hands for about four centuries. The first step taken by the new government was to expel the Sardinian and Genovese population, and Alghero—or Alghè, in *Algherese*—grew to become a proud Catalan colony.

Dimly lit streets cut through the center from the Baroque church of San Michele to the cathedral, but Alghero's most romantic walking itinerary is along the ancient twelfth-century ramparts, from Torre de l'Esperó Reial to Torre della Polveriera. At night you can watch the

reflections of the city lights dance on the black water there or, closer to the port, sip cocktails outdoors at the Café Latino, which may be Sardinia's most picturesque watering hole.

Couples in the market for a love token will find fertile shopping grounds in Alghero. The area is home to a unique coral with colors ranging from ox-blood to the lighter *pelle d'angelo* (skin of an angel). The coral grows more than 300 feet (100 meters) below the surface, and for centuries young divers from Alghero have risked their lives to harvest it. Its fan-shaped branches are broken off and carved into beads, earrings, and lucky charms. Pendants made from coral are believed to be extremely effective against the evil eye— particularly those of envious ex-lovers, so if a jealous ex lurks in your background, you might want to consider investing in the red jewelry. If you do buy coral, make sure you get a certificate guaranteeing it is from Sardinia.

Boats leave Alghero regularly for excursions to the Grotta di Nettuno, passing along fifteen miles (twenty-four kilometers) of spectacular scenery. Sheer cliffs jut out from the sea, past Capo Caccia and around to Cala d'Inferno, or "Hell's Inlet." Inside this mass of rock is the underground La Marmora Lake, formed some 135 million years ago. When the Duke of Buckingham visited the cave, he described it as "the miracle of the gods."

❧ STINTINO TO THE NORTHERN TIP ❧

At Sardinia's northwestern corner is a spur of land pointing at Isola Asinara. At the tip is Stintino, home to what many Italians consider to be their country's best beach. Although the Torre della Pelosa, a sixteenth-century tower meant to deter Arab pirates determined to collect Sardinian slaves, stands in the background, it is the sight of La Pelosa beach that will knock you out. The expanse of white sand descends gently beneath the waterline, like the hum of a piano recital's last chord. You can walk a few hundred feet out before the water reaches your hips. Locals also claim that the white sand gives sunbathers a unique tan that lasts longer and is a deeper brown in color. Unfortunately, word has gotten out, and the crowding is made worse by the fact that changing tides have carried away much of La Pelosa's, and nearby La Pelosetta's, precious sand, making the beach areas smaller.

For more privacy, make reservations to visit Asinara Island. Because it is a protected national park, authorities will only allow 300 visitors per day, and if you come in the off-season you could get this stunning island to yourself. Your only other companions will be the rare blue-eyed white donkeys that live here, after which the island is named. Asinara has a secretive and difficult past that has helped shape its current mystique. First it was a colony for people infected with cholera, and then until 1997 it was used as a penitentiary for Mafiosi and drug kingpins. Among the prisoners detained in 1938 was a real-life Venus from Ethiopia. Rounded up with other exiles, the daughter of Negus Ailè Selassiè was so beautiful she was nicknamed Melograno d'Oro (Golden Pomegranate). Tragically, she died only a few days before the Ethiopian prisoners were liberated.

Back on Sardinia, the road to Costa del Paradiso and the Gallura region passes Porto Torres and the citadel of Castelsardo. Along with Alghero, Castelsardo is likely to be the only other "old town" you'll see on the northern coast. Located on a huge rock that protrudes into the sea, Castelsardo is visually stunning, but not entirely inviting. Actually, it's a bit spooky. Its streets are quiet, and lead to an oversize stone castle. On Easter Monday Castelsardo celebrates the *Processione del Lunissanti*, a festival with roots in Spain, in which figures dressed in white robes with pointed hoods parade through candle-lit streets chanting Sardinian hymns.

Sardinia has myriad other folk festivals, such as Sassari's *Cavalcata Sarda* horsemanship test and the *Li Candereri* festival, when oversize candelabras are paraded through town. But the most curious of all is held on Carnival Sunday and Fat Tuesday in the town of Oristano. Also traced back to Spain and influenced by pagans, la *Sartiglia* (from *sortija*, or Catalan for "ring") is part equestrian event and part fertility rite. A horseman representing purity and bravery is selected and carefully dressed by virgins in a top hat and lace, with buttonless clothing sewn onto his body. He is then given a mask with a female face, and is thus transformed into an androgynous demigod figure. He is lowered onto a horse, not allowed to touch the ground because that would presumably deplete the magic power. In this complex ceremony, the androgynous hero gallops through town along with assistants who carry violets, called *sa pippia de maju* (May children), a symbol of spring and of fecundity. Later they ride to the cathedral square at breakneck speed and try to spear suspended stars with their swords. The success of next year's harvest rests on how many stars are collected, and the ritual is executed with extreme emotional intensity.

LAND OF SOFT ROCKS AND PINK SAND

While France's Corsica is rough and rocky past the Bocche di Bonifacio straits, Sardinia's Gallura region soothes the eye the way warm milk and honey soothe the stomach. The light seems softer here and is tinged with pink and gold. The sea is as tame as the Mediterranean will allow, and the curving rocks reflect the same softness as the clouds above. In fact, the granite is the most striking element of the panorama: It looks as if it has been sculpted by a superhuman Michelangelo.

A SARDINIAN CINDERELLA

Once upon a time, there was a widower prince who had a daughter named Zezolla. He cared for her dearly and entrusted her to a loving governess before remarrying. But Zezolla's step-mother was an abusive witch, and the desperate girl asked the governess for help. The woman advised Zezolla to kill her stepmother and convince her father to marry the governess instead, so she would become the girl's mother, which is exactly what happened.

But before long, the former governess's tenderness turned sour, and to make matters worse, she revealed she had six daughters of her own. The six girls moved in and won the prince's attention. Zezolla was relocated to the kitchen, given rags to wear, and became so covered in soot that her teasing stepsisters called her "Cenerentola" (ash-girl). One day a white dove flew to her and said: "If you should ever need to make a wish, ask the dove of the fairies on the island of Sardinia."

It so happened that the prince soon went to Sardinia for business and asked his daughters to draw up a list of presents. They requested gowns and jewels, but Cenerentola asked only that her father relay a message to the dove of fairies. Following her instructions, he went to a grotto, met with the fairy, and received in return a date tree, a bucket, a hoe, and a silk napkin. He gave the items to his daughter, who cared for the tree and polished its leaves with the napkin. A fairy emerged and asked Cenerentola to make a wish. She wished to be noticed.

Days later, the six sisters prepared to attend a party and dressed in their best clothing. Secretly, Cenerentola visited the fairy, who transformed her into a ravishing beauty. That night a bachelor king saw her and fell in love, but Cenerentola did not reveal her identity. Other parties followed, and each time the king fell deeper in love. He ordered his servants to uncover who she was, but Cenerentola fled, leaving behind a magnificent shoe. The king prepared a feast and ordered all the women to try the shoe. It only fit Cenerentola, and she was crowned queen.

Those familiar with the G-rated version may be shocked to learn Cinderella murdered her stepmother. This version is told by Giambattista Basile, a count from Naples who traveled across Italy to collect folktales for his book, Il Pentamerone, published in 1634. Originally entitled Lo Cuntu de li Cunti ("Story of Stories"), it contained fifty fables to be told in five days. Number six was "Cenerentola," and others include first-generation accounts of Rapunzel and the goose with the golden eggs. The stories, each with a moral, were wittily written for adults in strict Neapolitan dialect, which explains why they remained preserved against manipulations over time.

A lone lighthouse on the windswept Capo Testa marks the northern tip of Sardinia. The winds and currents have done their most impressive work here, molding a lunar landscape that is best admired in Cala Luna, also called Valle della Luna. Since the 1960s the valley has been a converging point for hippies and spiritual pilgrims, many of whom live in tents between the rocks. It's not hard to understand why the Valle della Luna is said to have a special energy: It looks like a birth canal from which the rest of the world came into being, with soft, flesh-toned walls open to the sea from the valley's V-shaped opening.

A few miles in either direction of Capo Testa is the perfect place to hunt for secluded beaches. Even in high season, with a little climbing or swimming you can find a secluded inlet for sunbathing with as little on as you wish. Breathtaking beaches, such as Rena di Ponente, are to be found in Baia di Santa Reparata, and the Tibula beach, otherwise known as Spiaggia dei Graniti, is not to be missed. Tibula was the name of an ancient Roman colony and mining town where granite was carved into columns and then shipped to remote parts of the Empire. Sloppy miners tossed their defective work into the sea, and today Roman columns lie on the beach and can be seen underwater. Some of the columns in Rome's Pantheon come from nearby, as does the granite base for the Statue of Liberty in New York harbor.

YOU CAN'T MISS THEM

Scattered around Sardinia are some 7,000 *nuraghe*, the mysterious truncated towers built by the Sharden people, who were among the first settlers here and after whom the island is named. Almost nothing is known about this herder/warrior tribe or why they settled here, and less is known about the odd cylindrical buildings they built with so much zeal. Some are 4,000 years old, with thick walls that suggest a military function. They may have served as places of worship to bring people closer to the sun, and some say they are ancient tombs. One expert believes that given the prehistoric population's obsession with giants, the *nuraghe* were protective shields against the oversize feet of passing monsters.

In the south near Cagliari, at Barumini, a whole complex of connecting *nuraghe* forms a small citadel. Near Oristano mind-boggling "wells" have been cut into the earth, presumably built with techniques borrowed by the ancient Egyptians. Water was allowed into the mines, and if it froze during the winter, the pressure caused the huge blocks of rock to shatter into more manageable pieces. The *nuraghe* at di Santa Cristina are among the most puzzling, because the huge gaps in the earth suggest female organs and may have played a part in fertility rites. The underground village of Tiscali is another famous stop (and after which Italy's top Internet company is named). An enormous sinkhole created a cavern in which this entire village was built, hidden from the eyes of its enemies. Located near Dorgali, it makes a good destination for hikers in the canyon of Gorropu.

Romantics with a passion for archaeology should visit Li Mizzani, near Palau, or Li Lolghi and Coddhu Ecchju near the town of Arzachena. It is said that if you lie on the flat rocks of the *Tombe dei Giganti* (Giant's Tomb) for a few hours, magical curative powers will be passed on to you. Believers flock from all over to rest on the rocks as a cure for rheumatism and muscular and bone problems. For the locals, "muscular problems" also includes both broken hearts and impotency, and couples have been known to sneak here after dark to test the magic for themselves.

One of the biggest towns is Santa Teresa di Gallura. Founded in 1808, it has more character than the other modern seaside towns. Its attractive main square provides good options for a nightcap. Santa Teresa also is a good base from which to explore the area, including the twenty-three islands of the Arcipelago de la Maddalena, a nature reserve since 1996.

Because the archipelago and its treasure trove of hidden beaches is not accessible by land, you should either rent a private motorboat or join one of the commercial boat tours. Organized trips leave from Palau in the morning and offer a good general overview of the La Maddalena Archipelago. The boat makes its way past the islands of Santo Stefano (where the United States has a naval base), Maddalena, and Caprera toward the pools of limpid water between the smaller Budelli, Razzoli, and Santa Maria islands. After lunch, it chugs over to the island of Spargi, where you can take a nap on the gorgeous Cala Corsara beach.

The little island of Budelli is home to la Spiaggia Rosa, what may be Europe's most heavily guarded beach since the Allied landing. Over the centuries, crushed shells and coral have washed up on the beach, turning the sand a brilliant shade of pink. The sand is so unique that people began collecting it to make "beach-in-the-bottle" souvenirs. The sand loses its color when removed from saltwater, so the keepsakes are no longer made, but tragically the damage is done—the "Pink Beach" won't reach its former hues for many more centuries. To allow nature's magic to continue, guards armed with whistles patrol the beach perimeter, and no one is allowed on shore.

The boat tour ends with a vacationers' version of the Rorschach test, this one in the rock formations: You may be persuaded into seeing a "witch's head," a "bear," and—this is a stretch—an "English terrier." There is one particular rock that needs no second-guessing. Located on the backside of Razzoli—and not always included on the tour, if the winds are too strong—it has different names like la Cosa (the thing) and il Rapace (the ravenous one). In short, it's a phallic-shaped rock that stands proudly erect, pointing to the heavens. When I told the skipper that I was writing a romantic guide and wanted to see the notorious Rapace for myself, she deftly replied, "Cara mia, that thing is anything but romantic."

❊ LA COSTA SMERALDA ❊

The Emerald Coast owes a lot to the bikini. Before the French fashion house Chanel turned suntanning into the latest rage by showcasing darker models on its Paris runways, this corner of Sardinia was nothing more than rocks and grazing goats. Its beaches were deemed utterly useless. But as bathing suits grew smaller and beach crowds grew bigger, an elite group of entrepreneurs turned Sardinia's natural resources into gold.

Gold is now the coast's primary color: from the bleached blondes who accent their golden tans with gold-rimmed sunglasses, to the boutiques in posh Porto Cervo displaying windows filled with precious metals as if they were candy. Even bathroom fixtures are gilded. If to you the word *vacation* involves mints on pillows, white terrycloth bathrobes, sommeliers, and gloved waiters, this is your place.

Both Porto Cervo and Porto Rotondo, further south, represent Italy's most incredible experiments in urban planning. Porto Cervo was designed for the jet set, with a build-it-and-they-will-come attitude. And they came. Starting in 1961 Porto Cervo became Italy's "in" resort, and some five years later a group of businessmen from Venice built another town inspired by the Lagoon City—complete with a San Marco square—and called it Porto Rotondo. Both are textbook examples of a new school of architecture called neo-Mediterranean (now duplicated in Miami and Montecito), and in both cases the principal point of entry is by sea—the idea being to step off the yacht for a night on the town.

SPRINKLE ON THE LOVE DUST

Sardinia's cuisine is inspired first by shepherds, then by fishermen. Myrtle, or *mirto*, is often paired with grilled meat, and the bitter berry is also fermented into a tasty after-dinner drink, or *digestivo*. *Carta da musica* (music sheets) is a thin, crackerlike bread. Sardinia produces a cheese so "aged" that live worms wiggle inside it; their enzymes are said to improve the taste, and diehard cheese fans wouldn't dare pull them out. All of this can be washed down with an assortment of Sardinian wines, such as Cannonau, Torbato, Vernaccia di Oristano, and my favorite wine, named after the Monica grape.

In Alghero the specialty is lobster, or *aragosta alla catalana*. Among Sardinia's most important fish dishes is *bottarga*, or lobster eggs pressed and dried in the sun like raisins. It looks like a powder, or may be shaved off in flakes, and it is used on pasta. Bottarga has a strong taste and smell, and—you guessed it—is considered highly aphrodisiac.

Other love foods include *panes de isposus*, or sweet bread made for newlyweds, and many treats associated with folk festivals. For example, Siurgus Donigala celebrates the Feast of the Bachelors in mid-October, when eligible young women bake bread and cookies in fantastic shapes. They join the bachelors in a party that lasts three days and nights. (If the right amount of wine is introduced, few people remain single at its conclusion.)

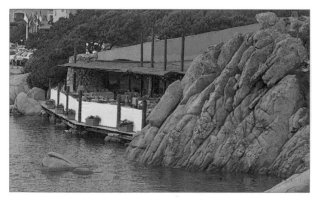

❧ Down to the Golfo di Orosei ❧

South of the glamorous Emerald Coast the number of tourists decreases, while the number of romantic beaches grows. There are incredible stretches of sand south of Olbia, with views of Isola Tavolara and the smaller Isola Molara. (Both islands can be visited, and Tavolara has great hiking trails, although half the island is home to a military base and is off limits.) Look for Sassi Piatti beach, where rock formations have created pools of water that change colors throughout the day. The road snakes by Capo Coda Cavallo, with more fantastic beaches, and then past San Teodoro and Siniscola. This last town is home to a rare microclimate that has created deformed lemons. Called *citrus monstruosa*, or more commonly *pompia*, it looks like a cross between a grapefruit and some kind of pockmarked squash. Although its skin is wrinkled, rough, and generally unsightly, the fruit is candied to make one of Sardinia's most expensive and celebrated desserts.

The highlight of the eastern coast is the Golfo di Orosei. Bulky mountains crowd up against the shore, forming hidden beaches and marine caves accessible by boat. Boats leave regularly from Cala Gonone to beaches south of here, such as Cala Mariolu, Cala Sisine, and Cala Luna. Of these, the most stunning is Cala Luna—some say it is Italy's most charming beach. I once saw an aerial photograph of a sailboat anchored in this inlet, in which the water is so transparent that the shadow of the boat on the seafloor and the entire length of the anchor chain were visible.

Boats to Cala Luna also stop at the Grotta del Bue Marino. As famous as the Grotta di Nettuno on the other side of Sardinia, this immense cave is named after seals that once came here to mate. They made so much noise, people believed that strange marine oxen (*bue*) lived inside. Only a few miles of what is presumed to be a vast underground network of caves have been explored. Guided tours take you past the stalagmite and stalactite formations, providing an ideal way to escape from the midday sun.

CUPID'S CORNERS

La Guardiola
Piazza del Bastione, 4
07031 Castelsardo
Tel: (+39) 079 470 755

This is the best place on the island to indulge in a potently aphrodisiac meal. La Guardiola is not for amateurs: the shellfish appetizer is served raw. The queens of this gala gastronomic event are *fasolari*, brilliant red shellfish surrounded by a colorful assortment of ladies-in-waiting, including *tartufi* (clams with ribbed shells), *mandorle di mare* (small and sweet-tasting mussels) as well as *bocconi* (sea snails, with a distinctive odor). Oysters are added for an aphrodisiac overdose.

Andreini
Via Arduino, 45
07041 Sardinia
Tel: (+39) 079 982 098

Andreini is the most classically romantic restaurant in northern Sardinia, and the best place to get an authentic taste of the region's earthier cuisine. The menu is rich and familiar, drawing on fresh, locally farmed ingredients such as pecorino cheese, suckling pig, and fennel, and the chefs recommend light and delicious regional Cannonau wines to accompany the food. The dining room is charmingly old-fashioned, with elaborate table settings and a warm décor of comforting houseplants and antique furniture—a meal here restores romance to the minutiae of dining out.

RENTING A BOAT

It's hard to imagine a vacation more romantic than one spent beach-hopping by yacht in Sardinia. Those interested in chartering a boat can select from sailboats with a skipper and cooking crew, to smaller motorboats for one-day trips. For more information and details of pricing, log on to www.sardiniayachting.it or www.sardegnacharter.it. The latter also offers sailing courses and windsurf rentals. Luxury yacht rentals can also be organized through www.bluewaycharter.it or www.sailing-it.com, which both operate nationwide. Another fun option is Pescaturismo (www.pescaturismo.com), which allows you to ride along with fishermen.

BEST BEACHES IN NORTHERN SARDINIA

ALGHERO: La Bombarde, with cold currents; Porto Ferro, great for windsurfing

STINTINO: La Pelosa, la Pelosetta

SANTA TERESA DI GALLURA: Capo Testa, Baia di Santa Reparata, Spiaggia delle Granite

ARCIPELAGO DE LA MADDALENA: Budelli, Cala Corsara on Spargi

COSTA SMERALDO: Poltu Li Cogghi (also called Spiaggia del Principe), Liscia Ruja

AROUND SAN TEODORO: Capo Coda Cavallo's Cala Brandinchi beach, Sassi Piatti beach, the island of Tavolara

DORAGLI: Cala Gonone, Cala Mariolu, Cala Sisine, and especially Cala Luna

HOTELS

Hotel Cala di Volpe
07020 Porto Cervo, Costa Smeralda
Tel: (+39) 0789 976 111
Fax: (+39) 0789 976 617
www.luxurycollection.com

Of the luxury hotels on the Costa Smeralda, this is the most celebrated. The hotel, built to look like a fishing village, is a prime example of neo-Mediterranean architecture, with colorful stuccoed torrettes and balconies. The inside houses Sardinian antiques, and many of the rooms are painted in colorful, traditional hues. There is water-skiing, tennis, squash, and the gorgeous Spiaggia dell'Elefante is reserved for hotel guests only.

Hotel Su Gologone, Ristorante Tipico
08025 Oliena (Nuoro)
Tel: (+39) 0784 287 512
Fax (+39) 0784 287 668
www.sugologone.it

I fell in love with Su Gologone the instant I pulled into the driveway, hidden in a green oasis at the base of a dramatic wall of mountains. Past the lobby is a dreamland courtyard where red hibiscus drapes over whitewashed walls, and copper pans glimmer in the sun. The colors are Mexican, the smells are tropical, but the feel is authentically Sardinian.

This may be the only place on the sunny island where you actually hope a random rain cloud will force you indoors. The sixty-five rooms are drenched in rustic charm, and the country theme is repeated in the excellent hotel restaurant, where smoked cheeses hang from wood beams, and ancient cooking utensils adorn the walls. A fire burns at the far end, with skewered meat roasting against the hearth. Small weddings may be organized on the charming terrace.

TUSCANY:
LAND
OF
RUBY
NECTAR

UN CAVALIERE TRA DUE DAME

FA LA FIGURA DEL SALAME

*A gentleman caught between two women
is like a sausage.*

Tuscan proverb

uscany's epic beauty is the stuff of myth. Say the word *Tuscany* and snapshots of idyllic Italy come to mind: sun-drenched farmhouses framed by vineyards and sensuously curved hills.

When Renaissance master Leonardo da Vinci set out to paint a portrait of the world's most famous femme fatale, the Mona Lisa, he gave lengthy consideration to the appropriate background. It had to enhance her physical beauty but not overwhelm it, and the scenery had to evoke the viewers' collective, and perhaps unconscious, idea of paradise. His solution was to paint the landscape that was closest to his heart, the land where he was born: Tuscany.

There is a raging battle among Tuscan towns today, which each claim that the slivers of countryside framing Mona Lisa were snatched from their backyards. In all likelihood, in a stroke of genius to be expected from a man of his acrobatic intellect, da Vinci borrowed separate snippets of scenery—a rock, a dirt road, a river, and a bridge—and assembled them to form a whole. The bridge could be the Buriano Bridge near Arezzo, and the rivers could mark the confluence of the Arno and the Chiana.

Da Vinci made geomorphic maps of the Arezzo area and was fluent in the contours of the land. But the painting's special depth, atmospheric intensity, reddish rocks, jagged spires, and twilight otherworldliness suggest illusion. Much like *la Gioconda*, the portrait of a Florentine merchant's wife, part imaginary and part real, whose modest smile has disarmed men for centuries, Tuscany is a land that straddles the line that divides reality from imagination.

For those who have visited Italy once before on the "grand tour," a second visit provides the opportunity to indulge their bucolic selves, and Tuscany is perfect for this. Rented farmhouses provide a base for exploring by car, bike, scooter, or on foot. Two of Italy's top ten most beautiful leisure drives—the *Chiantigiana* and the via Cassia—are here. Or rooms can be reserved at former monasteries and castles, where activities include horseback riding, cooking lessons, and winetasting. Tuscany is an enological mecca, and one of the most romantic activities is to help with the September harvest. (Legend says grapes picked with the delicate touch of young lovers give the wine a fuller flavor.) Tuscany also is ideal for the artistic-minded, who come to paint or photograph the soft curves and amber sunshine of the Tuscan countryside.

But Tuscany is also a land of a great paradox: How can a land with such soft feminine appeal be so masculine in spirit? With art superstars such as da Vinci and Michelangelo, the

genius of Galileo and Dante Alighieri, the clairvoyantly astute Medici family, the political pundit Niccolò Machiavelli, and other historic swashbucklers, Tuscany never did have much need for heroines. Its folk traditions are demonstrations of masculine might, and its history is all about flexed muscles. Its emblem is the statue of David—a symbol of Italian virility. If one could assign a sex to Tuscany, it would be male.

❧ FLORENCE: RENAISSANCE BEAUTY ❧

"Florence is as romantic as a reference library," warns one popular guidebook. Nothing could be further from the truth. Yes, visitors may be overwhelmed by the long list of art to see here, but this is the capital of the Renaissance, and its urban fabric oozes with the romantic ideals that ushered Italy from the miserable darkness of the Middle Ages. It is a monument to humanism, light, laughter, and love.

Florence is a city to be taken in at once, and on foot. The center of this universe of red brick and marble is the Duomo cathedral, and chances are you will gravitate toward it first. The church's mammoth dome, designed by Filippo Brunelleschi according to calculations no

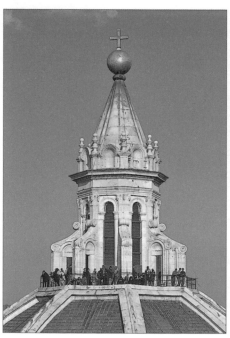

one has fully understood since, casts a long shadow over the city. The geometric pattern of the cathedral's exterior is made with red, green, and white marble, a curious nod to what would later become the Italian tricolore, or flag.

From the Duomo, walk ten minutes (follow the pedestrian flow) to the Palazzo Vecchio on the piazza della Signoria. In front stands a reproduction of the Renaissance heartthrob David—a timeless measure of male beauty that proves Italians have not changed much since their ancestors. When Michelangelo completed the original in June 1504, it was carried to the square—on the backs of forty men—and was placed so the sun could hit it full on. Michelangelo was just twenty-nine years old when he created David, and his masterpiece provoked such jealousy that guards were put in place to stop rowdy gangs from throwing rocks at it. The original statue remained on the square until 1882, when it was moved to the Galleria dell'Accademia (where you can admire it today).

I would like to make a special recommendation for lovers: Make time in Florence for shopping. If you are engaged and searching for wedding bands, there is not a more beautiful place to shop for them than Florence's Ponte Vecchio. The covered bridge that spans the Arno River was the only one in Florence not destroyed during World War II. Its shops were first occupied by butchers, but Cosimo I, duke of Tuscany, was so fed up with walking by pools of blood and animal innards that he passed an edict to replace them with gold merchants. Since 1565 Ponte Vecchio has shimmered with precious metals inside little stores that resemble jewelry boxes themselves. You will find wedding bands, engagement rings, and other love tokens for sale, and merchants who will happily engrave or satisfy special orders.

Besides its world-class goldsmiths, Florence boasts artisans who make hand-worked paper from thick fibers dipped into large vats of colored dye. Another variation of carta fiorentina, as it is known, is inlaid with gold and floral motifs. The city is full of cartolerie, or stationery shops, and all will design wedding invitations or personal stationery.

Florence is also known for its excellent antiques and high-quality leather. This is the headquarters of Gucci, and plenty of retail outlets offer leather footwear, purses, colorful gloves, jackets, and belts. Near the Ponte Vecchio is the Mercato Vecchio, also known as the Straw Market. It is located inside a loggia erected in the mid-1500s and originally sold fine silks and gold. Today the quality of the offerings is of a lower grade, but couples are drawn here for the Porcellino statue.

This statue of a bronze boar has had its snout rubbed so many times, it shines brightly. According to legend, put a coin in its mouth, and if the coin falls between the gratings below, your future will be full of romance. (If it doesn't—try again, until your wallet is empty.) Legend tells of a Tuscan boar that had the unexplained ability to transform himself into a dark and handsome (and presumably hairy) man at night. Each evening, dapperly dressed, he sauntered into the city, and soon he met a beautiful girl. Given his beastly physical appearance at sunrise, the lovers enjoyed limited time for love. The girl grew frustrated, and eventually coaxed the boar into divulging his secret. But he warned her that if she shared this secret with anyone else, he would be frozen into bronze. She told her mother first, and by the top of the hour half of Florence knew her daughter's new boyfriend was really a wild animal, and he was turned into this statue.

On the other side of the Arno River is the appropriately named Oltrarno. Originally a working-class neighborhood, it is where you'll find Florence's most genuine flavor. A labyrinth of *vicoletti* opens onto dimly lit workshops, where furniture restorers and artisans carry on traditions passed down for generations from Renaissance-era maestros. Sounds of hammering, shaving, and the hum of craftsmen singing as they work fill the air. The Oltrarno's Borgo San Frediano, and the little streets that radiate off of piazza Santo Spirito, are a quintessential example. During the day you'll find some of the finest antiques boutiques in Italy, and at night you can seek out the quaint eateries and hole-in-the-wall taverns. Aside from the streetlights, the neighborhood has not changed in centuries.

The Oltrarno is also where the oversize Palazzo Pitti stands; it is connected to the Uffizi by way of the Vasari Corridor, built over the Ponte Vecchio to save the nobility from having to rub elbows with the peasants. Behind the palace are the Boboli Gardens, well worth a visit for its ponds, flowers, parks, and cherub statues. Don't miss the nude Bacchus statue near the exit. A dwarf-sized, overweight Bacchus rests his wine-filled belly on the shell of a tortoise. You can't resist a chuckle, although Bacchus's inebriated expression suggests he gets the last laugh.

High above this side of Florence is a balcony with stunning views of the Renaissance skyline. Piazzale Michelangelo, laid out in 1869, is a favorite with young Italians who can't bring their dates home, where mamma undoubtedly also makes her abode. They come here instead to kiss in parked cars.

Northeast of Florence is the town of Fiesole, which is so near the city it is considered a suburb. Travel the few miles it takes to get there, and you will be catapulted into a charming small-town landscape that inspired E. M. Forster's *A Room with a View*. Literary thread for Boccaccio's *Decameron* was also gathered here.

FROM THE UFFIZI, WITH LOVE

Florence's Uffizi museum is Italy's most important painting gallery. Designed in the mid-sixteenth century by Giorgio Vasari as public administrative offices for Cosimo I—hence *uffizi*, for "offices"—it almost immediately doubled as an exhibition space for the Medici family's growing art collection. These walls enclose hundreds of priceless paintings and sculptures, and a full-day visit is required to do the collection justice. Among the various Madonnas and portraits of illustrious personalities are works that have special resonance with lovers.

First and foremost is Botticelli's *Birth of Venus*—the Uffizi's single most important work. The goddess of love was ushered to earth on a shell, according to the myth, created after the phallus of heaven fell into and fertilized the sea, the womb of the earth. Completed in 1485, it is seen as an allegory linking the physical world with the spiritual one. Also housed here is Botticelli's *Allegory of Spring*, in which some 190 different flower species are represented as symbols of marriage. The complicated painting depicts Venus, or "true love" (in the center,

with Cupid overhead), along with the Three Graces (who represent her beauty) and the nymph Chloris, who is pursued by Zephyr (lust) and is transformed into Flora (fertility). Or to put it plainly, it's about sex.

Titian's *Venus and Cupid* and *Venus of Urbino* are also on display here, as well as the *Venus de' Medici*, a third-century BC statue from Greece that became part of the Medici collection. The statue has had great influence on the image of femininity, long revered as the most beautiful of the Venuses and described as a "miracle of art."

If spending the day in the museum does not sound that exciting, consider this bit of trivia: According to a study by Rome's Institute of Psychology and Psychoanalysts, museums are aphrodisiac. Apparently something in the dust, the smell of old canvas, and the artwork itself stimulates Eros. The institute polled 2,000 Italians, and twenty percent of them admitted to having an "erotic" experience inside a museum. The phenomenon (or the problem, according to museum janitors) has been dubbed the "Rubens Syndrome." A junior Italian culture minister, who admitted to making love inside a museum, explains: "People who like to go to museums feel love. Love for art and love for eroticism are, therefore, completely compatible and transferable." The institute ranked Italy's sexiest museums, and the Uffizi came in fourth, after Genova's Palazzo del Principe Doria, Milan's Pinacoteca di Brera, and Turin's Galleria d'Arte Moderna.

For more information and to see an excellent online catalogue of the collection, go to www.uffizi.firenze.it.

On the Road: La Chiantigiana

To most Tuscans, the number "222" is synonymous with lazy afternoons driving with the windows down, long lunches, and encore servings of wine. The *strada statale* 222 road, known as la Chiantigiana, wiggles its way south of Florence and cuts through the heart of Chianti. The whole length of the route, spanning from Florence south to Siena, is a mere forty miles (seventy kilometers). Yet there is enough to digest along the way—in terms of both scenery and outstanding food and wine to make the voyage last two or three pleasurable days. To many, even that's too short, so they ditch the car and hit the road on a scooter or bicycle to prolong the *Chiantigiana* experience.

This is Chianti, and thanks to its wine, no other pocket of Italian geography enjoys more powerful name recognition. The thickly wooded Chianti Mountains are as gentle as they come. With elongated slopes ranging from 1,300 to 2,300 feet (400 to 700 meters) in altitude and plenty of southern exposure, they are ideal for growing wine grapes. Rows of vineyards have been cut sharply from the forests that hug the hills. Where nature's woods remain intact, wild boar and rabbit roam, and keep Tuscan chefs on their creative toes.

San Casciano marks the full-blown Chianti countryside. Slightly north is Sant'Andrea in Percussina, where Niccolò Machiavelli lived while writing *The Prince*. The first big town on SS222 is Greve, in Chianti. Greve is one of the flagship cities of the "Slow City" movement, which followed in the wake of the "Slow Food" movement to safeguard the nation's gastronomic traditions (see www.slowfood.com). Slow Cities pledge to grant more permits for *osterie*, or traditional neighborhood eateries, ban neon signs, combat noise pollution, plant more trees, and develop bicycle paths instead of traffic thoroughfares. Those efforts have paid off, making Greve not only charmingly intact but an excellent base from which to explore the surrounding area.

Greve's main square, lined with butcher shops and restaurants, is Piazza Matteotti. It has a triangular shape and an arcaded walkway at its perimeter, and in the center stands a statue of Giovanni da Verrazzano, the same explorer who gave his name to the Verrazzano Bridge in New York, as the first European to pass through the New York narrows in 1524. (Fellow explorer Amerigo Vespucci was born in the fortified hamlet of Montefioralle, just a few miles away.) A tiny sinuous road with tight curves climbs from Greve and cuts through more beautiful scenery to Panzano. This detour is worth taking, because it leads to a dirt road and the Badia a Passignano—one of Tuscany's most photographed castles. The eleventh-century abbey rises from a patch of pointed cypress trees and is now owned by the Antinori family, who use it as a wine cellar and make an excellent Chianti Classico.

In Panzano make time to pay a visit to Italy's most famous butcher. The "Poet Butcher," as Dario Cecchini is known (see chapter twelve), rose to stardom during the bovine spongiform encephalopathy, or "mad cow," scare a few years back. Cecchini defied a ban on the delectable *fiorentina* T-bone steak, cut as thick as a phone book, and staged a mock funeral in which a steak was placed in a coffin and paraded around town, accompanied by a band and mourners in black. His manifesto, he explains, is the preservation of gluttony and *ciccia*, or the kind of body fat that softens a woman's curves.

Following the road for another twenty minutes or so by car, after a bend the hilltop hamlet of Castellina in Chianti suddenly comes into view. The town is a great place for an afternoon stroll and winetasting. An oversize tower dominates its Piazza del Comune, and the town's heavily fortified walls suggest Castellina found itself too often on the battlefront between the warring armies of Florence and Siena. Today the Castellina countryside is one of the preferred spots among Americans looking to rent a farmhouse for the summer.

To the east are the towns Radda and Gaiole, both generously endowed with a good selection of country homes available to rent. They are also abundant with wine bars and restaurants, since this area is the source of some of the best of Chianti's wines (see "In Vino Veritas," on page 129). Less than a mile before Castellina, you'll see the turnoff for Radda (take Route 429). From here you can explore the romantically secluded Etruscan tombs around Volpaia, which start just a few miles to the north. Gaiole is yet another Chianti jewel nestled within a wild and rustic setting. Couples can put some mileage on their hiking shoes on the trails that cut through the forests and start at the Vallombrosan Badia a Coltibuono abbey, located just over two miles (four kilometers) north of Gaiolo. South of the town is the Castello di Brolio, one of the few Tuscan castles open to the public. The original building was almost completely leveled in the late 1400s, but it was rebuilt in 1860 by Baron Bettino Ricasoli, the man credited with putting Chianti Classico on the enological map.

VIA FRANCIGENA

Of all the roads that lead to Rome, one in particular carved a corridor of commerce and communication that forever enriched central Italy. The via Francigena spans the entire length of Tuscany and is the key to understanding the region today. The ancient trade route draws a line across Europe, from London, through France, the Swiss Alps, and down the Italian peninsula to the seat of Christianity in Rome. A millennium ago thousands of pilgrims, merchants, and clergymen walked this route, traveling twelve miles (twenty kilometers) per day on their holy journey to receive indulgences from the pope.

Wherever the via Francigena veered, it left a path of gold. The road generated a booming economy, and towns such as Lucca, San Gimignano, Monteriggioni, and Siena, which had the good fortune to be located on its course, were ushered into the economic stratosphere. Merchants brought exotic ingredients from faraway lands, such as chocolate, that were eventually incorporated into local cuisine. Almost all the manmade beauty you see in this part of Tuscany came thanks to these poor souls marching to Rome for their ticket to paradise.

Only about twenty percent of the via Francigena exists today, and it is a popular hiking path, albeit one that starts and stops in random places. Brown signs with a picture of a pilgrim mark its course; detailed maps are available at local tourism offices.

From Castellina, leaving SS222 in the direction of Poggibonsi, drive west to reach San Gimignano, a leader in the pack of Tuscan tourism towns. San Gimignano has plenty to offer you and your special someone. The town is packed with picturesque rustic eateries, bijoux buildings, quiet corners, towers with panoramic views, and places offering excellent gelato, and it also is a gateway to more beautiful countryside to explore by car or on foot.

This is a modest town with great aspirations, which makes it simply magical for romantics. *La città delle torri*, also called Tuscany's "medieval Manhattan," holds first prize as far as Italian skylines are concerned. From afar, its erect towers look like a cluster of cypress trees pointing to the heavens. Back in its heyday, in the twelfth and thirteenth centuries, a whopping seventy-two towers stood proudly in the city—certainly an awe-inspiring sight at the time. And just as New York's skyline later grew taller and more elaborate as the city became wealthier, San Gimignano rose vertically thanks to the city's position on the via Francigena. Traditionally, the tallest buildings in medieval towns were the town hall or the church steeple, in which the tower is a symbol of the population's collective might. But San Gimignano's skyscrapers were altars to the individual, in much the same way the Chrysler building, the Empire State building, and Rockefeller Plaza celebrate the affluence of a single business interest. And, not unlike in New York, San Gimignano's towers eventually became a vulnerability: warring neighbors and fighting fractions found wicked delight in watching those symbols fall.

At the center of town is Piazza della Cisterna, with a functioning thirteenth-century well, and the Torre del Diavolo, or "devil's tower," which earned its name when its owner convinced his neighbors that it mysteriously grew by itself. Adjacent is the Piazza del Duomo and the Collegiata, and within the wall-to-wall frescoed cathedral is the Cappella di Santa Fina. Santa Fina, San Gimignano's patron saint, affixed herself to oak planks in a rat-infested room from age ten to fifteen after her mother scolded her for accepting a *melarancia* (a mythical cross between an apple and an orange) from a young admirer. Unable to articulate his love for her, he gave her the red passion fruit instead. Hers (and his, for that matter) is not one of Italy's happier love stories.

Further to the south, on the Si-Fi highway, is another mandatory stop: Monteriggioni, a surreal vision that stands like a crown on the crest of a hill. Its circular walls boast fourteen perfectly preserved military towers that encircle a small but enchanting town center. Dante was so impressed with Monteriggioni he described it as a hellish "well" filled with swimming creatures in the *Divine Comedy*. For a romantic vista, walk to the back of the town to where a stone entranceway creates a fitting frame for the country landscape.

SIENA

At the end of the SS222 is the romantic valentine at the heart of Italy. Some may question Florence's allure for lovers, but no couple can resist Siena's spell. The city is smaller, pinker, prettier, and in many ways friendlier than its archrival to the north. It is certainly more self-reliant and self-contained. Most important, Siena is a city of passion, which it celebrates with fiery fervor in the elaborately choreographed Palio horserace, staged twice a year on July 2 and August 16. But the truth is, the Sienese live with the Palio lodged in their hearts every day.

Of all of Italy's folk pageants and parades, none is more complicated or genuine than the Palio. It is an allegory to love with a succession of time-honored traditions, all frozen in medieval glory, that in many ways mimics a colossal wedding celebration. There is rivalry, seduction, competition, victory, and long days of banqueting, drinking, and merrymaking to follow. *Per forza e per amore* (for strength and for love) is the battle cry, and the rules of engagement are anything goes. The winner doesn't receive a trophy or a cash prize. Instead, the top award is a painted banner of the Virgin Mary. The race is carried out in her honor, as she is the undisputed incarnation of love.

But just as important as love, the Palio race is also a colorful and musical reenactment of ancient, passionate animosities. Here the enemy is not Florence or Pisa, or any other group of outsiders. Instead, it is a rivalry with the person next door. Siena is divided into seventeen *contrade*, or neighborhoods, that trace their roots back to the twelfth century and vaguely represent the military groups that protected the city from its enemies. Newborn babies are baptized in their *contrada* fountain, couples are married at the *contrada* church, and the dead are buried with their *contrada* flag. The rivalry between Siena's neighborhoods is as fierce as the loyalties within them. Walking through the city streets, you will see plaques on street corners marking the borders of the *contrada* districts. Symbolized by animals or objects, they are: *Aquila* (eagle), *Bruco* (caterpillar), *Chiocciola* (snail), *Civetta* (owl), *Drago* (dragon), *Giraffa* (giraffe), *Istrice* (porcupine), *Leocorno* (unicorn), *Lupa* (she-wolf), *Montone* (ram), *Nicchio* (shell), *Oca* (goose), *Onda* (wave), *Pantera* (panther), *Selva* (forest), *Tartuca* (tortoise), and *Torre* (tower).

The *contrada* also represent the seventeen teams that compete for the Palio victory. The first race is held on the Feast of the Virgin Mary (July 2) and the second on the Day of the Assumption (August 16), but the preparations—and plotting—leading up to the race last all year. Each team selects a horse and a jockey, but the horse is the real hero, adored and pampered by the *contrada* it represents. In fact, getting the jockey across the finish line isn't the point, and many of the bareback riders fall off their horse before the end of the race anyway. A few days before the race, the horse is taken inside the local *contrada* church for a pre-race prayer; it is said to be a good omen if it leaves droppings at the altar.

After several trial runs and a parade of drummers and flag carriers in medieval costume, the horse race is staged. The race is short, two minutes at the most. Some 30,000 Sienese and foreigners cram into the center of Piazza del Campo (considered Italy's most beautiful square, along with Rome's Piazza Navona) wearing team colors, waving banners, and bellowing traditional songs. After the race, the euphoric winners sponsor a series of banquets and street parties, well supplied with wine and music, which drag on until September. The second-place team's hatred for the winning *contrada* lasts until next year's race. As in love, being number two is far worse than being last.

ON THE ROAD: LA CASSIA

More beautiful than the SS222, in my opinion, is the via Cassia (SS2), which heads south of Siena toward Rome. With Siena at your back, the thick forests of Chianti give way to long views of the undulating Tuscan plains. The road leads you past fields of sunflower with their heavy heads bowing down, red poppies, machine-manicured rows of barley, and neatly wheeled bundles of

hay that look like giant scattered marbles. You'll see the quintessentially Tuscan farmhouse and lone cypress tree. The imagery is so iconic as to seem unreal. On this ancient Roman trading route, you'll want to stay in the slow lane. Even Italy's Formula One driver Giancarlo Fisichella confessed that when he first drove via Cassia, he left a piece of his heart behind.

The best part of the drive is the first fifty miles (eighty kilometers) south of Siena to Lago di Bolsena. Time permitting, you could also opt to hook up with the via Cassia later, and in this case, there are two options. First, to the southeast of Siena, Route 438 crosses a lunar landscape known as the Crete Senesi, where deep gullies cut into white clay hills. Within the Crete territory and surrounded by pine trees is the Monte Oliveto Maggiore. This Benedictine monastery is open to the public, and a handy little side shop run by the monks sells everything from homemade digestivo drinks to herbal cough syrup and love potions. One of these little bottles makes a great souvenir of your Tuscan getaway.

The second option is to head southwest of Siena, along the winding Route 73, to the Abbazia di San Galgano. The detour is highly recommended for couples for the sheer poetic impact of this romantically ruined abbey. The abandoned San Galgano would make a great setting for a profound declaration of the heart. The abbey was once among Italy's greatest

Gothic buildings in the French style, but today it stands as an eerie reminder of the forces of fire, wind, and rain. It was built in the 1200s, but over time it was sacked and destroyed. The last mass was held in 1786, during which the roof came crumbling down. The visitor today is confronted with almost cartoonish skeletal remains: high arches, stone columns, a dirt floor instead of pavement, and the blue sky for a ceiling.

Just a short walk away is the Cappella di Montesiepi, where Saint Galgano Guidotti stabbed a stone with a sword in renunciation of his warlike ways. You can see the sword sticking out of the stone in Italy's own take on the Knights of the Round Table fable.

If you choose not to take either detour, stay on the via Cassia, passing the first major town after Siena, Buonconvento, packed tight within red brick walls, and on to Montalcino, where the real romantic action is.

Montalcino marks the western front of Tuscany's holy trinity of hilltop towns. The other two are Pienza and Montepulciano, and between the three you'll find more winetasting opportunities than you can take advantage of. This is the picturesque Tuscan countryside of postcards and calendar covers. Montalcino's claim to fame is the Brunello grape, a Sangiovese clone, which goes into the robust Brunello di Montalcino. It stands among the belpaese's top wines. The DOCG Brunello di Montalcino must age four years—five for the riserva—whereas Rosso di Montalcino ages in barrel for one year, making it a less weighty, and less expensive, alternative (for more on the DOCG seal of quality, see "In Vino Veritas," on page 129). Brunello di Montalcino has a great capacity for aging in the bottle, whereas the Rosso di Montalcino is best consumed within four or five years of the vintage. You'll find many wine bars in the vicinity of the shield-studded Piazza del Popolo, where you can sample either version. Reward yourself with a glass after a climb up to the Rocca fortress (there's an excellent enoteca inside, too) to admire the magnificent views.

If you exit the via Cassia at San Quirico d'Orcia (east on Route 146), Pienza is about six miles (ten kilometers) further. It's worth noting that only a few miles south of San Quirico d'Orcia is the hamlet Bagno Vignoni. There is no other town in the world quite like it. Famous for its thermal spas, the town features a huge pool of steaming water as its main square. Although you can't swim in the pool today, little streams of mineral water provide a place to soak tired feet. In the gully below are more natural hot springs for full-body immersions.

Pienza was built as an experiment in humanist ideals during the Renaissance. It was designed as a utopian city, in which its buildings and public squares were calculated to be the perfect fit for its inhabitants: not too big as to be daunting, but big enough to reflect mankind's soaring aspirations and know-how. If you stand on the central Piazza Pio II, you'll see that Pienza does shine as a città a misura d'uomo (a human-sized city). It's also a city of the heart, and a stroll through its quaint streets lined with flowerpots is like a stroll along a lovers' lane: There's the via del Bacio (the road of the kiss), via Buia (road of darkness), via della Fortuna (road of luck), and the via dell'Amore (road of love).

Further east, about a twenty-five minute drive through spectacular scenery, is the hilltop of Montepulciano. This is another ideal place for lovers to linger, although you'll have to face the climb up to Piazza Grande for a cool drink at an outdoor café. As you huff and puff your way up, keep in mind that a brave few opt to make the ascent more difficult than it already is. On the last Sunday of August, Montepulciano puts on the *Bravìo delle Botti*, in which team members from the town's rival neighborhoods race to the top of the town rolling 180-pound (eighty-kilogram) wine barrels uphill on the cobblestone streets. The winner usually makes it up in less than ten minutes, and is then doused in the local Vino Nobile di Montepulciano wine. The *Bravìo delle Botti* is a perfect example of a fertility rite, Tuscan-style, in which macho bravado and the mantra "no sweat, no glory" are the mating call.

Continuing northeast past Montepulciano and Valdichiana, you eventually encounter the former Etruscan city Cortona. This *città d'arte* basks in the limelight today thanks to Frances Mayes's memoir *Under the Tuscan Sun*. Further north still is Arezzo, featured in Roberto Benigni's Oscar-winning film *La vita è bella* (*Life Is Beautiful*). Arezzo also holds one of Europe's best antiques markets on the first Sunday of the month in and around its Piazza Grande, where you can buy linens, farming tools, furniture, and decorative knickknacks.

Umbria and
Saint Valentine

Once in the shadow of its neighbor, Umbria has come into its own. Unlike rambunctious Tuscany, this region is a quiet and soulful world apart. Perched on a tall plateau, Perugia is its capital: Originally one of twelve cities in the Etruscan federation, it grew in might and wealth and blossomed into a Renaissance metropolis. Umbria is Italy's greenest region and the most geographically isolated, the only one without access to either the sea or international borders.

Umbria was originally inhabited by a mysterious and peaceful race called the Umbrii. The gentle temperament of the Umbrii survived that of their aggressors, and the region went on to produce numerous religious celebrities: Saint Clare and Saint Benedict, founder of monasticism, Saint Rita, patron of impossibilities, and Saint Valentine all left their mark on Italy's "green heart." And it was from these hills that Saint Francis of Assisi (1182–1226) preached love of nature, chastity, and spiritual enrichment through poverty, while the Tuscans were busy fighting or scheming to get rich off of the pilgrims. The importance of the saint, known as il *Poverello* (the "little poor one"), in the Catholic Church is unparalleled, and his shrine in Assisi is the country's second most important holy site, after the Vatican.

Of all the saints to come marching out of Umbria, only one is celebrated throughout the world and across religious lines: Saint Valentine, the patron saint of engaged couples, travelers, young people—and inspiration for this book. On February 14, Saint Valentine's Day, lovers exchange poems, red roses, chocolates, and heart-shaped cards with amorous declarations known as valentines. Many become engaged on this date, others get married, and all couples find creative ways to say "I love you."

Not much is known about the former priest and physician, other than that he was born in Terni, Umbria. Some accounts say his birthday is February 14, 175 AD, and others that he was martyred on February 14 at the ripe old age of ninety-eight. The Catholic Church's official register lists three Valentines, so details of his true identity remain fuzzy. One version says Saint Valentine became the patron of lovers and sweethearts because he skirted the law of Rome and performed secret Christian marriages. Consequently, he was arrested, and while in prison, Valentine concocted an ointment made from magic herbs to miraculously heal the blind daughter of his prison guard. The guard and his family converted to Christianity, and Roman authorities were so angered that they ordered Valentine beaten and beheaded. Another version has it that the saint and the young woman fell in love, and moments before his death, he sent her a love note signed "your Valentine."

Valentine's Day may also have derived from the Catholic Church's co-opting of a pagan celebration. February 15 marks the bizarre feast of the pagan deity Lupercus. On that day a jubilant crowd assembled to watch a dog be sacrificed. The blood from the sacrificial knife was smeared onto the foreheads of sprightly youngsters, and the dog's hide was ripped into long strips called *februa* (also related to the word February). The youths ran about and slapped women with the furry whips, in a gesture believed to make them more fertile. At nightfall the names of young maidens and bachelors were drawn from a love urn, and the couples were encouraged to pair off as lovers under the cover of night. The Catholic Church outlawed the Lupercalia in 496 AD, cleverly replacing it with Saint Valentine's Day.

The city of Terni, about sixty miles (100 kilometers) north of Rome, has done its best to reinvent itself by adopting the sobriquet "City of Love" and capitalizing on its patron and protector, Saint Valentine. It stages a month-long celebration of love in February. On the first Sunday of the month, some 200 couples travel from far and wide to attend the Feast of the Promise at the nondescript Basilica di San Valentino (where the saint's remains lie in a crystal coffin under the altar). During the ceremony couples are blessed and make a pledge to get married within the year. The next two Sundays celebrate married couples who have hit their twenty-fifth and fiftieth anniversary marks. There is also a film festival dedicated to love stories, music, food, and an annual goldsmiths' exhibit for those looking to pick out wedding rings. Foreign couples are welcome to attend and are encouraged to participate in the *Festa della promessa.*

PA PA PA PAPPA AL POMODORO

Tuscan cuisine has scaled the culinary ranks thanks to the region's complex history and civilization. One of Tuscany's most cherished treasures is its golden olive oil, which strikes a happy medium between the lighter and darker varieties of the peninsula's geographic extremities. Among the first courses in the regional cuisine are *tagliatelle* and *papardelle*, ribbonlike pastas, white beans, *acqua cotta* (bread and cabbage in broth), and *pappa al pomodoro*—a porridge-like tomato soup whose singsong name is a children's rhyme. Gamey meat dishes include rabbit, wild boar, and pheasant. And, of course, there's the succulent *florentina* T-bone steak from cows raised in the fertile Valdichiana. As the activist butcher in Panzano in Chianti will remind you, indulging in earthly pleasures is no sin.

CUPID'S CORNERS

I n honor of Tuscany's celebrated wines, I'm devoting Cupid's Corners to the best wine producers, enotecas, and wine bars of the region. Almost every producer offers tours, tastings, and often meals and accommodation, so follow your nose—and your heart—and have fun exploring the most beautiful and romantic vineyards in Europe. Because the vineyards are lost in the rolling Tuscan countryside, it's best to call or look online for accurate locations and travel instructions.

IN VINO VERITAS

It has been noted that the beauty of Tuscany reaches its maximum form of expression in a glass of red wine. This ruby nectar is sensual, subtle, and soothing to the senses. Of all of Italy's aphrodisiacs, none rushes through the bloodstream and hits your heart faster than the so-called "juice of passion" (see chapter twelve). Because of its inebriating and euphoric effect, *vino* is named after Venus, goddess of love.

Ninety percent of Italy's wine and food tourism is focused on Tuscany, and great strides have been made over the past years to promote Tuscany's wine tourism. The Movimento del Turismo del Vino (www.movimentoturismovino.it) coordinates the Strade del Vino, or "wine road" tours, organizing guided cellar visits, tasting tours, and meals with wine and food pairings. You can also visit wineries on your own with the help of the excellent *Italian Wines*, published each year by Gambero Rosso. If a particular producer does not have a tasting room, keep in mind that Tuscany's best vintages are archived at the local *enoteca* where you can swirl, sniff, and sip to your heart's content.

Tuscany is a producer of quality wine, of which forty-five percent is DOC or DOCG standard. *Denominazione di origine controllata* and *denominazione di origine controllata e garantita* are two classifications modeled loosely on the *appellation contrôlée* laws of France. These regulations provide the framework for quality control in Italian wine. Tuscany currently has six DOCG wines: Brunello di Montalcino, Carmignano, Chianti, Chianti Classico, Vernaccia di San Gimignano (Tuscany's only white DOCG wine), and Vino Nobile di Montepulciano. The many DOC wines range from Bolgheri to Morellino di Scansano, to Rosso di Montalcino and Rosso di Montepulciano.

This region is also the home of the notorious "SuperTuscan" wines that are held in high esteem by connoisseurs but ironically don't carry a DOC or DOCG classification. This is because winemakers add foreign grapes such as Cabernet Sauvignon and Merlot to their blends in order to make them more suitable for barrel aging. These originally experimental wines, such as Tignanello by Antinori and Cabreo by Ruffino, are among Italy's very best today, as is Sassicaia (which now enjoys DOC status) from the Bolgheri area of southwestern Tuscany.

Chianti Classico

The heart of Chianti Classico is the area around Radda and Castellina. Once known as a cheap drink served in hay-wrapped flasks, today the wines of Chianti are among Italy's most sophisticated. Although his restaurant, Cantinetta Antinori, is in Florence (Piazza Antinori 3, www.antinori.it), Marchese Piero Antinori is the king of Chianti. He makes Chianti Classico, the flagship Tignanello, and Solaia—the 1997 vintage of which was named the world's best wine by *Wine Spectator* magazine, and finding a bottle of the stuff is almost impossible today. Another celebrated producer is Castello di Fonterutoli (Fonterutoli, Via Rossini 5, Castellina in Chianti, tel: + 39 0577 73571, www.fonterutoli.it), responsible for a ruby-red Chianti Classico Riserva, among others. Located in a 700-year-old abbey, Badia a Coltibuono (53013 Gaiole in Chianti, tel: +39 0577 74481, www.coltibuono.com) is known for reliable and good-value wines. In addition, you can also buy olive oil there and sign up for cooking classes. Two other notable producers are Barone Ricasoli at Castello di Brolio (53013 Gaiole in Chianti, tel: +39 0577 7301, www.ricasoli.it), which makes the outstanding Chianti Classico Castello di Brolio, and Felsina (Via del Chianti 101, 53019 Castelnuovo Berardenga, tel: +39 0577 355 117), with a Chianti Classico Riserva and the SuperTuscan Fontalloro.

For more information on Chianti Classico, go to www.chiantinet.it.

Montalcino

There are dozens of *enoteca* in town and many more vineyards in the surrounding hills where you can sample the delicious Brunello di Montalcino or its younger sibling Rosso di Montalcino. Castello Banfi (Montalcino, tel: +39 0577 840 111, www.castellobanfi.com) is well known thanks to its high-quality exports. This producer makes an excellent Brunello di Montalcino and a wide range of other wines, and there is a restaurant on the estate. Biondi Santi (Tenuta Greppo, tel: +39 0577 847 121, www.biondisanti.it) is considered the birthplace of Brunello. In 1870 the winemaker Ferruccio Biondi noticed that the Sangiovese grape of Montalcino had special characteristics that distinguished it from the Sangiovese of Chianti. Not surprisingly, only a lucky few can afford the top vintages today. Another producer is Fattoria dei Barbi (Podernovi, tel: +39 0577 841 111, www.fattoriadeibarbi.it), which also sells olive oil, grappa, and cheese and has an excellent restaurant.

For more information on Montalcino's wines, go to www.consorziobrunellodimontalcino.it.

MONTEPULCIANO

A favorite among Tuscan aristocrats and the Medicis—thus the name "noble"—Nobile di Montepulciano is still an elite wine. An outstanding producer is Avignonesi (via di Gracciano nel Corso 91, Montepulciano, tel: +39 0578 757 872, www.avignonesi.it), with weekday tastings and tours. The Vino Nobile and the Riserva Grandi Annata are both remarkable. Poliziano (via Fontago 1, Montepulciano Stazione, tel: +39 0578 738 171, www.carlettipoliziano.com) is known for reliable wines that won't break the budget, although some of the top Vino Nobile is pricey. If you get the chance, don't miss Montepulciano's *vin santo*, a specialty sweet wine pressed from sun-dried grapes.

For more information on Montepulciano's wines, go to www.consorziovinonobile.it.

TUSCANY: LAND OF RUBY NECTAR

LIGURIA: THE LAND OF POETS

INTU MEZU DU MÄ GH'È 'N PESCIU TUNDU

CHE QUANDU U VEDDE Ë BRÛTTE
U VA 'NSCIÙ FUNDU

INTU MEZU DU MÄ GH'È 'N PESCIU PALLA

CHE QUANDU U VEDDE Ë BELLE
U VEGNE A GALLA

Out at sea is a round fish that sinks to the floor
when he sees an ugly girl

Out at sea is a puffer fish that floats to the top
when he sees a pretty girl

Song from folksinger
Fabrizio de André's *Creuza de mä*

Those with a penchant for poetry will feel drawn to Liguria. Sandwiched between the French Riviera and Tuscany, its coastal geography reads like verse, from the Gulf of Paradise to the Bay of Silence and the Bay of Fables, and on to the appropriately named Gulf of Poets. Colorful boats bobbing in snug harbors provide cadence, and fishmongers bellowing out prices at the neighborhood market add rhyme. Pastel buildings basking in the sunshine resonate harmony.

Liguria is divided in two parts: the Riviera di Ponente runs from the French border to Genova, and east of that lies the Riviera di Levante. Italy's gardening capital, or the Riviera dei Fiori, is on the Ponente side, as the patchwork of greenhouses surrounding Ventimiglia testify. Men should take note of the two important specimens of romantic flora that originate here. Fragrant acacia (or mimosa) colors Liguria's mountains with bright yellow in late winter, and March 8 marks the *Festa della Donna*, when Italians give the fuzzy flowers to the women in their lives as a sign of appreciation. Liguria is also home to a special rose that produces a long, elegant stem. "Long-stemmed roses" might be sold around the world, but the originals are only found here.

Dividing the two sides of Liguria is a city that was at one time the world's biggest maritime powerhouse. Genova snakes along the coast for eighteen miles (thirty kilometers) and is barely two miles (three kilometers) across at its widest. Its layers of history rarely fall into neat lines: Cupolas cast shadows on condos, and towers lean against ancient walls. Nicknamed *la Superba*, Genova fell on hard times after 1492, when native Christopher Columbus, the son of a local wool merchant, discovered the New World. Some 500 years later, and thanks to an ambitious public-works agenda, Genova is back on her feet and ready to enchant you. The "superb one" ranks with Naples and Marseilles as one of Europe's most seductive port cities.

This chapter details the eastern half of the Italian Riviera, a golden belt of sun-and-sea wonderlands such as Portofino, the Cinque Terre, and Portovenere. They were built wherever nature afforded the room, and the tenacious inhabitants developed a strong bond with both sea and mountains. As the writer Stendhal remarked matter-of-factly: "This is a place where if a lemon falls from a tree, it ends up in the sea."

GOLFO DI PARADISO

The Riviera di Levante starts with the sun-drenched buildings of Nervi, Recco (home of excellent focaccia), and Camogli. The latter, whose name comes from *Casa Mogli* (home of the wives) because the fishermen left their spouses alone so often, is a good place to begin a romantic tour of the coast.

If absence makes the heart grow fonder, Camogli's women devised a unique way to show their affection. On the second Sunday of May what is claimed to be the biggest frying pan in the world, at twelve feet (four meters) in diameter, is carted to the town square, where it is used to cook two tons of sardines to tender perfection—the equivalent of one day and one night of fishing. The bounty is distributed free as a sign of the city's collective generosity, and the words "*San Fortunato, pesce regalato*" ("free fish for the saint of luck") are repeated. The *Sagra del Pesce* was first celebrated after World War II, when young fishermen miraculously returned home unscathed after inadvertently drifting into a minefield. Like many Italian festivals involving fish, its roots can be traced to pagan rituals, in which Venus (the goddess of love and the protector of fishermen) is celebrated with a display of abundance and prayers that the sea will be equally generous the following year.

At the end of the Gulf of Paradise, bulky mountains edge up against Mount Portofino. Although it only takes about one hour to climb to the summit, most people opt to see the stunning scenery from sea level. Boat tours leave Camogli regularly to make a thirty-minute trip to the Abbey of San Fruttuoso. On the way you pass Punta Chiappa, where the water magically alternates shades of blue. The abbey is a truly magnificent sight. Built in 711, it is topped by a Byzantine cupola and surrounded by cloisters behind a thin strip of beach, in a seemingly inaccessible spot. Snorkelers will want to swim to the famous Cristo degli Abissi—a bronze statue of Christ, his arms outstretched, that sank eight fathoms beneath the sea in 1954. It is a bizarre underwater scene.

PORTOFINO AND SANTA MARGHERITA

Portofino derives its name from Portus Delphini, or "port of dolphins," and was once an irresistible hideaway for illicit trysts and paparazzi-dodging movie stars, who arrived by yacht or in sleek sports cars. The brawny mountains that protected Italy's most famous nook provided a seclusion that made it a promised land for a diamond diaspora. Here Richard Burton proposed to Elizabeth Taylor, and Humphrey Bogart wooed Lauren Bacall. Grace of Monaco, Greta Garbo, and Frank Sinatra were often seen sipping cocktails. Legend has it that Rex

Harrison was having a drink with the Duke of Windsor when he suddenly excused himself to buy cigarettes. He spied actress Kay Kendall, and never returned to his seat.

Today Portofino does not merit more than a day trip, unless you're lucky enough to have reservations at the posh Hotel Splendido. Cars are rarely permitted along the narrow road into town, and even if you do get in, you will pay as much for parking as you would for dinner in other towns. In general, the relationship between quality and price is badly distorted in Portofino. A better bet, and a personal favorite, is Santa Margherita. Don't miss the Basilica di Santa Margherita in the town center. This rococo explosion, set against a whirlwind of frescoed facades, is a decadent feast for the eyes.

RAPALLO TO BAIA DELLE FAVOLE

Rapallo, tucked within the dramatic recesses of the Gulf of Tigullio, is one of the most famous resort towns on the Riviera di Levante, and an exceedingly pleasant place to while away a vacation. The services are excellent, there is a celebrated golf course, and the beach is large enough to accommodate most everyone. Like the rest of Liguria, the sea is warm until October, so you can enjoy the surf well into the off-season.

Rapallo's main attraction is the *funivia*, or cable car, that climbs roughly 2,000 feet (650 meters) to the sixteenth-century Santuario di Montallegro. According to legend, the Madonna appeared to a shepherd here on July 2, 1557, and miraculously left behind a Byzantine icon symbolizing the "Holy Virgin in Transit," which unexplainably "flew" here from Dalmatia. Each year the town celebrates the event from July 1 to 3. This is one of Italy's most evocative events, with fireworks exploding over a glittering sea, the embers slowly falling from the sky while hundreds of little boats with red lanterns and candles bob in the distance.

Lavagna, about six miles (ten kilometers) south of Rapallo, is a town that loves a good wedding party. In fact, it is so hooked on nuptial events that it organizes one each year on August 14 known as *Torta dei Fieschi*. A wedding cake is prepared for the occasion, according to a recipe you won't ever find in a cookbook: It calls for 4,000 eggs, 150 kilograms of sugar, 150 kilograms of flour, 140 kilograms of fresh whipped cream, 50 kilograms of almond paste, and 120 liters of rum. When assembled, the finished product weighs several tons and measures twenty feet (seven meters) high and a foot (three meters) wide. It was Count Opizzo Fieschi, a man with deep pockets and a heart as big as his sweet tooth, who first ordered this cake to be prepared on August 14, 1230—the day he married a noble woman from Siena named Bianca dei Bianchi—declaring to the townsfolk that the cake represented the immensity of his love for her. In further demonstration of his amorous largesse, he distributed free slices to all the citizens of Lavagna. Today this

CITIES OF ILLUSION

Much of what makes Liguria's towns so appealing to the eye is optical illusion. Lacking the resources and materials to adorn buildings with marble and stone window framing, artisans blended ingenuity and creativity to perfect the art of trompe l'oeil.

Nervi and Santa Margherita are two prime examples of such "painted cities," as they are known. Ornate details on the buildings—from green shutters left seductively ajar, to balustrades and nymph statues over doorways—have all been applied with a brush. One building near the town of Rapallo has a painted cat watching traffic from a third-floor window. The black-and-white feline looks so real, you almost expect it to tilt its head and blink its green eyes. Some buildings are so draped in illusion, you need to run your hand against the walls to remind yourself that they really are flat. "One would need to paint with gold and precious gems," said Impressionist painter Claude Monet when he came to Liguria.

Trompe l'oeil was introduced in the late 1400s, when noble families from Genova employed the talents of the best artists to decorate their palazzi on both the inside and outside. By the 1800s the trend had spread to the middle class, who opted to beautify real estate with low-cost three-dimensional motifs rather than real marble to create columns, capitals with floral carvings, and cornerstones. Maintenance is taken care of with a second coat of paint. It's no coincidence that the most elaborate buildings face the sea—like a movie set designed for passengers on passing ships.

The few artisans who still practice this fresco technique are treated with special respect. A trompe l'oeil signed by a famous painter makes a home's value skyrocket, and property owners exchange gossip about who painted which buildings the way Beverly Hills wives drop the names of their interior decorators.

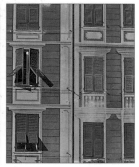

ritual is repeated, but with a twist. The oversized triangular *torta* is paraded through town by cake bearers dressed in medieval costume, and lottery tickets are handed out to locals and tourists alike. Men get blue cards and women get pink ones, and every pair has a matching codeword. The men and women must compare cards with the thousands of people crowding the main square in order to find their partner-to-be. If holders of matching cards are lucky enough to find each other, only then are they entitled to a slice of cake.

Further down the coast is another inviting inlet known as the "Bay of Silence." Past a small peninsula lies a second bay that Danish storyteller Hans Christian Andersen dubbed the "Bay of Fables," and now each year a children's literature festival is held here to honor the man who found words to describe these fairy-tale surroundings.

THE CINQUE TERRE

A regional highlight are the Cinque Terre—five fishing villages with maximum postcard potential, crowded into impossibly snug spots. The Apennines do not gracefully slope down to the flat beaches that mark the beginning of Tuscany; instead these mighty mountains literally offer a cliffhanger finale to the Ligurian territory. Among this dramatic landscape of gnarled black rock and sheer seawalls, the Cinque Terre cling. While the mountains shielded residents against invaders from the north, and offered refuge during repeated Saracen attacks by sea, they also imposed an exceptional isolation. Since the Middle Ages, the "five lands"— Monterosso al Mare, Vernazza, Corniglia, Manarola, and Riomaggiore—were only accessible with difficulty by boat or foot, and over the years the communities developed their own identity, dialect, cuisine, and traditions—despite each being separated by only a few miles.

The most popular way to visit the area is to take the vintage train that clatters its way from one station to the next on a convenient timetable. This allows you to squeeze all the towns into a one-day visit, skipping or revisiting towns as you like; or you can stay onboard and breeze through all five in under thirty minutes, looking out the window to catch the key panoramic points. Another quick option is to view them by boat; guided trips leave La Spezia throughout the day and offer glimpses of hidden coves and cobalt-colored pools.

True romantics will not want to miss the famous seven-mile (twelve-kilometer) footpath that links the five areas. It is strenuous in places, but generally affords a leisurely stroll, providing options to hikers of all levels. Descending from the north, the first of the Cinque Terre is Monterosso al Mare. This is the only town with a long pebbled beach, and is the wealthiest of the five thanks to its fishing industry. A newer quarter called Fegina is separated from the old town by the hilltop Convento dei Cappuccini, built in 1622, and the eighteenth-century Santuario di Soviore. Monterosso al Mare's tiny streets are home to a growing number of *enoteca* (particularly good is the Enoteca Internazionale) that feature Sciacchetrà, a local wine pressed from raisins, in both a sweet and a dry version.

Ninety minutes away on the footpath (which starts at sea level and climbs up to Porto Rocca) is what many consider to be the most beautiful of the five towns. Vernazza is built on a tiny spit of land extending into the sea and has the area's only true harbor. The church of Santa Margherita di Antiochia, built in 1318, stands tall near a collection of inviting outdoor cafés shaded by yellow umbrellas. Vernazza is a perfect lunch spot, and some of the area's best restaurants are located here, such as Trattoria Gianni Franzi and Gambero Rosso. The local specialty is *acciughe*, or marinated anchovies.

Leaving Vernazza, the path hugs the coast for another ninety minutes to Corniglia, past the eighteenth-century Cantina Mananan, where you can stop to dine or rent a room to stay the night. This is the most strenuous part of the walk, because unlike the other towns, Corniglia is located on a cliff some 300 feet (100 meters) above the sea. But the olive groves and vineyard-lined path on the way to town are stunning. Wine has been made here since antiquity, and the virtues of this nectar were carved onto terracotta vases discovered near Pompeii. In 1340 the

THE WALK OF LOVE

The most celebrated leg of the Cinque Terre's footpath is the so-called Via dell'Amore, or "Walk of Love," that connects Manarola and Riomaggiore. This short path, which takes about twenty minutes for those not inclined to linger, tucks into hidden coves, extends over scenic overlooks, slides under dangling overhead rocks, and opens out breathlessly to steep drops and a foaming sea.

The Walk of Love was built in the early 1900s, when the engineers who installed the railroad that links the five towns through miles of solid rock needed a safe place to store their explosives. Two tiny footpaths led to this secret place. After the railroad company left, local residents calculated they could walk from one town to the other if the paths touched. Two young men were given the princely sum of 10,000 lire (about $5 today) to remove the last of the rock and carve a new channel of communication.

Appropriately called Strada Nuova back then, the story goes that the path sparked numerous new love affairs, and that even the two men who completed the project may have been compelled by a motivation stronger than money. Today the path is still a lovely spot to exchange some affection.

GREEN GOLD

In the Cinque Terre, all agriculture is confined to steep terracing, and only a handful of crops are viable, such as citrus, grapevines, and olives, sometimes planted just two feet apart. Near vertical groves let the crops smile at the sun longer and allow for warm rays to caress each specimen on all sides.

What sets Liguria's oil apart is the difficulty associated with its farming: no machines can be used to harvest the olives, and workers must negotiate the zigzagging elevations. Ingenious farmers have employed gravity to take care of a large part of the harvest. Orange netting is installed to collect fallen fruit and helps avoid the bruising that causes a bitter taste. The thick and syrupy extra-virgin olive oil of the Cinque Terre has an acidity of .80 percent and is lower in color intensity than most others. It's a sensuous treat not to be missed.

poet Petrarch spoke of "vines lit up by the kindly eye of the sun and most pleasing to Bacchus." Corniglia also offers a famous staircase: Thirty-five flights and a total of 377 stairs connect the town to the train station below, where you can start your journey back.

One hour further on by foot, along a stretch that overlooks beaches accessible only by boat, Manarola sits on the black rock that characterizes this part of Liguria and is the second largest of the five lands. Its name derives from Manium Arula, a Roman temple built for the souls of the dead on the site, a historical tidbit that seems lost on its sunny residents.

The last town to the south, and the most visited of the Cinque Terre, is Riomaggiore. It is situated around a quaint harbor and divided into two parts that straddle the Maggiore River. Its charm has been slightly dampened by concrete construction at the outer edges, but its center boasts the same picturesque appeal as the others.

❦ GOLFO DEI POETI ❦

It is impossible to pinpoint Italy's most romantic spot, but Portovenere is surely a top contender for the title. Named after the goddess of love herself, romance is part of its urban makeup. A temple to Venus once stood on the tip of the promontory that reaches toward the island of Palmaria. Those who worshipped the goddess centuries ago scampered along the exposed rock to steal kisses and exchange flirtatious glances, just as they do today. Even Christianity could not diminish the power of Venus here. A curious little church with zebra-like black-and-white stripes, built in 1277, now stands where the temple once did, and when I first saw it as a young girl, I vowed I would be married there.

Others who have fallen under Portovenere's spell include Lord Byron and Percy Bysshe Shelley, after whom the Gulf of Poets is named. Shelley rented the Casa Magni in nearby Lerici, and Byron wrote his famous *The Corsair* inside a grotto that collapsed in the 1930s. An avid swimmer, Byron regularly kicked his way past sapphire-colored inlets and rocks covered in green moss to visit Shelley on the other side of the bay. Shelley died in a boating accident near Livorno in 1822. Later D. H. Lawrence moved near here for one year to write. And in 1975 the Italian Nobel Prize–winner Eugenio Montale (who had a summer home in Monterosso al Mare) handed out scraps of paper with his poetry scribbled on them as gifts to local shopkeepers.

> See the mountains kiss high Heaven
> And the waves clasp one another;
> No sister-flower would be forgiven
> If it disdained its brother,
> And the sunlight clasps the earth
> And the moonbeams kiss the sea:
> What is all this sweet work worth
> If thou kiss not me?

—from *Love's Philosophy*, by Percy Bysshe Shelley

CUPID'S CORNERS

RESTAURANTS

Focacceria della Manuelina

Via Roma, 278
16036 Recco
Tel: (+39) 0185 74128
Fax: (+39) 0185 721095
www.manuelina.it

You can't come to Liguria without trying the
region's delicious focaccia, an oven-baked flatbread.
Manuelina is a historic focacceria (as well as an
elegant restaurant and hotel) open since 1885.
Ask for the focaccia all'olio, crispy flatbread slightly
charred at the edges topped with dribbles of
extra-virgin olive oil, salt, and chopped rosemary,
or the focaccia col formaggio, stuffed with oozing,
piping-hot cheese. It's culinary perfection as far
as bread is concerned.

Da Giovanni

16030 San Fruttuoso, Camogli
Tel: (+39) 0185 770047
Fax: (+39) 0185 770047

The difficulty getting here is what gives Da
Giovanni its romantic edge. You can hike or go
by boat—either way, your appetite will be roused
once you see this charming restaurant nestled
beside the San Fruttuoso abbey. Monks came
here for spiritual cleansing and communion
with God. But any ascetic intentions will col-
lapse at the first whiff from the kitchen: Da
Giovanni is all about celebrating indulgence.
Baby octopus is cooked in the oven with wine
and pine nuts. Waiters who descend from the
fishermen that fed the abbey's monks serve
shellfish and lobster with a wink and a smile.
After lunch, you'll want to take a long nap on the
beach. Better yet, there are a few spartan but very
private rooms for overnight stays.

Paracucchi Locanda dell'Angelo

Viale XXV Aprile, 60 (Fiumaretta)
19031 Ameglia (La Spezia)
Tel: (+39) 0187 643912
Fax: (+39) 0187 64393
www.paracucchilocanda.it

I'm usually not one for minimalist settings
outside of Milan, but this hip hotel, cooking
school, and world-class restaurant is an
exception. Built in the 1970s by Vico Magistretti,
one of Italy's most innovative architects, it was
designed to reflect the white mountains and
blue seas. The restaurant is run by Marco
Paracucchi, who took over for his father, Angelo,
a famous chef and cookbook author in Italy. The
family also offers one-week cooking courses that
cover culinary theory and practice. The menu
changes regularly, but the dishes are always
surprisingly simple. Menu eye-poppers include
involtino di scampi e melanzane (prawns and
eggplant rolled together) or chitarrucci agli scampi
e olive taggiasche (pasta with prawns and local
Ligurian olives). Dessert includes a scrumptious

mousse di castagne con salsa ai cachi (chestnut mousse with persimmons). An excellent wine selection accompanies every course.

Ristorante Ca'Peo
Via dei Caduti, 80
16040 Chiavari a Leivi
Tel: (+39) 0185 319696
Fax. (+39) 0185 319671
www.capeo.it

A meal at this elegant and expensive restaurant, with breathtaking panoramic views of the Gulf of Tigullio, is well worth the trip (reservations are mandatory). Franco Solari and his wife, Melly, will dazzle you with one of the most memorable meals in Liguria. Feast on flat noodles made of chestnut flour and pesto made fresh in a mortar and served with potatoes and broccoli, ravioli filled with mullet, or roasted porcini mushrooms in a potato pie. Follow the main course with local cheeses, including sarazzu (very ripe ricotta) or dessert such as home-made chocolate pie, apple flambé with marron glacé ice cream, or berries and pudding. The cantina houses more than 250 Italian wines, including Ligurian varietals. Lazy lovebirds can spend the night by renting one of the farmhouse suites.

LA CUCINA PROFUMATA

Ligurian fare is known as la cucina profumata, or "fragrant food." While fish is clearly a central ingredient, the region's most prized culinary creation is pesto, named after the mortar and pestle used to grind the garlic, pine nuts, olive oil, cheese, and basil that comprise the green sauce. Pesto has a long shelf life, which made it appealing to sailors at sea, and those on shore leave may have indulged in totem herb basil's aphrodisiac properties (see chapter twelve for a recipe). Wild herbs are used in sauces called tocchi, because they add a "touch" of taste to a meal—and, according to locals, a touch of virility.

Genova's geographic positioning enabled it to influence much of what the rest of the nation ate. Ligurians, whose ancestors once inhabited southeastern France, had dabbled in foreign tastes long before Christopher Columbus opened taste buds to the New World. The tube-shaped pasta called macheroni made by the Genovese in the thirteenth century quickly spread to other Italian ports of call. Popular pasta now includes trenette, slender noodles which are usually paired with pesto, and trofie, or spiraled pasta. Other goodies include farinata, or chickpea flatbread, and oven-baked focaccia.

Fresh fish, ranging from prawns to datteri di mare, or date mussels (so rare that fishing them is banned), is grilled, marinated, or stewed. Cappon magro, a labor-intensive seafood salad, calls for more than a dozen types of fish. Codfish is a culinary point of reference, much like in the rest of the Mediterranean basin. It is cooked with a Ligurian twist to make stoccafisso, or cod stew with white wine, nuts, olives, potatoes, and herbs. Baccalà (see chapter twelve) is a menu staple, and its presence demonstrates the influence of the ancient god Bacchus.

Hotel Cenobio dei Dogi

Via Nicolò Cuneo, 34
16032 Camogli
Tel: (+39) 0185 7241
Fax: (+39) 0185 772796
www.cenobio.it

Operated by the same people who own the nearby Hotel Portofino Kulm (the two hotels are connected by shuttle bus), Cenobio dei Dogi enjoys the more romantic spot of the two. As it should: It was once the summer residence of Genova's doges, who settled for nothing less than the best. The leisure palace dates back to 1565 and is surrounded by a lush garden on a tiny bay at the foot of Mount Portofino.

Grand Hotel dei Castelli

Via Penisola, 26
16039 Sestri Levante
Tel: (+39) 0185 485780
Fax: (+39) 0185 44767
www.hoteldeicastelli.com

This stone castle-turned-hotel earns romantic points thanks to the legend behind its location. Once upon a time, there was a little spot along the Ligurian coast where the sea was bluer and the sun shined longer. Mermaids chose it as their place to meet and gossip. Young and handsome Tigullio happened to see Segesta, the most beautiful of the mermaids, and he fell madly in love. One night he tried to kidnap Segesta so that she would be his

forever. But jealous Neptune, god of the sea, learned of the plan, and just as Tigullio extended his arm to grab the mermaid, Neptune turned it to stone. The little isthmus under the Castello dei Cipressi (with twenty-nine romantic guest rooms) is said to be Tigullio's petrified arm, frozen in love.

Grand Hotel Miramare

16038 Santa Margherita Ligure
Tel: (+39) 0185 287013
Fax: (+39) 0185 284651
www.grandhotelmiramare.it

This Belle Époque building overlooking the Gulf of Tigullio is the perfect refuge for romantics. Laurence Olivier and Vivian Leigh spent their honeymoon here in 1947, and countless couples have followed in their footsteps. The hotel is available for large weddings and receptions, and organizes honeymoon holiday packages. Back when wealthy foreigners did a mandatory "grand tour" of Italy, it was fashionable to have a Miramare sticker attached to their steamer trunk.

Hotel Splendido

Salita Baratta, 16
16034 Portofino
Tel: (+39) 0185 267801
Fax: (+39) 0185 267807
www.splendido.orient-express.com

The staff won't blink an eye when they tell you this is the world's most romantic hotel. While that may be a matter of interpretation, without a doubt this sixteenth-century former monastery is an institution

to love. The most famous stars of the silver screen have stayed at this luxury hotel, including Brigitte Bardot, Clark Gable, and Humphrey Bogart. Splendido started attracting its A-list crowd in 1952, when the Duke of Windsor became the first to sign the guestbook.

Splendido offers a honeymoon package in which guests sail on a thirty-four-foot sloop to secret swimming holes; champagne and flower petals on the bed are arranged for their return. All guests can enjoy a range of activities, such as a hiking excursion to collect herbs with a botanist who explains their special properties, followed by cooking lessons. At €2,000 per couple per night, it is pricey. A slightly more affordable branch called Splendido Mare opened in 1998 on the Portofino waterfront.

Hotel Stella Maris
Via Marconi, 4
19015 Levanto
Tel: (+39) 0187 808258
Fax: (+39) 0187 807351
www.hotelstellamaris.it

This is an adorable little hotel that has unexplainably been bequeathed only two stars. Located near the Cinque Terre, and an excellent base from which to explore them, Stella Maris boasts eight rooms, many of which have gilded chandeliers and ceilings frescoed with cupids and angels that smile down on antique queen-sized beds. There are an additional eight rooms in a nearby building, and the hotel is a favorite among honeymooners. You won't find a place with more atmosphere and genuine warmth, and the in-house restaurant serves delicious seafood.

Villa Pagoda
Via Capolungo, 15
16167 Genova-Nervi
Tel: (+39) 010 3726161
Fax: (+39) 010 321218
www.villapagoda.it

About 200 years ago a rich merchant from Genova fell in love with a young woman from China he met during one of his voyages. Upon his return to Italy, he built his summer residence Villa Pagoda as a tribute to her exotic beauty. In the years that followed, this five-story palace surrounded by lush gardens in the picturesque town of Nervi

(immediately south of Genova) became a favorite haunt of artists and intellectuals. It wasn't until the Cavaliere family stepped in that Villa Pagoda was reborn as a four-star hotel. Now a member of the Romantik Hotels association, this is an ideal hideaway for couples seeking to avoid the glaring glitz and glamour of the Riviera. There is private access to the beach, and each room is carefully decorated with the same antiques and precious textiles that the Genovese merchant collected during his trips abroad.

Locanda di Palazzo Cicala
Piazza San Lorenzo, 16
16123 Genova
Tel: (+39) 010 2518824
Fax: (+39) 010 2467414
www.palazzocicala.it

If you plan an overnight stay in Genova, reserve a room at the urban-chic Palazzo Cicala. This 500 year-old building has been recently modernized with Philippe Starck toilets, Ron Arad sofas, and Achille Castiglioni hanging lamps. Ask for room 6, the most romantic thanks to its low ceilings and cozy atmosphere. The hotel is also affiliated with the hip dining spots Cantine Squarciafico (www.squarciafico.it) and Mentelocale Restaurant in the Palazzo Ducale.

VENICE,
VERONA,
AND
VENUS

Baso no fa buso, ma xe scala
per anda suso

A kiss won't take you all the way,
but it's the stairway for going further.

Venetian proverb

he Veneto region is home to two of the country's most romantic cities, Venice and Verona. Together they form Italy's romantic heartland, with Venice as the honeymoon capital, and Verona as the wedding capital.

In Venice newlyweds steal kisses in gondolas sliding past the Bridge of Sighs on their pilgrimage to the Lagoon City. Daring couples can choose to spend a night in the Grand Canal *palazzo*, rumored to be haunted by the ghost of a peasant boy buried alive in the building's thick walls by the father of the young girl he fell in love with. If masks and costumes turn you on, Venice's February carnival should not be missed. During the celebration revelers employ pointed glances and silent gestures to slip undetected in and out of each other's grasp.

Although Venetians are known to be suspicious of the tourists who inundate their unique city—a local motto, "*chi ama el forestiero ama el vento*," admonishes that one who loves a foreigner loves the wind—keep in mind that practically anyone born outside the city is considered a foreigner of sorts. The city and its former republic became part of a united Italy rather recently, in 1866, and that was only after they'd been defeated by Napoleon, were made part of the Hapsburg Empire, and consequently fought three wars for independence. All of this has contributed to the unique feel of the city today, which in some areas seems to be a nearly deserted small village, perfect for intimate conversations and furtive kisses, and in others appears to be the center of the world, with beautiful couples showing off during their evening stroll between an aperitif, a theater show, and dinner.

The absence of cars and other traffic from Venice's thoroughfares is one of the first differences visitors notice. At the height of its naval power, the city's vast reign was referred to as the *Serenissima Repubblica*—and that was well before cars were invented, so you can just imagine how peaceful it seems in comparison with the contemporary world. This rare peace is conducive not only to serenades and lingering along the canals to watch the gondolas quietly glide past, but also to the curious, very private mode of conversing one must adopt here, as any word said too loudly immediately carries across the stones and water to your neighbor's ear—which is inevitably closer than you expect.

The city is divided into six regions called *sestieri*—San Marco, San Polo, Santa Croce, Dorsoduro, Canareggio, and Castello—each with its own lore, character, and landmarks. The festival of its patron, Saint Mark, on April 25, is also the day on which it was founded in 421 AD, settled by refugees fleeing barbarians. While Venetians tend to have the closed manner one would expect from the descendants of refugees, for centuries they also were the merchant masters of a large commercial seafaring republic, and therefore have a cosmopolitan and utterly unique air impossible to find elsewhere. From Marco Polo's expeditions to Lord Byron's verses written for his many lovers here, the city has perennially opened itself to new ideas, culture, and, of course, relationships.

Venice's Captivating Passages

Adding to the enchantment of this serene city is the fact that everything has a special name. Take for example the car-free routes: A street, which elsewhere in Italy is called *via*, locally is baptized *calle*; a canal filled in to create a street is dubbed a *rio terà*; a street that runs along a canal is a *fondamenta*; and some lanes that run along the lagoon's shore are called *rive*. I highly recommend that visitors take part in the traditional aperitif hour, and when you do, instead of ordering a glass of wine by requesting a *bicchiere di vino*, ask for a red or white *ombra*, or "shadow"—an allusion to the fact that wine merchants unloading barrels and flasks from ships by Saint Mark's Square would set their goods in the shadow of the bell tower, to keep the wine cool and out of the sun.

Venice's narrowest street is near the Fondamente Nove in Canareggio; Calle Varisco is reduced to twenty-one inches at its most extreme. Two other notably constricted lanes are close contenders: the twenty-three-inch wide Calesela De l'Ochio Grosso in Castello, and the Ramo de Ca'Zusto in Santa Croce, where locals will warn you that attempting to pass through it in twos can be difficult or—given the right company—a most delightful new experience.

A City of Devilish Temptation

Castello is the *sestiere* perhaps least overrun by tourists and the richest in popular lore. A tale of the devil in a dress helps to explain the existence of Ponte del Diavolo, or "Devil's Bridge" (also known as Ponte della Tentazione, or "Temptation Bridge"), which one crosses, curiously enough, while en route to Calle dei Preti—Priest Street. A sixteenth-century legend holds that a certain young Tonio was determined to join the priestly fold when, while crossing the bridge on his way to dedicate his life to religion, he encountered a buxom young temptress who invited him to enjoy earthly pleasures with her, rather than waste his vitality on more celestial aspirations. Church superior Don Marco Fornaro—luckily or not, depending on one's view— witnessed this and confronted the woman while brandishing a crucifix, forcing her to reveal her true devilish nature. An alternative history, retold in anecdotes of libertine Venice, attributes the bridge's name to the simple fact that it connected the monastery of San Severo to the nunnery of San Zaccaria—two famously promiscuous cloisters.

THE ART OF FLIRTATION

A French fan maker noted the following guidelines for his small masterpieces, as employed in the hands of Venetian women:

> Twirling a closed fan, held in the left hand: "I am looking at you."
> Holding a fan closed in the right hand, in front of one's face: "Follow me."
> Covering one's left ear with an open fan: "Don't give away our secret."
> Tracing lines with a closed fan on the palm of one's hand: "I hate you."
> Tracing lines on one's cheek: "I love you."
> Touching the end of the closed fan with one's fingertips: "Let's talk."
> Holding the fan still on one's right cheek: "Yes."
> Holding the fan still on one's left cheek: "No."
> Opening and closing the fan: "You're cruel."
> Letting the fan fall to the ground: "We'll be friends."
> Slowly fanning oneself: "I'm married."
> Quickly fanning oneself: "I'm engaged."
> Bringing the handle of the fan to one's lips: "Kiss me."

Nearby, in the same *sestiere*, you will find Calle de le Moschete; this would appear to indicate a "street of flies" but, as with most curious street names here, actually refers to something rather more flirtatious. *Moschete* in this case are the small "flylike" faux moles, more attractively known as beauty marks, that Venetian women dispersed across face, neck, and bosom as amatory aids, and which were fabricated in several small workshops along this street. They were available in star, crescent moon, circle, diamond, and heart shapes, and strict names and meanings were attached to each depending on where they were placed. Similarly intricate rules existed for another tool of flirtation—the hand-held fan. Fans of silk, parchment, and painted paper were a key to communication during courtship and between potential couples, and this rite can still be observed during the more silent moments of today's carnival. While the carnival masks are famous for their clear role in both hiding and revealing identities, these fans and their subtle movements were equally vital.

If you happen to visit Venice during the carnival, you will see the festival's most skilled masqueraders employing these intricate rituals of communication, and the many beautiful fans available in shops throughout the city make it possible for you to add this to your own repertoire.

❧ LOVE AND PINING ❧

Naturally, when discussing love and the Lagoon City, Giacomo Casanova inevitably comes to mind. This famous writer, whose works record in detail his mastery of the art of seduction, was born here in 1725, and although his many affairs (not to mention his incarceration for having written openly about his conquests) eventually led him far away, one of the *palazzi* he lived in

MARY, LOVELY MAIDENS,
AND MARIONETTES

The Festa delle Marie is just one part of Venice's centuries-old obsession with feminine beauty. What is now basically a beauty pageant each carnival, in which twelve of the city's most beautiful girls parade about, began as a remembrance of a marriage ceremony in the church of San Pietro, in Castello. During the wedding Narentian pirates invaded the church and massacred nearly everyone. Clever as they were, the pirates spared twelve lovely maidens, gathered the church's treasures, and loaded everything into their boats. It didn't take long for the surviving Venetians to get back on their feet and into their fastest ships, soon overtaking the Narentians off the coast of present-day Caorle and saving their young women in the area of coastline now known as Porto delle Donzelle, or "Port of the Young Women." Since then, this day has been celebrated as the Festa delle Marie, because February 2, the day the brides-to-be were saved, is also the day of Saint Mary's purification.

This festival has gone through several metamorphoses in the centuries since its inception. Initially, two young women from each of the six *sestieri* were chosen to honor Mary, escorted in a grand procession of decorated gondolas to the church of San Pietro. They were richly adorned in new gowns, lavished with jewels, and given treasures, so that by the end of the celebration they were ready to marry, complete with a dowry provided by the city government. This annual ritual soon grew out of hand, as jealous fights broke out between the families of the few women chosen, and by 1272 the number was reduced from twelve to four women, and soon thereafter reduced again to three. Not long after that, it was decided that the number should return to twelve, but instead of live brides, twelve statues carved out of wood, called *Marione* or "large Mary," because of their larger-than-life scale, were used. The city's enterprising craftsmen were quick to start carving tiny versions of these statues to sell as souvenirs at the festival, and their nickname for these small reproductions, *marionette*, now lends its name to all small theatrical puppets. This procession is the root of the carnival festivities that now last a full week, and sometimes a few days more.

remains one of the most interesting examples of Gothic architecture in its transition toward the Renaissance style. Palazzo Bragadin Carabba, in Castello on Calle Bragadin 6050, was his home for nine years. Two centuries before he moved in, this was also the place where women's earrings made their first appearance in the city, to great clamor among the ever fashion-minded crowd, during the marriage reception of Matteo Bragadin's niece. Although Casanova's innumerable conquests probably would make it possible to inscribe historical plaques to him on almost each canal and *calle* throughout the city, this spot certainly merits a visit.

Another special place for couples is the Ponte dei Sospiri, or "Bridge of Sighs," among the most famous to span the city's canals. Originally the bridge earned this name because it led from the courthouse to the prison and execution chambers, thus providing the last visit between the condemned and his beloved. But this sadder history has been replaced by a more romantic attribute—it is one of the more stunning bridges under which couples ride in gondolas, sighing with delight at the overwhelming beauty.

SAINT MARK, HOLINESS, AND A PENCHANT FOR DRAMA

The theme of annunciation lies at the core of the city's founding mythology about its patron, Saint Mark. According to the story, on his voyage from Aquilea to Rome, the saint stopped for rest at the island of Rialto, one of the first parts of the city to be settled, but in his time still a wilderness. An angel appeared to him in a dream and foretold the building of a marvelous city right where he slept. Part of the pronouncement was that this future city would hold his remains, as he would be its patron.

A reenactment of the scene of the Annunciation as it appears in the gospel of Luke, including priests who play Saint Gabriel and the Virgin Mary, became a key part in an exclusively Venetian festival. This rite, the *Festa delle Marie*, has a long, rich history that is as inextricably bound to legend as the city itself. Its rites and processions transformed the city, its government order, and the inhabitants, eventually becoming the riotous carnival that continues to this day.

The festival at the root of carnival, which began as a chance to pay homage to virtue and innocence, rapidly became a forum for citizens to thumb their noses at ordinary rule, criticize their rulers, and above all for young women to liberate themselves from the strict scrutiny of their guardians, flirtatiously flaunting their vanity, attracting male attention, and distracting all from the ostensibly holy reason for the celebration. This is just further proof that Venetians not only have a serious penchant for allegory, but also that they easily confound allegory and reality. This is a trait particular to this city and is evident not only in the carnival processions, but also in some great literature written here. Couples looking for suggested reading and viewing to enrich their trip are encouraged to check out the works of Casanova, Lord Byron, Aretino, and the films of Luchino Visconti for a crash course in the major role metaphor assumes in this city's life. In addition, the creation of self-aggrandizing myth and skill in the masquerade—in turning reality into fiction and vice versa—all play part in any consideration of the city.

THEATRICAL TEMPTATIONS

Most visitors to Venice will certainly be familiar with the famous Gran Teatro La Fenice, originally built in 1790, partially destroyed by fire in 1836, and burnt completely to the ground in 1996. After a major reconstruction it is now once again open to the public, and no matter how many photos you have seen or how many recordings of performances there you have heard, nothing can beat attending a live performance. Prepare to have your breath taken away. Although skeptics claimed any reconstructed version would never be as beautiful as the original, it is worth bearing in mind the theater's name: *La Fenice* is the phoenix. Just as any great love affair—be it between two people, or a city and its theater—is reborn after disaster, this theater has become even greater each of the two times it has risen from the ashes.

LOVELY SPOTS ON THE ISLANDS OF THE VENETIAN LAGOON

Aside from the thousands of islets that contribute to a most singular horizon, the lagoon around Venice has four main islands, each with its own distinct feel.

Lido, the famous seaside resort of Venice, features dunes and open beaches within view of the city; only a short *vaporetto* ride away, it is perfect for when the romantic alleys, canals, and bridges of the city begin to seem perhaps a little too intimate. The Alberoni beach offers the best breathing room, and couples looking to stay in Venice and get the best sunset and sunrise views over the Adriatic should consider staying at the Grand Hotel des Bains or the Excelsior. Aside from its beaches, Lido also has orchards, more open-air markets, gardens, and an *agriturismo* catering to those looking for something off the beaten path.

For those intrigued by the innumerable glass treasures found in almost every Venetian shop window, Murano, to the east, offers visits to the breathtaking glassworks. Burano, meanwhile, is known for its *merletti* and *pizzi*—masterpieces made in lace—and the local women can still be seen producing work of the highest quality.

Torcello is the furthest, and in many respects the most interesting, of the islands. It is also the most solitary and lends itself perfectly to couples looking to get away to a world of their own. Remains of Venice's ancient Roman heritage, overlooked everywhere else, can still be found, as can one of novelist Ernest Hemingway's preferred eating spots, the Locanda Cipriani. Their signature *riso alla torcellana* is the perfect prelude to a secluded romantic evening.

STOLEN KISSES

For centuries a kiss given in a church or house doorway, the quick snipping of a small braid of hair, or the swift theft of a jewel were considered acts with which a matrimony could be sealed. The parents of the girl were forced to give their consent, or their daughter would face great difficulty finding another husband. In some instances, however, the act of stealing a kiss, which stood for a symbolic abduction of sorts, offended the honor of the young woman and relit old interfamilial disputes, causing anger and new vendettas that required swift resolution—often through "honor-restoring" bloodshed.

While wandering through Castello, you may come across a curious passageway in Calle del Cafetier. At the Fava, a curious cross between a dark courtyard and a dead-end alley, you will find a stone with a cross and the inscription Dio ti vede, or "God is watching." Right across from this is another stone with a drawing of a deathlike figure. Local lore claims these two stones were placed here as an effective device to deter sinful nighttime rendezvous in what is otherwise a most perfectly romantic, private spot. For those keen on the historical theme of love and death, and undeterred by the superstitions, a walk here is highly recommended.

The Veneto coast, on the northern shore of the Venetian lagoon, offers many beaches and hamlets for those wishing to break out of the classic tourism canon and explore the *terraferma*. More than seventy-five miles (120 kilometers) of coastline await, including the beach resorts Bibione, Albarella, Caorle, Eraclea Mare, Lido di Jesolo, Litorale del Cavallino, Chioggia, and Rosolina. Most visitors coming from Venice are surprised by the lush greenery found so close to the lagoon's coast. Mediterranean pines line fine sands, providing a shady haven for summer siestas protected from the sun. For couples who find camping and a natural environment more romantic than the stones and palaces of Venice itself, this is the place. A prime example is Jesolo, which offers some ten miles (fifteen kilometers) of golden beach stretching from the edge of the Venetian lagoon to the banks of the Piave River. The town itself has a distinct flavor, showing its roots in the rule of the Hapsburg Empire in both the architecture and cuisine. Here the gastronomic specialties center on the river, sea, and the inland countryside. The waters of the lagoon create a sweet climate most favorable to a key local delicacy, eel. For a meal spiced up by the bitter leaves of radicchio, claimed to have aphrodisiac properties, visit the nearby town of Oderzo.

❧ Verona ❧

Verona is the setting of Romeo and Juliet's tragic love story, and a visit to the Shakespearean site of Juliet's balcony is a mandatory stop on any romantic itinerary. Tradition dictates that lovers inscribe their initials on the chalky walls near the world's most famous balcony. It is said that by doing so, even the most capricious lovers are guaranteed long-lasting love. It may well be true, since couples flock to the city. Verona holds Italy's record for most foreign weddings, and has earned its reputation as the city of love.

Verona's romantic attractions go far beyond being the stage for one of the world's greatest love stories. Its ancient Roman, medieval, Gothic, and Renaissance layers have left something to appeal to the lover in everyone. The Roman amphitheater stages Shakespeare, opera, and classical music festivals, which you can enjoy before heading for a candlelit dinner at any one of the many charming nearby *trattorie*. The ancient Roman arena, located in the heart of the city, is an unforgettable setting for the operas and concerts offered throughout the summer season. While many of the operas performed each year—such as *Nabucco*, *Aïda*, and *La Forza del Destino*—are mainly historical works, others, such as *La Traviata*, tell the tale of the world's most melodramatic lovers.

For those looking for a romantically pastoral place to whisper sweet nothings into one another's ears, the Giardino Giusti is perfect. A short walk across the Adige River from the city

center, this is one of Europe's most famous gardens, replete with a large sculpture inspired by a theater mask just below a panoramic point offering an unsurpassed view over the city and surrounding hills. Goethe was inspired to write about the lovely large cypress tree just to the left of the entrance, and a small bush labyrinth makes a perfect spot for coquettish couples who like to play hide-and-seek.

While Verona provides a rich core of romantic spots, the small towns of the surrounding region supply many other sweet possibilities, making a trip out of town worthwhile.

MALCESINE

During the golden age of the Venetian Republic, Malcesine was an important trading center, where boats full of riches sailed on Lake Garda. The strikingly romantic landscape surrounding this small town just outside of Verona provides superb scenery—views that left Goethe astonished, and were subsequently described in rapture-filled sections of his romantic writings.

VALEGGIO

Located just fifteen miles (twenty-five kilometers) outside Verona and a mere stone's throw from Lake Garda, Valeggio is the medieval town that best shows the strong traces of the area's mixed Lombard and Venetian heritage. For centuries, it marked the border of the two regions and was therefore a crossroads where travelers could always find good food and a safe place to sleep. Today Valeggio remains a restaurant-rich town, noted for its hospitality. It is a good place to stop for a meal and immerse yourself in an enchanting atmosphere.

MONSELICE

For those wishing to stay inland, take a trip to quaint Monselice, in the vicinity of Padua, which sits on the slopes of the Euganei hills and is full of Renaissance palaces, such as Villa Nani Mochenigo and Villa Duodo. For wine lovers, sipping a glass in one of the area's many romantic cantinas and vineyards is an absolute must.

ARQUÀ PETRARCA

Nearby, the medieval hamlet Arquà Petrarca is famous as the final resting place of the fourteenth-century poet Petrarch. Fans say his verses on love have yet to be equaled in the six centuries since he so eloquently poured his heart into ink and paper, and his books and works can still be found in the house where he resided in the center of town.

ABANO TERME

The Greek root of Abano, which means "relieves pain," indicates perfectly the town's fame as a spa center and thermal health retreat. According to local myth, Abano was founded by Hercules, who stopped in these hills to recover from his strenuous labors in Spain. The virtues of the town have been extolled for centuries: The Roman epic poet Claudian dedicated more than 100 lines of praise to the baths at Abano. This ancient volcanic zone and its surrounding Colli Euganei Nature Park include more than 40,000 extremely fertile acres where one can pay a visit to numerous hot springs and vineyards. The region is dotted by picturesque little villages for exploring, and castles dating back to the Middle Ages have been converted into hotels with incredibly romantic views, both inside and beyond their walls. Contemporary vineyards and farmhouses also offer romantic retreats, where the ancient local traditions survive in a bucolic setting.

 PADUA

Padua, just twenty miles (thirty kilometers) inland from Venice and a famed university town since 1222, should be on everyone's itinerary, not only for its noted intellectual inspiration but also for its lesser-known amorous ambiance. The Scrovegni chapel houses Giotto's magnificent thirty-six frescoes from the twelfth century, the university still holds Galileo's chair, and Andrea Mantegna's fifteenth-century paintings may be admired in the church of the Eremitani. For an unforgettable lunch, make reservations on the daylong boat trip from Venice to Padua. A complicated canal system spanning some thirty miles (fifty kilometers), complete with locks and pools, connects the two cities. The boat stops at celebrated Palladian villas along the way, and you'll be treated to a lavish lunch served on board.

CUPID'S CORNERS

As anyone who has visited will tell you, Venice and Verona are dripping with romance, and the sense of a rich and sensual cultural heritage pervades the region. Just being in Verona can put anyone in an amorous mood, and walking the bridges and sculling the canal of Venice is about as beautiful a way to spend a day as you can find. With that in mind, I've chosen to single out just a few places that stand out even in this, the most romantic region of Italy.

RESTAURANTS

Locanda Cipriani
Piazza San Fosca, 29
30012 Torcello
Tel: (+39) 041 735 433

Hiring a launch to take a lover across the lagoon is romantic enough, but setting foot on the island of Torcello and arriving at this restaurant is breathtaking. Locanda's walls are covered in memories of visitors past, including sketches from Charlie Chaplin, a painting by Marc Chagall, and photographs of the restaurant's most loyal devotee— Ernest Hemingway. The food is rich and delicious, and drinking wine by the restaurant's fogher (a regional outdoor fireplace) and sitting in one of the various dining rooms is an unmitigated pleasure.

HOTELS

Hotel des Bains
Lungomare Marconi, 17
30126 Venice Lido
Tel: (+39) 041 526 5921

Now more than a century old, the Hotel des Bains remains the grandest hotel in the city. Memorably captured as the setting for Thomas Mann's haunting novella of beauty and mortality, *Death in Venice*, the hotel transports guests to the era of the Grand Tour, to an aristocratic way of life, and to an atmosphere of dignified and sensual romance. This is simply the place for serious honeymooners.

Venice Metropole
Riva Degli Schiavoni, 4149
30122 Venice
Tel: (+39) 351 21 464 74 30
metropole.hotelinvenice.com

Facing the lagoon as it meets the Grand Canal, and steps away from Piazza San Marco, the Metropole is a pristine relic of Old World Venice. Beautifully decorated interiors and a charming private garden make it a romantic oasis at the heart of the city.

LOVE
ON
THE
LAKES

AMATEVI COME COMPAGNI DI VIAGGIO,

CON QUESTO PENSIERO D'AVERE
A LASCIARVI,

E CON LA SPERANZA DI RITROVARVI
PER SEMPRE.

Love each other as companions in a journey,

with the thought that you will have to
part from one another,

and with the hope of being reunited forever.

Alessandro Manzoni, I promessi sposi

**A**ny scenographer knows that in theater, the stage on which the drama unfolds is key. It must be layered in planes that guide the eye to a focal point. The operative word is perspective, and its visual impact reaches the maximum in Italy's lake region.

The dizzying presence of two converging perspectives grants a heightened sense of dimension. First is the perfectly horizontal line of the lake surface, extending as far as the eye can see. Second is the sudden vertical rise of the mountains that flank it like a corridor and force your gaze to the sky. If you look at a topographical map of northern Italy, you see how the land butts up against the Swiss and Austrian borders. Within these deep folds are seven lakes that run north to south and become pencil-thin where the mountains are highest. These lakes are Italy's most visually dramatic natural stage.

Lake Como, for example, is an expanse of water with a sapphire color unique to glacier lakes, which undulates thanks to gentle winds or the passing of a ferry. Rocky mountains press on the water from all sides, and the lake is as deep as the mountains are high in many places. Follow these jagged lines to a scenic crescendo: the snow-capped peaks of the Alps that seem to point beyond the limits of our atmosphere. At the water's edge, and wherever nature has afforded the room, are lavish summer villas and towns—all with the inevitable church steeple towering high above the roofline.

It's no wonder this epic setting inspired Italy's greatest love story. Alessandro Manzoni's I promessi sposi, translated as "The Betrothed," is the nation's most significant literary work, second only to Dante Alighieri's The Divine Comedy. The gripping 700-page tome tells the story of lovers Renzo and Lucia, who are separated and prevented from marrying. Set in the turbulent early seventeenth century, when the state of Milan was occupied by the Spanish Habsburgs, the frustrated pair endure obstacles including a corrupt nun, a mean-spirited priest, kidnappings, plague, and famine before destiny reunites them. Love conquers all, and good prevails over evil are the themes of this thinly veiled political novel. It was first released in 1827, but Manzoni published a new edition in 1840 in which he changed the language to a more vernacular form, making it one of the first works written in modern Italian.

In addition to giving his country a love story that has been read by nearly all its citizens since it became part of the school curriculum, Manzoni, an avid gardener, is said to have left

something equally romantic to his beloved lake region: the acacia flower. Thanks to special microclimates and the particular alchemy of the soil, the shores of the lakes are splashed with color from a remarkably rich variety of flowers, plants, and trees: pink and white azaleas, purple rhododendron, the orange of citrus trees, creamy magnolias, violet wisteria, red and yellow tulips.

To see this symphony of colors, you must visit in the spring, mid-May being the best time for azalea viewing. If you come in the fall, however, you have picked the perfect time for a tour of Piedmont's wine. As the summer heat subsides, the first fog starts to descend on the fertile le Langhe area. Grapes are ready to be harvested, hazelnuts hang heavy from trees, and white truffles appear in the forests, for the lucky few who know where to find them.

A section on Milan has also been included here, for those flying to Malpensa International airport—or for those tempted by an Italian shopping detour.

✿ LAGO DI GARDA ✿

The largest of the four lakes covered in this chapter is Lake Garda, which straddles the regions of Lombardy, Veneto, and Trentino. Lemon and olive groves, palm trees, and balmy weather make it the Amalfi Coast of the Alps. Dreamy villas, beaches, perfect windsurfing and sailing conditions, nightclubs, and the Gardaland amusement park (Italy's answer to Disneyland) also mean it's a favorite destination for Germans and northern Europeans, who zip down through the Alpine pass to this Mediterranean wonderland.

If you drive up the lake's eastern shore—from Peschiera near Verona, to Riva, some thirty miles (fifty kilometers) to the north—the flat landscape eventually gives way to cliff-hugging mountain roads and tunnels. Past the unsightly Gardaland is the lakefront town of Lazise, with its colorful collection of Venetian-styled buildings and a fantastic castle. Next is Bardolino, which shares its name with the fragrant red wine produced here. Both towns are fun to explore on foot, but couples looking for a more romantic stroll should head straight to the cypress-lined Punta San Vigilio; a lakeside footpath to the cape starts north of Bardolino.

A Latin inscription inside the chapel of San Vigilio reads *en somni explanatio* ("here your dreams are explained"), and this sums up the spot's impact on the senses. A path leads to the privately owned Villa Guarienti and the Baia delle Sirene (Mermaid's Bay) on the other side of the promontory. Offshore you can see the rock of Scoglio della Stella, named after the nymph Stella, who refused the amorous attentions of the local god of flora and fauna. Since he could not have her, the story goes, he turned her into a stone so that he could admire her beauty for eternity. Another lovely path heads north, through the olive groves, to Torri del Benaco.

At Torri del Benaco, you can catch a ferry to the western shore, or continue your drive north, past Pai and Brenzone to Malcesine—where a rainbow of buildings and castle enclose a tiny harbor. A unique microclimate in Malcesine nurtures so many different species of flora that the area has been called "Italy's botanical garden." One of the best ways to enjoy the panorama is by taking the cable car up Mount Baldo for bird's-eye views of the lake and surrounding mountains. Slightly past Riva to the north is the beautiful Castello d'Arco and another good opportunity for hiking.

Driving on, after another violent tango with Italy's best-engineered road, you'll reach Gargnano. The writer D. H. Lawrence lived here for a spell in 1912 and found some inspiration for *Twilight in Italy*. The town often hosts sailing regattas. To the north, you can admire the recently refurbished Villa Feltrinelli (now a luxury hotel, and available for weddings) with its star-shaped windows and peach Art Nouveau facade. Dictator Benito Mussolini was put under what amounted to house arrest here by the Nazis at the end of his reign.

Past Gargnano, the muscular mountains finally relax and the landscape becomes gentler and flatter. The last leg of Lake Garda begins at Toscolano-Maderno, where you may be tempted to spend long hours on what many say is the lake's best beach and enjoy the views of the fairy-tale Venetian-Gothic villa that adorns Isola di Garda (a private home, believe it or not).

The romantic highlight of Lake Garda is the razor-thin Sirmione peninsula that extends three miles (five kilometers) into the water from the southern shore. At the tip of the peninsula are the evocative remains of a first-century villa known as the Grotta di Catullo. The medieval town of Sirmione is a maze of tiny streets from which you emerge on the waterfront in any direction. A celebrated spa here emphatically underlines the locals' love affair with water, as does the Rocca Scaligera, which ranks among Italy's most picturesque castles because it appears to float on the lake.

✵ Lago di Como ✵

Lake Como is heralded by many as the most beautiful of Italy's lakes. The thin, elongated lake has two branches: Lago di Como, which spans from the city of Como to Colico, and Lago di Lecco, which joins it from the east. A romantic eye might see it as a dancer with her slim legs frozen in an elegant leap, not unlike one of the frolicking figures in Henri Matisse's *Dance*.

The best approach to take is to drive up the western shore, along the via Regina. Named after the beloved Lombard queen Theodolinda, who charmed this part of Italy with her fair skin and light hair in the early seventh century, the road has existed since antiquity as a major artery connecting the fertile Lombard plains to the Alps. Starting at Como, known for its factory outlet stores packed with silk and cashmere goods, the road immediately becomes an astounding journey through charming villages, past Versailles-like palaces and artfully landscaped gardens, and to some of the most breathtaking vistas to be found anywhere.

The best photo ops on the old via Regina are doubtless found in Argegno, a quaint town about twenty minutes north of Moltrasio, with a bridge spanning a waterfall and a road that leads to the so-called "Balcony of Italy." Even better views can be had from the town's cable car into the mountains, or from the *strada panoramica* that rises to 4,300 feet (1,325 meters). The next village north is Sala Comacina, whose Comacina Island is home to Roman ruins and the Baroque oratory of San Giovanni. Once an important military installation, today the lake's only island is a peaceful and romantic hideaway (boat service runs regularly).

At Tremezzo, the two branches of the lower lake converge. Villa Carlotta and its stunning gardens (see box below for more information) is the most accessible of the area's residences. From both Tremezzo and Cadenabbia, a few miles north, you can catch a *traghetto* (car ferry) to Bellagio and Varenna (on the lake's eastern flank). But boats run more frequently from Menaggio, the next town up the road, and this lively town, with a graceful town square littered with café tables, makes a good place to linger for a while over coffee or ice cream.

Menaggio, Varenna, and Bellagio mark the three corners of what must be cupid's inner sanctuary. Water meets mountain, and mountain meets sky, and the light touch of humankind has succeeded in further enhancing nature's masterpiece. Bellagio has become an emblem of sorts of what we consider beautiful—or *bella*—but its name comes from the Latin *bi lacus*, because it overlooks two lakes. Bellagio glows in pink and peach stucco, and cafés, restaurants, and shops line its waterfront. It is among the mandatory stops on a romantic tour of Italy.

Not nearly as popular, Varenna sports value-added attractions for couples. From the ferry docking area, you can walk to the center of town along the appropriately named *strada dell'amore* (path of lovers), which hugs the rock and is shaded by blossoming flowers. In the opposite direction from the port, you'll come across the puzzling Fiumelatte that at a mere 820 feet (250 meters) is Italy's shortest river. From March to October its water rushes down to the lake, but the rest of the year it is inexplicably dry. Leonardo da Vinci once crawled deep into the opening to see where the water goes during these months but failed to find an answer. Perched high above the town is the remains of Castello di Vezio. The hike up is invigorating, and very romantic. The peak affords a view of the roofs of Varenna and the shimmering lake. A tour of the castle includes a random collection of medieval artifacts, including an improbable male chastity belt.

LAKE COMO'S DREAM VILLAS

VILLA DEL BALBIANELLO: Balbianello is largely regarded as the most romantic of Lake Como's villas, thanks to its location at the end of a promontory south of Lenno and its views of Bellagio across the water. The gardens are the main attraction here, with brilliant splashes of azaleas and rhododendrons in the spring. The initial construction was completed in the sixteenth century, and the villa was refurbished 200 years later with loggias, terraces, and a portico with the pavement inscription *fay ce qui voudras*, or "do what you'd like." The villa does accommodate small weddings inside, or larger parties outside in a tent. Today is it owned by the Fondo per l'Ambiente (FAI) (www.fondoambiente.it; click on "i luoghi del FAI," or ask for more information by emailing them at proprieta@fondoambiente.it).

Villa Carlotta: The most photographed of Lake Como's luxury properties, Villa Carlotta is located on the western shore, near Tremezzo. Its sprawling, immaculately tended gardens are home to some 500 species of brilliant flowers and plants, and the eighteenth-century neoclassical home is now a museum with a fantastic collection of romantic art. Near the entrance, for example, you can admire Antonio Canova's marble *Cupid and Psyche*, locked in an amorous embrace. Although the property is open to the public, it does not host weddings. However, it will gladly accommodate couples looking for a breathtaking background for their wedding photographs (www.villacarlotta.it).

Villa Erba: This spectacular residence was built at the end of the nineteenth century by the Erba family and eventually passed into the hands of Carla Erba in the 1920s. She married Duke Giuseppe Visconti di Modrone and gave birth to Luchino Visconti, the legendary movie director who also made his home here. Located in Cernobbio, on the lake's western shore, the villa has two floors joined by a central staircase and a turret with panoramic views. Today, it also includes a conference center, and both the villa and the grounds are available for weddings, large or small (www.villaerba.it).

Villa d'Este: Without a doubt, this is one of Italy's most celebrated luxury hotels, built in 1568 as a summer residence and transformed into a hotel in 1873. The lakefront property includes twenty-five acres of Renaissance gardens where you can play hide-and-seek among

the cupid statues. Steep paths at the back of the garden lead to more fountains, grottoes, and "private love corners." Villa d'Este is efficiently set up to accommodate marriages (although they don't come cheap) and has a full-time wedding planner on staff (www.villadeste.it). The hotel also enjoys an unparalleled reputation among honeymooners.

VILLA MELZI: You can visit the hillside gardens of this villa near Bellagio, complete with water-lily pools and a Moorish-styled garden house. But the neoclassical home itself is closed to the public. Some time spent in the gardens should make a nice addition to your photo album.

VILLA SERBELLONI: Literally perched above Bellagio, this is thought to be the site of the summer home of ancient Rome's Pliny the Younger. It has the largest garden on Lake Como, teeming with magnolias, oleanders, and palms. The building is closed to the public, but meandering through gardens you'll feel as if you were on a honeymoon—even if that was years ago.

There are a slew of lesser-known villas on Lake Como available for weddings or receptions. Studio Brivio (www.comovillas.com) represents the following dream villas:

Villa Cademartori, near Blevio, on the eastern shore north of Como, has a lovely garden that extends to the lake shore, dotted with mossy satyr statues. The villa dates from the sixteenth century, and outstanding features include a tower and pastel-colored rooms.

Villa Parravicini Revel, a few minutes' drive from Como to the west, is a majestic neoclassical mansion built in 1770. The interior features frescoes on the ceiling and mosaic floors. Between the lake and the villa is a small but enchanting Italian garden.

Villa Pizzo (between Cernobbio and Moltrasio), built in the sixteenth century, is surrounded by olive trees, figs, and vines. It is christened after the promontory on which it stands—or *piz*, in local dialect. Located between Villa d'Este and Villa Fontanella, it was the beloved residence of the late designer Gianni Versace.

Villa Lugarna (near Menaggio), built in an English style, boasts grounds with caves, ponds, and waterfalls, and can be rented by couples for their honeymoon. It is not, however, available for weddings.

Another good resource for those looking to rent a wedding villa is www.dimorestoriche.com. Among the listings is the neoclassical Hotel Villa Flori in Como, with eighty-five rooms; and the Villa Camilla, which is surrounded by tall trees and a manicured lawn.

LAGO MAGGIORE

Lake Maggiore is the region's second largest lake, lapping at the borders of Lombardy, Piedmont, and Switzerland to the north. During the Belle Époque, its shores were among Europe's most fashionable playgrounds for aristocrats and the nouveaux riche. The grandiose buildings and casinos of Stresa—which once rivaled those of Monte Carlo—provide an enduring legacy. While Lake Maggiore may not have the overall panoramic punch of Lake Como or the soothing tranquility of Lake Orta, its little collection of islands is simply out of this world—precisely as their eccentric owners intended them to be.

If you come from the south, you first encounter the water at Arona. The main monument here, just outside of town (you won't miss it), is the 115-foot (thirty-five-meter) copper statue of San Carlo. You can climb up inside "Charlie," peer out through his eyes, and admire the technique used to fasten the huge metal sheets together that comprise the outer shell. This workmanship was copied later by those assembling New York's Statue of Liberty.

Following the lakeshore, you eventually hit Stresa, the most picturesque town here. Located at the southern lip of the Gulfo Borromeo and at the very heart of Lake Maggiore, Stresa made its way into Ernest Hemingway's novel A Farewell to Arms and has inspired other literary figures as well, such as Lord Byron. Lavish villas line the waterfront, and behind them is a cheerful patch of cafés, hotels, and shops. At the end of August the town is at its loveliest yet when it hosts a week-long music festival. From Stresa, you can catch a cable car to ascend the 5,000-foot (1,500-meter) summit of Mount Mottarone. Some claim you can see all of Italy's seven lakes on a clear day, but instead count on fabulous views of the immense Lake Maggiore. Midway up the mountain is the Alpinia Botanical Garden (also reached by the cable car), where amateur botanists can inspect some 700 plant species. The hardy can opt to climb the nine-mile (fourteen-kilometer) path to reach Mottarone's summit (you need about five hours from Stresa).

From Stresa's shores, those strange forms you see floating on the lake are the famed Isole Borromee. The closest of the bunch is Bella Island (boats leave regularly from Stresa to all three islands). Also known as Isola Inferiore, the island is dominated by a colossal Baroque—thing—that is in fact a palace and garden designed to look like a huge boat. The palace was begun in 1632, when Count Charles III Borromeo transformed a sleepy fishing village into a summertime retreat for himself and his wife, Isabella d'Adda, whose name it bears (hence "Bella"). The interior features a collection of art and tapestries (even a bed slept in by Napoleon and Josephine) and a knockout lower-level grotto completely plastered in seashells that are attached to the walls like mosaics. But it is the gardens that are the center of attraction: ten terraces at the "bow" of this rocky vessel, where beautiful flora wraps itself around statues of divinity and Borromeo family symbols.

The next island over is Isola dei Pescatori (Fishermen's Island), which to this Los Angeles native smacks of a movie set. Painted fishing boats bob offshore, their nets and buoys neatly stacked; the only portside commotion is the hungry crowd queuing up for the best restaurant tables. You'll have many Kodak moments on Isola dei Pescatori, but my hunch is none of them will involve fishermen.

The last island is Isola Madre, with an alluring sixteenth-century palace commissioned by Count Lancellotto Borromeo. (The Borromeo family reportedly still owns the fishing rights to the lake, which may explain the tourist trappings back at Isola dei Pescatori.) An elaborate eighteenth-century marionette theater with dozens of puppets attests to the family's preferred pastime.

Back on the shores of Lake Maggiore, and around the Gulfo Borromeo, is Villa Taranto. Scottish captain Neil McEacharn bought the property in 1931 and set out to create one of the most important botanical gardens in the world. It took him five years to tame the underbrush and design the park, with ten miles (seventeen kilometers) of paths, terraced pools, fountains, faux Greek temples, and nurseries. Botanists will be stunned by the sheer number of different plants, trees, and flowers—including some that are extremely rare in a world rapidly losing its plant diversity. From Japanese maples to giant Amazonian lilies, to 300 different species of dahlias, the garden is a flourishing testament to the lake's hospitable climate.

Near Pallanza, you can tour the Villa San Remigio, which, like Villa Taranto, is also a labor of love. Except in this case the mutual adoration was between two cousins, who met in their youth and stayed happily married for half a century. Together they created a monument to their emotions and gave whimsical names to the gardens: "Melancholy," "Memories," and "Sighs."

❧ Lago d'Orta ❧

Lake Orta is the smallest and quietest of the lakes covered here, and in my opinion the most romantic yet. At eight miles (thirteen kilometers) in length and just two miles across, everything about it is diminutive.

The famous philosopher Friedrich Nietzsche came to Lake Orta in 1882 with a traveling companion, the Russian poetess Lou Salomé, and it was here that he realized he was hopelessly in love with her. As the two were walking through the woods near Sacro Monte (above Orta San Giulio), he attempted a kiss. Surprised and frightened by the unexpected gesture, she refused the advances of the budding literary giant. "Sacro Monte: the most beautiful dream of my life," he reflected later. Burdened with a rejected heart, the writer suffered immensely, and when he wrote Thus Spake Zarathustra a few years later, he dated it Von Orta an (from Orta onward). He never did fall in love again.

The highlight of the lake is Orta San Giulio, located about one-third up the eastern shore. You know you're almost there when you see the minaret tower of Villa Crespi (now a hotel), which looks like it has been catapulted here from Constantinople. Leaving this Moorish fancy behind, the architecture turns Alpine, with slate roofs and frescoed walls. In town, the action is on Piazza Mario Motta. Cafés and restaurants line the square, and to the right is the adorable sixteenth-century Palazzo della Comunità. A frescoed second story stands over an arcaded loggia.

The most bewitching aspect of Orta San Giulio is the island that rises from the mist-covered lake surface directly in front of town. It's a sight you could admire for hours in the changing light. According to legend, dragons and monsters once infested the water around the island. Enter San Giulio (Saint Julius) in 390, who bravely fought off the demons and founded the basilica on Isola San Giulio. You can take a water taxi or row over to the island and visit the Benedictine monastery, where the dragons are immortalized in stone. The island's one restaurant ranks high on the list of Italy's most romantic places to dine.

❧ Piedmont Wine Country ❧

South of the lakes, between Turin and Genova, is a little swath of hilly territory that has been blessed by Bacchus. This is Piedmont's le Langhe, spanning from Asti (famous for its bubbly, Asti Spumante) to Alba and including the towns Barolo and Barbaresco—both of which have lent their names to world-class wines. The focus here is on eating and drinking—but romantics will surely find other activities to round out their visit.

Literally translated as "the foot of the mountains," Piedmont occupies a space of varied landscape, soil, and climatic conditions that prove ideal for some grape varietals. The most commonly planted red grapes are Barbera and Dolcetto, but the spotlight is on Piedmont's noblest grape—Nebbiolo, which is pressed into both Barbaresco and Barolo (dubbed "the king of wines and the wine of kings"). Notoriously difficult to manage because it does not always yield good color, this varietal is named after the *nebbia*, or "fog," of the foothills, and enjoys a powerful structure and excellent capacity for aging. Growers know to harvest it when the first fog starts to descend over le Langhe.

To taste these wines at the source, visit the elegant brick castle of Grinzane di Cavour, near Alba. It is both an *enoteca* and the meeting place of the "Order of the Knights of the Truffle and Wines of Alba"—a serious organization, indeed. Or better yet, enjoy the scenery and drive to Barbaresco (east of Alba) or Barolo (to the south). If you love the wine country, this is paradise. Gentle hills are given texture by trellises and vineyard rows, which inevitably frame a farmhouse or church tower. You can easily tour the area by car or bicycle in just a few days. The number of *agriturismi* (rural bed and breakfasts) and gourmet restaurants will leave you with *l'imbarazzo della scelta* (or "the embarrassment of having to choose").

 # Milano da Bere

Italy's second largest city may not fare well in a romantic classification of destinations. Surrounded by the most ghastly examples of the use of concrete, plagued by fog that in the summer is transformed into *afa*—an exceedingly hot fog relished only by masochists and mosquitoes—and generally disfigured by World War II bombing, not many lovers feel compelled to vacation here. And why should they, when Venice and Florence, the poster cities of romance, are just a few hours away? But savvy Milan does have one card up its sleeve that makes it irresistible to couples: shopping. If you're in the market for, say, a pair of Gucci sunglasses, a Prada purse, or an Armani suit—or simply want to impress your date with your purchasing power—Milan is where you need to be.

"Luxury goods" is part of the industrial world's lexicon thanks to Italy's capital of finance and fashion. A vigorous cash flow fuels a spend-it-flaunt-it attitude that makes designer labels a proud civic uniform. With an identity rooted in the notion of style, Milan is a magnet for the greatest minds of the fashion and design industries. The Lombard capital put *alta moda* icons on the fashion map, and each year the city hosts the Salone del Mobile design expo. Its stylistic contributions are as much a part of the Italian identity as Vespa scooters, pizza, or the Tower of Pisa.

BEAUTY IN THE
EYE OF THE BEHOLDER

Lucio, a fifty-nine-year-old retired factory worker, has an ugly nose. At two and a half inches (6.5 centimeters) in length, it is too big for his face, and his nasal topography is textured by pockmarks, pimples, bumps, and protruding veins that add shades of red and purple. A flap of skin between the nostrils gives the nose a prominent hook at its tip. His singular facial characteristic might not appeal to everyone, but in the town of Soragna (near Parma in Emilia-Romagna, and a ninety-minute drive from Milan), Lucio was crowned "King of Nasonia" for being blessed at birth with Italy's most beautiful snout.

The definition of beauty is elastic enough in Italy to include—and appreciate—what other cultures might deem physical abnormalities. And no Italian can resist praise for something as enviable as a big nose, because—like big feet—it is said to be indicative of the size of another part of the body.

In Soragna, contestants are judged not only for the nose's beauty, but for its size: Lucio's trophy-taking rhinological specimen measured nearly one and a half inches (3.5 centimeters) in width and drooped a mere three-quarters of an inch (two centimeters) from his upper lip. This unusual competition was initiated more than twenty years ago by four friends who met regularly at the town's tavern and spent a lot of time drinking and making fun of each other's noses. Held annually at the beginning of September, it attracts dozens of contestants—both men and women—who vie for the title.

First comes the smell test. Blindfolded contestants are passed a platter of local culinary specialties. Each contestant is asked to identify *prosciutto di Parma, culatello* (the center cut of ham), and *Parmigiano Reggiano*; Giuseppe, a seventy-three-year-old contestant boasting a "potato" nose, was booed off the stage when he answered "gorgonzola" in the cheese category. Then comes the moment of truth—the measuring tape. Each nose is carefully measured by the master of ceremonies with a caliper. The year Lucio won, a fifty-year-old woman named Lorenza nabbed the female championship with a proboscis measuring two and a half inches (6.2 centimeters) in length and nearly an inch and a half (3.4 centimeters) in width. Awards include supermarket coupons and the keys to the city presented by Soragna's mayor.

Before driving off in a horse-drawn chariot with his new queen and a regal court of seventy costumed locals, King Lucio I was asked if he would consider insuring his prized nose. He paused and gave a pensive look that suggested he might consider the idea.

The "Golden Square" of shopping, called the *quadrilatero della moda*, is marked by via Montenapoleone, via Manzoni, via Sant'Andrea, and via della Spiga. Once inside this aurous patch of urbanity that exists apart from the normal limitations of the material and economic universe, you'll either shop 'til you drop, or run to the nearest gym. If you are part of the first group, here is a list of your credit card company's new best friends: Alberta Ferretti, Bruno Magli, Chanel, Dolce & Gabbana, Fendi, Ferragamo, Gianfranco Ferrè, Giorgio Armani (he opened a superstore, aka an Armani mall, on via Manzoni), Gucci, Helmut Lang, Hermès, Hugo Boss, Krizia, Laura Biagiotti, Max Mara, Missoni, Miu Miu, Moschino, Paul Smith, Prada, Roberto Cavalli, Romeo Gigli, Trussardi, Valentino, Versace, Louis Vuitton, and Ermenegildo Zegna. Few people have the fortitude to "window shop" in Milan.

When your fashion frenzy is over, you can unwind and enjoy Milan's greatest contribution to civilization: the *aperitivo*. This is Italy's premier cocktail city, hence the phrase *Milano da bere* (drink Milan). Free finger foods called *stuzzichini* (they "tease" hunger) are doled out with sparkling *prosecco* or bittersweet Campari (a Milan native) served in its trademark triangular bottle. Precious cafés like the Art Deco Zucca or Bar Magenta (both near the Duomo) or ATM (built inside a former tram station and located in the Brera area) serve great *aperitivi*. Or, for a more bohemian flavor, meander down to the trendy Navigli neighborhood on the city's southern side.

For an unforgettable evening in Milan, reserve seats at the famed Teatro alla Scala opera house. The theater with Italy's best acoustics was inaugurated in 1778, and since then has staged the works of such opera greats as Vincenzo Bellini, Giacomo Puccini, and Giuseppe Verdi. The opera season opens on December 7, the feast of Milan's patron saint, Saint Ambrose. To get to the theater from Milan's Gothic Duomo cathedral, walk through the glass-roofed arcade of Galleria Vittorio Emanuele II. (Inside the Galleria, you'll see people spinning their heels on the design of a bull's testicles on the floor. Doing so is said to bring good luck—especially luck in love.)

TARTUFI, PESCE, AND PASSION

Thanks to the wealth that has poured into Lombardy and Piedmont, these regions nurture Italy's most talented restauranteurs and sophisticated palates, putting them at the forefront of *la cucina italiana*. They also boast regional gastronomic specialties, many from outside their borders thanks to the waves of workers who migrated here from the south. This culinary repertoire borrows flavors, most notably from France. For example, the olive oil used in cooking throughout Italy is often replaced with butter or cream here.

Lombardy's plains—*la pianura*—comprise Italy's farming heartland. To the north, the Alps block destructive frost, and to the east and west, lakes Maggiore and Garda soften the temperature extremes. But two-thirds of Lombard territory is locked within the fertile flat-lands of the Po River basin. Europe's biggest rice paddies are found here—giving rise to risotto *alla milanese*, or rice with saffron and bone marrow, a distant cousin to Spain's paella—and the clover- and barley-blanketed fields fuel a centuries-old dairy tradition.

From sharp gorgonzola to spreadable *stracchino* (named after "tired cows," or *stracchi*, in local dialect) to oozing *taleggio*, this is a cheese lover's mecca. Towns such as Cremona and Crema are even named after their dairy treats. In Piedmont it is not uncommon to find "drunk" cheese that has been aged in Barolo or Barbaresco wine and boasts a deep purple rind to prove it. The luscious mascarpone is said to have been named when an approving Spaniard pronounced the cheese *mas que bueno*.

Landlocked Lombardy and Piedmont are also good places to dine on freshwater fish. The lakes and rivers yield sturgeon and gray caviar in late November. Perch, trout, carp, salmon, and eel are also incorporated in lake cuisine: Don't miss the pink-colored trout that locals will tell you only live in lakes Garda, Como, and Maggiore. And if that doesn't tempt you, consider that this uniquely colored fish is also said to be an aphrodisiac. Other menu items not to miss are *luccio alla gardesana*, or pike with capers, and *coregone in crosta*, which is whitefish cooked with fennel and coarse salt.

Piedmont, on the other hand, provides fertile hunting grounds for the rarest culinary treat: the white truffle that appears after the fall rains. The precious fungi is shaved over eggs or used to flavor pasta and meat. The region is also home to the hazelnuts that go into Nutella, a chocolatey spread for toast, and *Baci*, or chocolate "kisses" filled with hazelnut cream and wrapped inside a love note (for more on both, see chapter twelve).

CUPID'S CORNERS

RESTAURANTS

Cracco-Peck
Via Victor Hugo, 4
20123 Milan
Tel: (+39) 02 876 774

One of the few restaurants in the region to have earned two Michelin stars, Cracco-Peck is the sophisticated lovers' choice in Milan. A collaboration between leading Italian chef Carlo Cracco and local gourmet food store Peck, the restaurant serves hearty, meaty dishes that are typical of the lake region: rich boar, suckling pig, or beef is cooked in wine, butter, and truffle oil, and veal *alla Milanese* is a popular favorite.

Boeucc
Piazza Belgioioso, 2
20121 Milan
Tel: (+39) 02 760 20224

This small, warm, and intimate restaurant is the oldest restaurant in Milan, and one of the city's hidden treasures. This spot has been catering to amorous local couples since the end of the seventeenth century, and neither the décor nor the menu has changed much over the years. Dark wood and brick walls give the place a cozy, coach house feel, and the fare is geared toward an appreciation of earthy, aromatic northern Italian cuisine. On quiet nights, this is the place to propose; on busy nights, this is the place to meet someone new while you're toasting with the neighboring table.

HOTELS

Villa Feltrinelli
Via Rimembranza, 38
25084 Gargnano
Tel: (+39) 0365 798 000
www.villafeltrinelli.com

This beautiful nineteenth-century art nouveau villa on the shore of the lake was only recently restored and converted into a hotel, retaining much of the soft, elegant furnishings and ornate décor of the original building. D. H. Lawrence lived nearby for a period in the early twentieth century, and the area immediately around the villa is the most beautiful stretch of the lake's coastline. A stay in the suite that occupies the villa's watchtower is unforgettable.

Grand Hotel Tremezzo
Via Regina, 8
22019 Tremezzo
Tel: (+39) 0344 42491

Situated on the shore of Lake Como, surrounded by its own large private landscaped gardens, and with 100 of its windows facing the lake, the Grand Hotel Tremezzo is irresistibly romantic and a perfect hotel for brief getaways.

Hotel du Lac et du Parc
Viale Rovereto 44,
38066 Riva
Tel: (+39) 0464 566 600

If you want to be pampered—or if you want to take your lover somewhere to be pampered!—this is the place. Large, grand, and ornate, the Hotel du Lac et du Parc rests in a beautiful stretch of garden on the coast of Lake Garda, with private beaches that extend down to the water's edge. The rooms are elaborately furnished and very comfortable, and the range of spa services available is enough to occupy an entire honeymoon.

LOVE ON THE LAKES

LOVE
AT
THE TOP
OF
THE
WORLD

UN CIÖN SOLO BAIA PÖCO

One dog alone doesn't bark much.

Ladino proverb,
meaning "two are better than one"

 he Italian peninsula was bequeathed a crown fit for a queen: The jagged, snowcapped peaks of the Dolomites reflect the rosy colors of dawn and sunny afternoon ambers as if they were made of precious stones. And of course, there are dozens of myths about the magical mountains that weave together the following themes: love, love lost, and living beings turned to stone.

The unique composition of the Dolomite mineral—calcium and magnesium carbonate, also known as magnesium limestone—gives the mountains warm coral colors and an ability to refract light in a special way. Covered in snow, they look like luminous crystals, and at times the purity of light is so remarkable, distant ridges come into focus in startling detail. The Dolomites stand apart not just for their color but for their razor-sharp contours. Over the eons, glaciers and blizzards have whittled away at the rock to create serrated crags and ragged spires that look like the spires of a Gothic cathedral.

The Dolomites are peppered with chalets and log cabins built on stilts and topped with granite roofs. These cozy havens come complete with pinewood paneling, roaring fireplaces, fur blankets, steaming meals, and spicy wine. Mountain devotees will be tempted by the excellent skiing and the endless miles of hiking trails to explore in the summer, with paths that skirt glacier lakes and cross fields of wild poppies, edelweiss, and buttercups fluttering softly in the breeze. (Overnight camping in tents can be arranged.) Or you can choose to stay warm under the blankets and watch the mountains change colors from your chalet window. No matter what activity you opt for, the snug surroundings of the Dolomites will ensure that sweethearts stay close.

THE LAY OF THE LAND

The Dolomites fan across two regions: Trentino and Süd Tirol (or Alto Adige, in Italian). These are two separate worlds, but the dividing line is cultural, not topographical. Trentino looks south for its identity, whereas Süd Tirol maintains an Austrian soul. Both enjoy measures of regional autonomy, but in many ways Süd Tirol is a nation apart. In its capital Bolzano (Bolzen), street signs are written in both German and Italian, and the cityscape is composed of gingerbread houses and cheerful beer halls—many of which make their own delicious

AMAZON WOMEN
AND HEARTS OF STONE

The people that populated the valleys were astounded by the beauty of their surrounding and fabricated wild myths, many based on Celtic fables from pre-Roman times, to explain it. Some involve dwarfs, hobbits, and trolls who scuttle about deep within the nooks and crannies, and other legends speak of Amazonian women so tall they could step over the mountains.

Of the many legends, one speaks of the king of dwarfs, who cared for a garden of roses dedicated to his queen. It was so beautiful that humans came to steal the carefully pruned bushes, but the clever king transformed his prized pink flowers into stone, to protect them for eternity.

Another story comes from the Cortina area and tells of a queen and her tribe known as *la reina de lis Croderes*. They were a race of people born without hearts. One among them, however—a young woman named Tanna—was mistakenly born with a heart. She fell in love with a man, and suffered the whole range of emotions associated with heartache. Sensing vulnerability, the queen arranged to have Tanna's heart turned to stone. But it had already grown so big, it was transformed into the Dolomites.

Let stories like these set the tone for your romantic retreat to this winter wonderland.

---

brews. Seventy percent of the local population prefers to converse in German, and in some remote mountain corners, Italian draws blank stares if spoken.

Sandwiched between the Austrian and Italian zones is a linguistic no man's land where the first language newborns learn is Ladino. The Rhaeto-Romance language is a twisted form of Celtic and, obviously, Latin, left by the Romans who conquered the area in 15 BC. There are Ladino television and radio stations, and primary schools teach the minority language to save it from extinction.

Chances are you will come to the Dolomites by way of the highway that heads north from Verona (A22) and zooms past Trento, Bolzano, and Bressanone to the Brenner Pass and Innsbruck, Austria. The mountain range is bordered by the Adige River to the west (where the A22 makes its ascent) and the Piave River to the east. Further east, the Dolomites become the Alpi Giulie Mountains and spill over into the Friuli-Venezia Giulia region, where the landscape eventually tapers out to the Slovenian border. To the northwest, the Dolomites hook into the Swiss Alps.

The space between the two glacial blue rivers is a jumble of complicated peaks and valleys, connected by hairpin mountain roads. The topography can be confusing, with a dozen verdant valleys radiating outward like the spokes of a bicycle wheel. Starting south at six o'clock and moving clockwise, they are: Val di Fiemme, Valle Travignolo, Val di Fassa, Val Gardena, Val di Funes, Val di Lusòn, Val Pusteria, Val di Landro, the Cadore area, Valle d'Ampezzo, and Val di Zoldo. Many more valleys furrow their way through the folds of the land. Below I have detailed the ones best suited for a romantic getaway.

VAL DI FIEMME AND VAL DI FASSA

These valleys are among those magical places where low-hanging fog tricks you into thinking you are surrounded by open horizons. But when that thick curtain lifts, you are suddenly dwarfed by the grandeur of the sheer rocky walls, invisible only a moment before. This feeling of suddenly being small must be why mountaineers here hold dearly to their tales of elves and hobbits.

Even the houses seem like they are something out of a bedtime story. Built on stilts to create a buffer against the cool moisture of the ground, and topped by an attic used to store hay—which also provides insulation—these wooden homes are called *tabià*. Many have been converted into mountain lodges, where you can warm your fingers around hot drink. In the larger towns, homes are adorned with frescoes of brave knights on horseback, dragons, and scenes from long-lost legends.

The Val di Fassa is my favorite valley here, because of its central positioning and proximity to so much great skiing in winter. If you make your base in Moena (famous for a stinky cheese called *puzzone*) or Vigo di Fassa, you can easily reach the slopes of Marmolada, Sassolungo, Sella, and the cable cars to connecting valleys. Marmolada is the highest of the Dolomites' seventeen major peaks. Moena and San Pellegrino also are good bases from which to reach the so-called *Trevalli d'Amore* (three valleys of love), a daylong skiing itinerary that covers sixty miles (100 kilometers) over three valleys.

✳ VAL GARDENA ✳

Val Gardena—or Ghërdeina, in Ladino—is home to one of the largest Ladina communities. The Gardena River runs down the middle of this open valley blanketed with pines and poplar trees. At its heart is Ortisei, a town of artisans specializing in woodcarvings that border on kitsch; pinewood is transformed into giant grizzly bears poised to kill or religious figures sporting facial expressions contorted by anguish and/or ecstasy.

Crisscrossing the eastern edge of the valley is a network of abandoned World War I railway lines, or the old ferroviaria della Val Gardena, which have been converted into mountain-bike paths and cross-country ski routes. Near the town of Selva di Val Gardena, you can take advantage of some of the most beautiful hiking in the Dolomites. Selva is called Wolkenstein in German, in honor of Oswald von Wolkenstein, a feudal lord whose family left behind fairytale castles huddled in the mountains like birds' nests and best reached on foot.

The highlight of this area is a group of rock pinnacles that encompass all the geological drama of the Dolomites. The Gruppo del Sassolungo includes Sasso Lungo ("long rock") at nearly 10,500 feet (3,200 meters), la Punta Cinque Dita, la Punta Grohmann, and Sasso Piatto ("flat rock"). Punta Cinque Dita ("five fingers point") is the most visually stunning—it looks like enormous fingers scratching and clawing at the heavens.

✳ VAL DI LUSÒN ✳

At the western mouth of the Val di Lusòn lies Bressanone (Brixen), the most romantic of Italy's Tyrolean towns. Its old main church, the Duomo, was given a facelift in the eighteenth century and boasts twin clock towers reminiscent of the architecture of Central and Eastern Europe, topped with tarnished copper spires that point to the sky like the surrounding mountains. Inside the fourteenth-century cloister you'll find a beautiful cycle of religious frescoes.

The best sightseeing in Bressanone is a stroll along the cobblestone streets of the historic center, past the *trompe l'oeil* frescoed facades (notice the elephant painted on the beautiful Hotel Elephant) and crenulated rooflines, cafés, and artisan boutiques. No matter how cold the mountain air proves, this cosmopolitan confection will warm your heart.

For one last stop in the area, visit the Abbazia di Novacella, just a few miles from Bressanone. Surrounded by vineyards, the abbey combines architectural styles from 1142 onward, and the inside of chiesa della Madonna is like a frosted wedding cake. It's a Baroque explosion of cherubs and cupids and pink and gold carvings splattered on the walls.

VAL PUSTERIA

Val Pusteria, above Bressanone, is the only major valley that runs west to east. It also represents one of Europe's most important watersheds. The 4,000-foot (1,200-meter) Sella di Dobbiaco marks a line from which water either runs south to the Adige River and the Adriatic and Mediterranean seas, or goes to the Black Sea via Austria, Slovenia, Croatia, and Hungary, where it pours into the Danube.

The many paths that branch off the Drava River here are a main attraction for mountain bikers; they slice through fields and forests with panoramic openings onto sun-drenched castles and abandoned mills. Depending on your pedal power, you can ride from 4,000 feet (1,200 meters) in altitude near San Candido, down to Lienz, Austria, which is at nearly 2,300 feet (700 meters). Cool off with a frosty mug of beer and head back to Italy by train. Other sites to round out a visit include the Castel Tures, near Campo Tures, and Lake Dobbiaco, where you can rent a boat and explore the shores for a private beach for a picnic.

VAL DI LANDRO

The Val di Landro is home to two beautiful lakes, smooth as glass, which like mirrors reflect all the details of the mountains beside them. One tale of origin tells of Misurina, the capricious daughter of King Sorapiss, who desired, at any cost, the magic mirror given to her father by the fairy of Mount Cristallo. What she didn't know, however, was that if the mirror was taken from her father's possession he would be transformed into a mountain. She stole it, and the king was turned to stone. Misurina was so distraught by her selfish act that her tears formed a lake named after her.

Lake Misurina, at nearly 6,000 feet (1,800 meters) in altitude, is home to spas and health centers, and is a magnet for ice skaters in the winter. The Gruppo dei Cadini Mountains located here have been favorites among mountain climbers since the 1800s.

CORTINA D'AMPEZZO

Cortina d'Ampezzo is to skis what Portofino is to yachts: Even the sound of its name evokes the pop of champagne corks and the cheerful chatter of famous ski bunnies such as Brigitte Bardot, Audrey Hepburn, Liz Taylor, Faye Dunaway, and other turtleneck-clad divas in sunglasses on a sunny terrace overlooking the slopes.

MAGIC HERBS

Millions of species of wild flowers and aromatic herbs thrive in the mountain microclimates. Some are used in local dishes, while others have been used as the base for medicines, libido enhancers, and even poisons.

Ancient tales tell of shy trolls called Sbilfs, who hide among the rocks and sow the earth with *semi*, or seeds, that they sprinkle from their pockets. Those seeds germinate to create a kingdom of magic botany.

In the Alpi Giulia (in the region of Friuli-Venezia Giulia) a common herb is the thin-leafed *sclopit*. It derives its name from the sound its seedpod makes when popped, and when cooked it tastes like spinach.

In Alto Adige the *tollkirsche* herb is a stimulant that is poisonous when eaten in large quantities (and therefore is said to be used in witchcraft). However, the plant also produces a little berry, and according to legend, if you keep one under your armpit for a day, you will break records in bed that night.

Cool a libido in overdrive by sipping broth from an herb called *libstock*. It has thin leaves with pointed tips that look like fingers and a palm, and it tastes like parsley; with some of this special potion, you'll be able to rest after the *tollkirsche*-induced marathon of the previous night.

The herb *sambuco* (elderberry) has so many magical qualities, villagers were said to kneel in front of it when they found it in the wild. Another love nectar is made from the tips of pinecones that are collected in May, when they are young and tender; they are boiled with sugar until a honeylike syrup is produced.

To get here, take the Great Dolomites Road, which snakes its way from Bolzano to Cortina and is among Italy's most scenic drives. First built in 1909, the SS241 is more than sixty miles (100 kilometers) of jaw-dropping panoramas, so take your time and enjoy the vistas along the way.

Cortina is nestled at the junction of the Bóite and Bigontina Valleys and embraced by the mountains Le Tofane, Cristallo, Sorapiss, and the Cinque Torri (five towers), which look as if they were painted red at sunset. The city hosted the 1956 Winter Olympics and is home to some of Italy's best skiing: There are thousands of runs in the network of valleys that branch off from Cortina, and most of the facilities have been modernized since the Olympics and are state-of-the-art.

But Cortina's daytime activities are not nearly as exciting as what it holds in store for nightfall. The concept of *après ski* was taken to new heights in chic Cortina. This is a high-altitude Beverly

Hills with a high-octane nightlife. Evenings start with the *struscio* (stroll) down the central corso Italia, which is lined with the same luxury boutiques as Milan's via della Spiga. Only the Italians—and maybe Mick Jagger, in one of his peacock moments—have the *struscio* down to a science. It is a time to see and be seen in suntanned glory, sporting furry boots, form-fitting nylon, and designer sunglasses that probably cost more than the entire ski trip. After an *aperitivo* comes dinner, and hands down, Cortina is home to the best and most expensive gourmet restaurants in the Dolomites. After hours, the beautiful people go dancing in places that were unfortunately bequeathed names like Club Vip and Disco Bar Clipper. If you're looking for a taste of *la vita mondana* (hobnobbing with people who think they are rich and famous—and may actually be), Cortina is the place.

OUTDOOR ADVENTURES

If you seek a thrill outdoors as well as indoors with your special someone, the winter sporting options in the Dolomites span the spectrum. There is downhill and cross-country skiing, luge, bobsled, skating, snowshoeing, ski jumping, snowboarding, and every other conceivable option.

When the snow melts, endless miles of hiking, mountain-biking, and horseback-riding trails are revealed. Some trails take several days to complete, and accommodations are a cozy tent or a different mountain *rifugio* each night. Climbing is another popular pastime, and free climbers are particularly attracted to this range.

The Dolomites also draw wind gliders and windsurfers. For those who prefer the water, pristine lakes offer opportunities for fishing, canoeing, kayaking, or sailing. There are even, surprisingly, golf courses.

SKIING

Trevalli d'Amore: The "three valleys of love" is a ski adventure in which you may never ski the same slope twice. The circuit takes a full day (get an early start) and covers sixty miles (100 kilometers) over three valleys (Passo di Valles, Passo San Pellegrino, and Col Margherita). There are more than two dozen lifts, including three cable cars, thirteen chairlifts (some that take you downhill in places too steep to ski), and eleven ski lifts, and twenty-five miles (forty kilometers) of trails. The course can be completed by intermediate skiers and above—there are a few black diamond slopes, and icy patches to watch out for. The trip is exhilarating and well worth every second: The views are unforgettable. You'll also have time for a few *grappa* breaks and a leisurely lunch at one of the stations (*rifugi*) along the way.

One pass (Dolomiti Superski, at www.dolomitisuperski.com) allows you to ski the three valleys either clockwise or counterclockwise, leaving from Moena or San Pellegrino in the Val di Fassa. Since this route is dedicated to *amore*, special promotional fares are available on St. Valentine's Day.

Cortina d'Ampezzo: Italy's first ski school was founded here, and Cortina hosted the first Winter Olympic games broadcast on live television. Many of the runs are hidden from the ski lifts, giving the impression that you are secluded with your special someone in the wilderness. You can take the cable car at Faloria, in the center of Cortina, and then the chairlift to Tondi di Faloria. For those who want to try something a little more unusual, possibilities include dog sledding, skijoring (imagine horse-drawn skiing), snow rafting, or parapenting (a form of parasailing).

LOVE LORE AND FESTIVALS

The Trato Marzo festival is celebrated on the last two days of February and the first day of March in Pinzolo, about forty miles (sixty kilometers) from Trento, to mark the beginning of the mating season. The town's bachelors are summoned to the main square, and with a rudimentary megaphone made from a tin can, the names of the women with whom they will be paired during the ritual are called out. There is a hitch: The bachelors proclaim their love to the most unlikely mate, such as the oldest woman or the ugliest spinster; or, as the case would be, the most hideous bachelor is paired with the town bombshell. Today it's a time for a hearty laugh, but years ago, when the preservation of the local gene pool was at the top of the agenda, the festival may have been less humorous. On the last day of the ceremony, couples who are truly in love proclaim their union and are officially *fidanzati*, or "going steady."

In Grauno, twenty miles (thirty-five kilometers) from Trento, a unique *carnivale* feast starts the day after the Epiphany. Young men chop down trees and drag them back to town. This must be done after midnight, otherwise the magic is said to be lost. Weeks later, on Fat Tuesday, a bigger tree trunk is dragged into town and satirical sketches involving the tree are staged to poke fun at various members of the community. A *colpevole* (guilty party) is picked from the crowd— almost always the man most recently married—and his task is to baptize the tree, which is dragged to a special spot and set erect. Everyone decorates it with good luck charms, and at night the tree is set on fire by the *colpevole* and his bride. The outcome of next year's harvest is determined by the behavior of the *bolife*, or sparks. If they fly high into the air, the harvest is doomed. If they stay close to the ground, they are said to be "heavy," and the harvest will be good.

Madonna di Campiglio: This is the most important resort in the Brenta Dolomites (take SS289 up from Pinzolo), and is perfect for skiers coming for a few days from Milan, Verona, or Venice. It is primarily a beginner and intermediate skiers' haven, with nearly 100 miles (160 kilometers) of well-groomed slopes—many of which start at the summit and terminate right in town—31 lifts, and even a ski jump. Madonna also attracts its share of spirited snowboarders.

Passo di Stelvio, for summer skiing: On the far western reaches of the Dolomites (accessible from Milan by the road that flanks the east side of Lake Como from Lecco), lovers with a passion for skiing can indulge year-round and ski on a glacier in T-shirts and shorts in July. The pass is open from May to November, and snow remains about eighteen feet (six meters) deep throughout the summer. It is slushy, though, so don't expect to break any speed records.

For hiking, mountain biking, horseback riding, rock climbing, or simply to admire the flora and fauna, the best option is to explore one of the eight national parks in the region. The High Trails of the Dolomites (Alte Vie delle Dolomiti) paths vary from 60 to 120 miles (100 to 200 kilometers) in length, and take hikers about two weeks to complete. The tourist offices or the Italian Alpine Club should be able to provide you with a map to the trails and mountain lodges.

AS ITALIAN AS APPLE STRUDEL

The food of the Dolomites shares little with the cuisine of the rest of the peninsula that extends south into the warm waters of the Mediterranean. The regional cuisine here has always borrowed heavily from Austria and, protected within the mountains' crags, has changed little over the centuries. The mountains are dotted with rifugi or baita—high-altitude hideaways that double as informal restaurants, where you can count on hearty portions being served to hungry mountaineers. Some even provide sleds, so you can race back down the trail you climbed to work up your appetite.

A local specialty is speck—a darker, more pungent prosciutto—which you will find in sandwiches, on pasta, or served in thin slices. The most popular first course consists of vegetable soups or cabbage soup with chunks of pork and beans, and the ball-shaped canederli. Also known as knödel, canederli are breadcrumb dumplings with chopped spinach or speck, boiled and topped with butter or cheese. Another version is flattened and fried with cheese. Other first courses are homemade ravioli stuffed with wild mushrooms (these mountains are full of porcini mushrooms after the fall rains). Polenta is topped with tomato sauce and sausage, wild mushrooms, or meat sauce (gulasch). Sauerkraut and sausage is also common. There is a special cumin-seed crunchy flatbread (völser schüttelbrot), pretzels, and above all excellent apfelstrudel (apple strudel). Other desserts are poppy seed cake, marillenknödel, a sweet version of the dumplings) served with stewed apricots, or a variation called schwarzbeerlaibchen with wild berries.

The Dolomites are home to some of Italy's highest vineyards, which make excellent red and white wines. Sometimes the red is warmed and spiced with cinnamon and served après ski. White wines include the excellent Gewürztraminer Aromatico (reputed to be a potent aphrodisiac) and Riesling Italico; they can be tasted at the vineyards that line der weinstrasse (the wine road) south of Bolzano. Distilled grappa will knock your socks off (and given the right company, possibly the rest of your clothing as well).

CUPID'S CORNERS

RESTAURANTS

Oste Scuro

Domasse 3
I-39042 Brassanone
Tel: (+39) 0472 835 343

Oste Scuro is a legend in Tyrol, the Dolomite region that most successfully mingles Germanic and Italian influence. The beautiful dark wood and tiled dining room maintains a formal but cozy atmosphere, while the typically German standup bar has a more relaxed feel. The menu is a perfect blend of Mediterranean and Germanic fare, incorporating the creamy cheeses, seafood, and fresh vegetables characteristic of South Tyrolean cuisine.

HOTELS

Elephant

Via Rio bianco, 4
39042 Bressanone
Tel: (+39) 0472 832 750

This charming inn, hidden in the cobbled streets of the medieval town of Bressanone, is the best place of its kind in the region. As reminiscent of the Austrian Alps as of its neighboring Italian countryside, the inn serves good, homey cuisine and is a great place to come home to.

Imperial Hotel Terme

Via Silva Domini, 1
38056 Levico Terme
Tel: (+39) 0461 706 104
www.imperialhotel.it

One of the grandest and most beautiful resorts in the Dolomites, the Imperial is a popular location for honeymooning couples and a great spot for a long, refreshing, romantic break. Set in its own 150,000-square-meter park, the hotel offers a plethora of spa services that only strengthen the sense of freshness, rejuvenation, and sensuality inspired by the lush natural landscape.

GETTING
MARRIED
IN
ITALY

EVVIVA GLI SPOSI!

Long live the bride and groom!

A traditional first toast made to newlyweds

For decades the bougainvillea-lined terraces of the Mediterranean and sensual contours of Tuscany have lured couples seeking nuptial inspiration. It's no surprise that Italy is among the world's most popular destinations for couples looking to get married. Each year approximately 6,000 foreign couples exchange vows in cities such as Florence, Venice, and Rome, and their numbers are growing rapidly.

Destination weddings are easier to stage now than ever before. Most villas, beachfront palazzos, vineyards, and hilltop hamlets for rent have English-speaking staff to help foreign couples, and the vast network of service providers ranges from photographers and caterers to makeup artists, florists, and transportation companies specializing in everything from horse-drawn carriages to gondolas. Dozens of online wedding consultants are eager to organize anything from a grand entrance by Ferrari or helicopter, to a fireworks display or a string quartet for cocktail hour. They can also make arrangements for English-speaking priests or rabbis. The nation's natural riches means wedding guests can climb a volcano in Sicily, view Tuscany by hot-air balloon, or spend a leisurely day winetasting. The low-hanging fog and romantic lap of the water in Venice make it the world's most celebrated wedding backdrop. Savvy city officials have done everything possible to make the marriage process easy for foreigners, and other cities are following suit.

Despite such improvements, destination weddings require long-distance planning, and that takes additional time, care, and perhaps money. Couples should start planning their wedding at least one year ahead, especially if they intend to secure one of the more popular villas. Destination weddings also mean staring down Italy's dizzying bureaucracy. Some couples get married at home and stage a symbolic wedding in Italy to avoid the hassle. Others, however, will insist on a real Italian church wedding, with a mass in Latin and a grand finale rendition of "Ave Maria." This chapter explains everything you need to know to prepare for your big day.

Matrimonio all'Italiana

No rite of passage is celebrated more enthusiastically in this ancient land than weddings. The concept of the *matrimonio all'italiana* conjures up images of countryside banquets with free-flowing wine and belt-loosening portions—and the cliché is almost always true. The occasion is so happy, not even bad weather can put a dampener on it: As the proverb goes, *Sposa bagnata, sposa fortunata* (a wet bride is a lucky bride).

Aside from the gastronomic excesses, Italian marriage traditions are similar to those in the United States. *La sposa* and *il sposo* agree to celebrate their union following a *proposta di matrimonio* (proposal) in which the prospective groom will *chiedere la mano* (ask for the hand) of his sweetheart. Both families are involved in the elaborate *piani di matrimonio* (wedding planning), but in Italy the bride's parents are not obliged to foot the bill. Instead it is commonly split between the families or paid for by whoever has more money. More important is a fund for the couple's new home, which is furnished before the wedding and slept in for the first time on the wedding night. The couple departs for their *luna di miele* or *viaggio di nozze* (honeymoon) after they have rested from the wedding.

Catholics opt for a church wedding, and after the ceremony the guests are transported to the reception site. This is when the wedding gifts are delivered, and the traditional wedding reception playbill is much the same, including the throwing of the garter belt and cutting of the cake. Unlike American weddings, however, Italians don't usually put on skits or slideshows to "roast" the couple. Instead guests eat, drink, and abandon themselves to an alcohol-induced chorus of "*evviva gli sposi, evviva gli sposi.*"

WEDDING SUPERSTITIONS

WALKING TO CHURCH: The bride should walk at least part of the way to the church, in order to watch out for omens. Seeing a rainbow is a good sign, for example, but having a pig cross your path is reason to cancel the ceremony. The bride must start her journey with her right foot.

THE BRIDAL GOWN: The bride should never wear her entire outfit until the wedding day. Early fittings should be done with at least one item, such as a shoe, missing. In ancient times, the bride made her own dress and saved the last stitch for immediately before she walked down the aisle.

BRIDAL FLOWERS: At one time, instead of flowers the bride carried herbs and wild garlic, because the smell was thought to ward off evil spirits.

BRIDESMAIDS: Although this tradition is more common in the United States than Italy, it has its origins in ancient Roman law. Ten witnesses were required at a wedding, and in order to confuse evil spirits intent on ruining the wedding, they dressed in identical clothing. At Italian weddings today, it is rare to see bridesmaids. Instead the couple has two or three close friends or relatives serve as witnesses.

THROWING RICE: This is an Italian tradition, symbolizing a showering of good fortune and money on the wedding couple.

HAVING THE BRIDE STAND ON THE LEFT: According to tradition, this allowed the groom to hold a sword in his right hand, in the event someone tried to steal his bride.

TOSSING THE BOUQUET OR GARTER: As in the United States, throwing the bouquet is said to determine who will be the next woman to marry, while throwing the bride's garter determines the next bachelor to marry.

WEDDING CAKE: A white cake symbolizes purity and virginity. In ancient times, however, a loaf of bread was used instead. The groom would break the bread over his wife's head in a symbol of husbandly dominance, and guests were left to scramble for the crumbs, which symbolized fertility.

CUTTING THE CAKE: This act is symbolic of the first task completed by the couple. In the past, however, the bride cut the cake alone and distributed the pieces to demonstrate her domestic disposition.

SLEEPING WITH A PIECE OF CAKE UNDER YOUR PILLOW: This tradition is still practiced today in some rural areas. It is said that an unmarried guest will dream of his or her future spouse if they sleep with a piece of cake near their head.

BREAKING A GLASS: As in Jewish weddings, some couples break a glass, with the number of shards representing the years of happiness the couple will have together. In the south, often a ceramic plate is used instead. Given the plate's thickness, it does not always break, and this is considered a sign of imminent infidelity.

WEDDING FAVORS: Favors have symbolized health, fertility, joy, and longevity. In Italy sugar-coated almonds called *confetti* are given; they are wrapped in individual bags called *tulle* and served from a large basket called *la bomboniera*. (See chapter twelve for more on almonds.)

WEDDING RING: A ring has long been a symbol of infinity, the sun, or the universe, and for perfection in general. It is traditionally worn on the left hand, because the Greeks believed a vein in that hand went directly to the heart.

⚜ RELIGIOUS CEREMONIES ⚜

Getting married in Italy is about more than just quality caterers and envy-provoking wedding photographs. Many couples choose Italy for its religious identity. Catholics lead the pack, attracted to the idea of celebrating their union in proximity of the Vatican and the pope, and some even travel to Rome to meet the pope at his regular Wednesday audience after they are married. Rome's churches host so many foreign weddings, many have started to turn couples away. It's best to book a church far in advance—especially if you dream of a ceremony at the Vatican itself.

To find out about English-language Vatican weddings, contact Rome's Santa Susanna church (www.santasusanna.org). Because the Vatican is not part of the Italian state, different paperwork may be required; the website of the U.S. embassy in Rome outlines what you will need (italy.usembassy.gov).

If you are looking for a simple ceremony, try Rome's St. Patrick's Irish church, where the rector notes that "couples are beginning to find the significance of the wedding vows is being lost in the trappings of big weddings at home, with money being lashed out on receptions, bands, even rehearsal dinners." On the other hand, if your desire to marry in Italy has

more to do with the scenery than piety, you may face obstacles. Because of the sudden boom in destination weddings, the church has started to crack down on what it calls "tourist weddings" performed in exchange for generous donations. Many priests refuse couples who are not parish members (such as on the island of Capri, and in Lake Como's Bellagio), while others require that they meet the couple at least six months in advance of the ceremony. In general, you will have a hard time convincing a priest to perform a ceremony outside his church. One way to avoid being confused with a tourist wedding is to talk to you priest at home and have him introduce you to one in Italy. Your local priest can also help find out what religious documentation is required (usually only baptismal and confirmation certificates).

If you intend to wed in a religious ceremony other than a Roman Catholic one, you will almost definitely be required to have a civil ceremony first to confirm the marriage's legality. This applies to unions of other Christian denominations and Jewish weddings, but also depends on where you get married. Most rabbis, for example, may only perform blessings or symbolic ceremonies, but the rabbi of Florence has the authority to perform civil weddings.

Couples looking to celebrate a Jewish wedding should know that Italy's religious community is almost completely Orthodox, and to marry in one of the country's historic synagogues, you must be Orthodox, too. The main synagogues are located in Rome, Florence, and Venice, and the couple should write a letter of introduction to the Italian rabbi, followed by a letter from their rabbi back home confirming they meet Orthodox requirements. Non-Orthodox Jews have an obvious alternative: They can bring their rabbi with them and organize a symbolic wedding wherever they please following a civil wedding at the town hall.

❧ RED TAPE AND CIVIL WEDDINGS ❧

The bureaucracy of marriage in Italy can seem daunting at first, but rest assured it gets easier as you move forward. One obvious step is to pay a specialized agency to untangle the knot for you (online consultants who do this are listed below). However, much of the paperwork must be completed in person, so it is important to understand the required steps and allot ample time. Two weeks should be enough to conquer the paperwork, if you make the necessary appointments beforehand. Unlike France, Italy conveniently does not require that you live in the country for any period of time before getting married there.

The best place to start gathering information is on the website of the Italian Embassy in the United States (www.italyemb.org). If you click on "Italy A-Z," you will find a link to "Information for U.S. Citizens Wishing to Marry in Italy." The American Embassy in Italy (www.usembassy.it) also explains the procedure and, better yet, lists the addresses and telephone numbers of the up to six offices you will need to visit. It also details the margins of time in which appointments are possible—sometimes as few as three hours each morning. Be forewarned that even "official" sources often post conflicting information, leaving you responsible to verify each step independently.

At the heart of the matter is your official declaration of intent to marry (*promessa di matrimonio*) made at the Marriage Office (*Ufficio Matrimoni*) of the Civil Registrar (*Ufficio di Stato Civile*) for the municipality or town hall where you intend to marry. You must make an appointment, to which you must bring two witnesses (with proper identification) along with the following documentation:

1. Valid U.S. passports. If you are a member of the armed forces, a military identity card will do.
2. Birth certificates that state the name of the mother and father. American birth certificates must be translated and authenticated for official use in Italy with an "apostille" seal (explained below).
3. Evidence of termination of previous marriages (a final divorce decree or previous spouse's death certificate) is required, if applicable. These must also be translated and legalized with an apostille seal.
4. Sworn statement of consent to marry from the legal guardians of minors, if applicable.
5. Affidavits stating there is no reason why you should not get married (you are not first cousins, for example). This is the most complicated step, because it requires two separate documents. They are the *atto notorio* and the *nulla osta*.

The *atto notorio* is an oath of your willingness to marry. It is obtained anywhere in or outside Italy, although the Italian embassy strongly suggests you get it before you arrive in Italy. To obtain an *atto notorio*, make an appointment with an officer at the nearest Italian embassy or consulate. You need two witnesses who are not your relatives to vouch that you and your spouse-to-be are not first cousins (inexplicably, some consular offices require four witnesses).

If, on the other hand, you plan on getting the *atto notorio* in Italy, you should make an appointment with the nearest *pretura* (lower court), town clerk, or notary public. Two witnesses must come and bring identity papers. There are taxes amounting to €40 that can be paid at a tobacconist shop. Don't get your *atto notorio* too far in advance, though, because they expire.

The *nulla osta* is only obtained from a U.S. consular officer in Italy, either at the U.S. embassy in Rome or at the Florence, Milan, or Naples consulates. It declares there are "no obstacles" to your marriage under U.S. law and costs $30 ($50 in Florence). No witnesses are required, but you will be asked to bring proof of U.S. citizenship. Appointments are not always necessary. Once you have obtained the *nulla osta*, bring it to the nearest *prefettura* (or Ufficio Legalizzazioni) to be authenticated. This costs about €10.

As mentioned previously, birth certificates, divorce decrees, and death certificates issued outside of Italy must be translated and stamped with an apostille. Also known as a "Hague certification," the apostille is a seal issued by the secretary of state notary public of the state that issued the document, and it authenticates the document for use abroad (see www.travel.state.gov to find out where to obtain it nearest you). You may also be required to have an Italian consular officer authenticate your documents.

It is worth noting that divorced women must wait 300 days after the divorce decree before remarrying in Italy.

Once your paperwork has been presented to the *Ufficio di Stato Civile*, the rest is easy. Italian law requires that banns, or public marriage announcements, be posted at the local town hall for two consecutive Sundays and for four days after the second Sunday before a wedding. (This gives members of the local community time to come forward if they suspect bigamy.) If you or your partner is a resident or citizen of Italy, the banns are required; they are almost always waived for foreigners.

You are now free to wed in a civil ceremony performed by the *Ufficiale di Stato Civile*, who is often the town mayor, or in a Roman Catholic ceremony. If you plan any other religious ceremony, your rabbi, priest, or minister will likely require that you first hold a civil ceremony to ensure its legality. If you marry in the Catholic Church, your priest is responsible for registering the union with the *Ufficiale di Stato Civile*, and there is no need to perform a civil ceremony.

In civil ceremonies—a popular choice with foreigners—the couple stands before the *Ufficiale di Stato Civile*, who wears a colorful sash across his chest. Although the couple can declare their own vows, the civil wedding is bureaucratic, and your guests will be treated to a long recapitulation of laws and their corresponding numeric codes. Non-Italian speaking couples are required to bring a translator (with valid identification); a good friend with a few semesters of Italian under his or her belt should make the cut. You are also required to produce two witnesses (*testimoni* in Italian), with valid identification, who will sign the wedding registry on your behalf. The *testimoni* play a very important role in Italian weddings and are comparable to the best man and maid of honor. The couple is given the option of signing a sort of prenuptial agreement called la *seperazione dei beni*, which determines how their finances and property will be shared. At the end of the ceremony, they receive two copies of the marriage certificate; additional copies are available for a fee (each one should be stamped with an apostille in Italy).

There are drawbacks to civil ceremonies. For one, they always take place in the local town hall's special marriage room. Some are very beautiful: The one in Venice's Palazzo Cavalli, for example. has views of the Grand Canal and the Rialto Bridge, along with a mooring point for couples arriving by gondola; in Florence, weddings take place in the Red Room of the beautiful Palazzo Vecchio. Others are what you'd expect an empty room at town hall to look like. Couples in Rome complained about the nondescript Campidoglio location—also because few guests could squeeze inside—and the city added a second, more attractive spot for civil weddings in a deconsecrated brick church near the Circus Maximus.

You'll also have to stick to office hours; otherwise, weddings get expensive. In Venice wedding times are Monday to Saturday from 8:45 A.M. to 1 P.M. A non-EU member pays €1,250 during those times (Italians pay nothing, by the way), and this increases to a whopping €3,100 if the ceremony is on a holiday. In Florence weddings take place on Wednesday, Thursday, and Saturday mornings, and the "tax" is €500. Time slots are tight, too. Expect to see the next wedding's crowd poised to enter as your party exits. To avoid the revolving-door frenzy, select a smaller *comune* for your ceremony. Try Siena over Florence, or Nemi over Rome.

Lastly, because civil weddings always take place at the town hall, forget the idyllic vineyard or villa ceremony—although there's no reason you can't have your reception wherever you'd like. That said, one enterprising American I know got married at town hall but convinced the *Ufficiale di Stato Civile* to show up at the reception—staged outdoors, with the rolling hills of Tuscany as a backdrop—to repeat the whole ceremony in a second, "fake" wedding for the benefit of the guests. After a civil wedding, you are free to organize a symbolic wedding or a religious wedding of your own.

If you marry an Italian citizen, you can request Italian citizenship after six months if you and your spouse live in Italy, or after three years if you live abroad. Women who marry in Italy keep their maiden names. American women can have their passports amended at a U.S. consulate immediately after the wedding to reflect their married name.

✣ ONLINE WEDDING RESOURCES ✣

The Internet is the driving force behind the exploding popularity of destination weddings. For $2,500 and upward, these online agencies will oversee every aspect of your wedding, from the caterers, florists, photographers, and musicians, to hair and makeup artists and transportation details. They will also help you prepare the necessary religious and civil documentation and can arrange for an English-speaking priest or rabbi, if desired. Some even help arrange insurance policies that cover everything from ripped gowns to unexpected cancellations. You may be overwhelmed by the number of consultants operating throughout the peninsula. To help you in the process, here are some of the best:

www.weddingitaly.com
www.gettingmarriedinitaly.com
www.italyweddings.com
www.italy-weddings.com
www.weddings-italy.com
www.ultimatewedding.com
www.weddinginflorence.com
www.blissweddings.com
www.thebookofdreams.net
www.confetti.co.uk

Some companies are more specialized. For one that has been assisting in arrangements since 1885 and focuses on Rome, see www.weddings-by-latour.com; for those interested in the southern regions, go to www.worldsislands/sicilywedding.htm. The company at www.iwillverona.it only operates in the city of Romeo and Juliet. Renting a villa or castle anywhere in Italy can be done via www.sogniitaliani.com (in English). Jewish weddings are detailed helpfully at www.destination-weddings-in-italy.com.

Online information is also available from city halls. Florence's www.comune.firenze.it informs couples that they may submit some documentation by fax (previously unheard of in Italy) up to four days before the wedding. Venice's www.comune.venezia.it allows users to schedule wedding dates with an online form. To find out about Capri weddings, you can try www.weddingincapri.com, or visit the town hall when you are there.

A NOTE ABOUT THE WEATHER

Italy is truly blessed in the weather department. The moderating influence of the sea and protection from northern winds by the Alps create a generally temperate climate. But the weather does change considerably, according to how far you are from the sea or mountains.

Winters are cold in the Alps, and cold and foggy in the Po River plain and the central Apennines, and snowfall is common; the Dolomites are awash in winter whiteness. Those same months, however, are mild to warm on the Ligurian Coast, the Amalfi Coast, and on the islands.

Summers are hot and dry in those areas—especially in arid regions like inland Sicily, Sardinia, and the south—but coastal areas are cooled by sea breezes. Meanwhile, cities like Milan and Rome are unbearably humid in those months, and Milan is plagued by bloodthirsty mosquitoes as well. Summer heat in Rome is somewhat tempered by the celebrated *ponentino* winds that brush over its hills; however, another wind, the sirocco from Africa, heats up the whole country in August. Not only does it bring temperatures well above 90 degrees Fahrenheit (30 degrees Centigrade), it also carries tiny grains of sand from the Sahara Desert that can leave a dirty film on outdoor patios. Despite its proximity to the sea, Venice is humid in summer and bone-chillingly cold in winter.

Between the extremes of winter and summer, spring and fall are glorious times when temperatures settle at perfect levels. Flowers bloom and trees give off fluffy white seeds that look like snowflakes dancing in the wind. It goes without saying that you'll want to circle these months on your calendar when planning your wedding.

One word of warning: Much of the nation experiences summer thunderstorms at the end of August, marking the beginning of fall. More rain comes in October and November, and then again in March and April. Venice is often flooded during those months: During *acqua alta*, tourists and locals must resort to stomping about the Lagoon City in rubber boots.

LOVE
AND
FOOD

EGO TIBI MONSTRABO AMATORIUM
SINE MEDICAMENTO, SINE HERBA,
SINE ULLIUS VENEFICAE CARMINE:
SI VIS AMARI, AMA

I will reveal to you a love potion
without medicine, without herbs,
without witchcraft:
If you want to be loved, love.

Philosopher Hecton of Rhodes,
early first century BC

ros and food, libido and appetite are tightly bound together, just like a husband and wife. The language of love resonates with food metaphors: A woman's lips may be described as ripe and red as a cherry, her skin as soft as a peach, and her eyes the shape of an almond. The sensations we derive from eating certain foods may mimic those of lovemaking: Blood races through the veins, cheeks turn rosy, and a good meal leaves an inebriating aura of warmth and lingering satisfaction. Long before Viagra, chemists and epicureans around the world dabbled in love potions and recipes meant to kindle carnal desires, provoke love and fertility, enhance physical pleasure, and cure impotency. In Italy, a land in which eating is itself an act of love, no additional magic herb, boar's hair, or duck foot is required. Instead, fresh ingredients awarded by the sun and sea are deftly manipulated to form the great symphony of tastes and textures that is *la cucina italiana*. If Italy is a choice for the soul, it is because all her edibles are aphrodisiacs—or so the chef will tell you, with a benevolent wink.

Like everything else in Italy, there is a prosaic reason why. One day, the phallus of the heavens fell from the sky and landed in the sea, the womb of Mother Earth. It fertilized the water and gave birth to a daughter named Aphrodite (in Roman mythology she is Venus). The goddess of love was ushered to shore on a shell, and wherever her feet touched earth, wondrous flowers and plants sprang to life. Those plants and herbs are known as "aphrodisiacs."

ALMONDS

Almonds are a symbol of love, joy, health, and fertility. Sugarcoated almonds, called *confetti*, are traditionally given to guests at Italian weddings. An ancient Greek story tells of a young man named Demophon who fell in love with a princess named Phyllis. Just as the two were about to marry, Demophon received news that his father had died, and he rushed to Athens for the funeral, promising a swift return. Time passed, and he never came back. Desperate and abandoned, Phyllis died of a broken heart, and in sympathy the gods transformed her into an almond tree. Shortly thereafter Demophon returned and learned of his lover's fate. He offered a sacrifice to the almond tree and proclaimed his undying love for Phyllis. At that moment, the tree erupted into a bouquet of delicate flowers, and almonds have come to symbolize immortal love.

If you are in Sicily in February, don't miss the *sagra del mandorlo in fiore*, or feast of almond blossoms, in Agrigento. Any time of the year, you can feast on the island's almond desserts, known as *pasta reale* or *frutta di Martorana*—colored almond paste that is transformed into miniature renditions of fruit, eggs, flowers, and fish. Or enjoy the flavor of almond extract added to milk in a delicious sweet drink called *latte di mandorla*, or to shaved ice in *granita*.

 ## APPLE

Before the "forbidden fruit" became associated with Adam and Eve, the apple—whose name in Italian, *mela*, is derived from *malum*, or "bad"—had already tempted others. In Greek myths, the athlete Atalanta had been warned not to get married and came up with a witty plan to avoid nuptials: She challenged her suitors to a foot race and said that any man who could beat her could have her hand in marriage. Hippomenes fell in love with Atalanta and asked Aphrodite for her help. The goddess of love gave him three golden apples, which Hippomenes threw onto the track. Unable to resist her attraction for the fruit, Atalanta stopped to pick them up and lost the race.

 ## ARTICHOKE

Artichokes are said to be the incarnation of a young nymph named Cinara, with whom the god Jupiter fell in love. When his jealous wife Juno found out about their affair, she tuned Cinara into a thorny artichoke, so her husband would never again be able to put his hands on her.

To some, artichokes are a symbol of the female sex, and to others they are proven aphrodisiacs. In the Middle Ages young girls were prohibited from eating them "because the flesh of an artichoke will provoke the temptations of the devil," and the personal doctor of France's Louis XIV observed that "artichokes make the blood boil and spark excitement before love."

Italy is home to numerous varieties, such as the small, violet-colored artichokes of Tuscany, or the *romanesco* (larger and rounder). When in Rome, don't miss the *carciofi alla giudia*, served in the Jewish quarter, in which the artichoke is fried to look like a giant flower in bloom.

 ## ASPARAGUS

Asparagus has long been considered a potent aphrodisiac, one that was downright dangerous if eaten in large quantities. Love potions were carefully measured to include just the right doses. Asparagus push from the earth like phalluses, and for that reason a man who eats a lot of asparagus is said to have many lovers. Don't miss the white asparagus of the Friuli Venezia Giulia region in northern Italy each spring.

BACCALÀ

Named after the god Bacchus (this was apparently his favorite dish), codfish has always been associated with decadence. Baccalà is dried codfish preserved with salt, and has a longer shelf life than most of today's canned goods. It was therefore immensely popular with Bacchus's disciples, principally bachelors, sailors, and anyone else who didn't have a mother or wife to prepare meals for them. Like most recipes involving fish in Italy, it is said to have aphrodisiac properties. Baccalà can be stewed either in a white sauce with potatoes, called stoccafisso, or with tomatoes, garlic, parsley, and black olives.

BASIL

Since the 1600s basil (a proven stimulant) has been thought to bring passion and happiness to those who munched on its leaves, and one saying has it that a plate of pasta without basil leaves is "like a beautiful woman with no soul." Basil's association with love goes back to Boccaccio's *Decameron*. Upon discovering their secret affair, Isabetta's brother kills her lover Lorenzo, buries his body, and fabricates a story to explain his disappearance. But the ghost of Lorenzo appears before Isabetta and tells her the truth, revealing where his body was buried. At night she goes to his grave and uncovers her lover's corpse. Unable to carry it away, she grabs his head and hides it inside a pot of basil, watering the plant each day with her tears. It's no wonder the aromatic herb is an important symbol of passionate love in Italy. If a woman places a plant of basil at her window at night, it is said she is ready for a visit from her lover.

BERGAMOT

The extract of this green-colored citrus that flourishes in Calabria (especially around Tropea) is used in perfumes and teas. Scientists have identified it as one of the smells that triggers our libido. According to one study, oddly enough, researchers found that bergamot brings out the memory of the clothing that your former lover kept in the closet and makes you nostalgic for that person. Consequently, it is thought of as an ideal medicine for couples in crisis.

BERRIES

Strawberries, raspberries, blackberries, and cherries are fruits that have been equated with carnal love and fiery passion, thanks to their vibrant colors and sweet taste. In paintings they are sometimes also depicted as metaphors for the blood of Christ.

CAPERS

Thanks to that seductive touch of spice you feel on your tongue when you bite into one, capers have been included in Italy's family of aphrodisiac foods. You will see caper bushes growing out of rocks and walls in the south, and the tiny fruit is carefully preserved in vinegar or coarse salt, to be added to a vast array of pasta and meat dishes. Don't throw around the word "caper" easily when you are traveling; in some areas, an ugly woman is a *cappero*.

CHILI

Your heart will skip a beat when you add chili, or *peperoncino*, to your meal. Hot peppers release endorphins to block pain and yield a sensation of pleasure. Their heat, suggestive shape, intense red color, and the fact that eating them causes a jolt to the body—with familiar side effects that include flushed skin, racing blood, and sweating—has reinforced the myth of chilis as Viagra *naturale* for men.

With more than 2,000 types of chili that vary in size, shape, color, flavor, and potency, Italians place *peperoncini* in high regard—so much so that the *Accademia Italiana del Peperoncino*, or the Italian Chili Pepper Academy, was founded in 1994 to safeguard the nation's chili-pepper culture (www.peperoncino.org). The annual Peperoncino Festival in chili capital

Diamante, Calabria, celebrates the hotter side of life through erotic art, racy cinema, cabaret, and spicy satire.

Chili peppers are eaten fresh, dried, whole, crushed, and in powder form. Calabria is famous for a soft sausage called 'nduja that is packed full of crushed chili. Chilis are made into a soft spread for toast and are even used in desserts. The *crostata del diavolo* (devil's cake) is a piquant pie made with peppery pastry and filled with chili jam and orange marmalade. Vanilla gelato can be topped with chili flakes, orange-peach syrup, and candied orange peels.

 ## CHOCOLATE

If we could take a bite of love, it would probably taste like chocolate. The world's most cherished aphrodisiac is said to contain the same substances produced naturally by our brain when we fall in love.

In Piedmont, *burro di cacao* is added to hazelnut paste to make Nutella (which has been described by the *New Yorker* magazine as "Eros in a jar"). If you find a bar in the dead of winter that makes a good hot chocolate (ask to have it topped with fresh *panna*, or whipped cream), you're in for an unforgettable treat. Italian hot chocolate is very dark and so thick your spoon will stand upright in it.

For one week in October, the Umbrian city of Perugia hosts its Chocolate Festival (www.eurochocolate.perugia.it), in which white and dark chocolate are presented in every conceivable form—from model chocolate racing cars, to bathtubs flooded with chocolate syrup. Event organizers even sponsor a program called *nozze al cioccolato* that arranges custom "chocolate honeymoons," which include visits to chocolate factories, chocolate landmarks, and lots of tasting time.

 ## COFFEE

Like chocolate, coffee is a stimulant thanks to the caffeine. The ancients considered it a sacred beverage that was served sparingly, and only on rare occasions. Modern Italians also consider it a sacred drink, but consume it in large quantities: One recent study found that eighty percent of Italians drink up to three *espressi* per day, and fifteen percent drink up to six. But its aphrodisiac nature may be exaggerated, since forty percent of those polled said they drink it alone.

Here's what you have to choose from:

ESPRESSO: A syrupy shot of coffee with thick body and persistent taste thanks to the way the beans are roasted. Must be served piping hot, otherwise the taste is sour. Most people drink it in a ceramic cup warmed by the steam of the coffee machine, but some prefer the feel of glass on their lips and ask for it *al vetro* instead.

CAPPUCCINO: A shot of *espresso* with frothy milk served in either a cup or glass. If the barman is in love with you, he will tilt the froth while pouring so that it forms a little heart in your cup. It is consumed at breakfast and is sometimes topped with cacao powder.

CAFFÈ CON MOKA: This is coffee that Italians make at home with their handy *cafetiera* pots.

CAFFÈ CON PANNA: Coffee served with whipped cream.

CAFFÈ CORRETTO: Coffee with a shot of cognac, brandy, whiskey, or grappa.

CAFFÈ AMERICANO: Coffee lighter in color and served in a larger cup. It has just as much caffeine as an *espresso*.

CAFFÈ MACCHIATO: Espresso that is "stained" with a bit of milk, making it easier to go down.

CAFFÈ LECCESE: A cup of hot *espresso* with sugar already dissolved inside, poured over ice. The result is a cool beverage with the taste of just-brewed coffee. Sometimes almond milk, or *latte di mandorla*, is added.

CAFFÈ FREDDO: Refrigerated coffee, chilled for hours before serving.

CAFFÈ DECAFFEINATO: The decaffeinated version.

CAFFÈ SHAKERATO: From the verb "to shake," this is hot *espresso* and sugar poured into a cocktail shaker filled with ice and shaken until a natural froth is formed.

 ## CRUSTACEANS

In Italy anything that comes from the sea and has a shell is associated with the birth of Venus, goddess of love. Crabs (*granchio*), crayfish or lobsters (*aragosta*), prawns (*scampi*), and shrimp (*gamberi*) contain phosphorous that is food for our brains and hearts. The ancients harvested and drank the bluish blood of live shrimp, because it was believed to enhance the sexual drive.

 ## EEL

These slimy creatures thrive in the Po River Delta in northern Italy, where there are dozens of little islands that disappear in high tide. Eels are diced up and marinated and eaten on Christmas Eve as a symbol of rebirth and renewal. They are rolled in cabbage leaves and stewed, their livers are turned into eel pâté (twenty eels are required for just one serving), and they are culinary specialties of Florence (baked with sage and red wine) and Venice (with lemon). The *anguilla's* backbone, head, and skin are boiled into eel broth called "fisherman's tea," which is said to fortify a man's procreative powers.

 FENNEL

Fennel is strongly associated with homosexuals in Italy, who are affectionately (and sometimes not so affectionately) referred to as *un finocchio*. Wild fennel is used in many southern dishes, while anise, made from fennel extract, is a strong stimulant discovered by the Greeks and Romans. It is said to be hallucinogenic when digested in large quantities, and some cultures use it with or instead of opium. People in the south of France mellow out with an anise-based *apéritif* called *pastis*, and the Italian equivalent is *anisetta*, a specialty of the Marches region.

 FICAZZA

The food with Italy's sexiest name—because it evokes vulgar slang for both the male and female gender—is best described as fish "jerky" and is considered a potent aphrodisiac. The eggs of female tuna are left to dry in the sun and are pressed into little brown bricks. You slice *ficazza* as if it were a hardened loaf of bread and eat it as an appetizer or with pasta.

 FISH

The sovereign ruler in the realm of aphrodisiac foods is fish. When heaven's phallus fertilized the sea in ancient mythology, it gave birth to the goddess of love and many, many species of fish. In some Italian dialects a penis is referred to as *un pesce*, and in painting and sculpture of all eras the fish is a symbol of fertility. Venus was known as the protector of fishermen, and symbolism of the fish is strong in Christianity as well: Pilgrims were referred to as *pisciculi*, and baptisms occurred in a *piscina*, or "pool." In fact, the Greek word for fish, *ichthys*, is an acronym for Savior Jesus Christ Son of God.

    Some 20,000 kinds of fish live in the Mediterranean and make up an important component of the Italian diet. On your culinary tour you will surely run into *acciughe* or *alici* (anchovies), *branzino* (sea perch), *cernia* (a fish with a large head), *dentice* (a flat fish similar to bream), *merluzzo* (codfish), *orata* (bream), *pesce spada* (swordfish), *rombo* (flounderlike fish), *salmone* (salmon), *sardine* (sardines), *scorfano* (scorpion fish, used in soups), *sogliola* (prized horizontal fish), *spigola* (sea bass), *tonno* (tuna), *triglie* (red mullet), and *trota* (trout, especially the unique pink trout from the lake region). Squid (*calamari*) and caviar are also aphrodisiacs.

GARLIC

A rejuvenator with essential oils that have an antibiotic effect, garlic is heralded as an all-round wonder drug for a long list of maladies. The ancient Egyptians and Romans pressed it to make a love tonic mixed with coriander. The malodorous brew was believed to spark lustful behavior and could cure impotency brought on by witchcraft.

GELATO

Gelato is an aphrodisiac because, well, everyone loves it. Real Italian gelato is not "ice cream," because there is no cream in it. Instead fresh strawberries, pistachios, or whatever the flavor of the day might be are mixed with milk and sometimes egg in a blender until a homogenous liquid is formed. One *gelateria* on Rome's Piazza Navona serves Viagra-flavored ice cream. (There's no real Viagra in it. The bright blue "Viagra Man" and pink-colored "Viagra Lady" only pay homage to the drug.) Others serve wine gelato (with flavors ranging from Barbaresco to Chianti), and as mentioned above, a *peperoncino* gelato has hit the market.

GRAPPA

Forget wine. By the third shot of *grappa*, you will have sussed out the true meaning of love—and will have had some fun along the way. *Grappa* is a distilled spirit made from the skins and seeds of discarded wine grapes. It can be flavored with peach, berries, pears, myrtle, or herbs.

HONEY

Honey is most definitely born from nature's loving affection. To ancient Romans, who added honey to their wine to increase its aphrodisiac mileage, bee stings were arrows shot into the flesh by cupid. You will find excellent honey is produced in Tuscany, Puglia, and Sardinia, because the aromas of those sun-kissed regions are locked within its sweet consistency.

LAUREL

Apollo fell in love with the nymph Daphne, but his amorous sentiments were not returned. To escape Apollo's unwanted advances, Daphne was transformed into a laurel bush. The god of the sun took the rejection in his stride and vowed that laurel would forever be a sacred plant in his loving eyes. Because he was also god of beauty, music, and poetry, laurel became associated with poets and scholars who were distinguished by a head wreath made from the pungent leaves.

LEMONS

Lemons were said to be a gift to humanity by the gods on the occasion of Juno and Jupiter's wedding. Because a lemon tree uses all its energy in producing its crop, and because some species flower year-round, it is a symbol of faithfulness in love and continues to be a common gift for couples. Arabs were the first to bring lemons to sunny Italy, and before the fruit edged its way into cuisine, they were used as potpourri, perfume, a disinfectant, a cleaner, and a medicine against poison. With fruit the same color as the sun, they were considered too precious to eat.

But why not drink them? *Limoncello*, the syrupy lemon liqueur also known as *limuncello*, *limonello*, or *limonoro*, has blossomed into Italy's most popular after-dinner drink. Campania is home to five varieties of lemons: The *femminello comune* is oval shaped, with a smooth, bright yellow rind, and is very sugary; the *monachello* is slightly larger, with many seeds, and is pale in color; the *lunario* comes in varying shapes, and has a very thick rind; the *l'ovale di Sorrento* has pronounced crannies in its rind; and the *sfusato amalfitano* also has a thick rind, but is seedless.

MOLLUSKS AND SHELLFISH

To fully understand why shellfish provoke desire, one must return to the story of the goddess Aphrodite's birth. She appeared out of the sea on a shell (depicted as the lower half of a scallop shell in Botticelli's *Birth of Venus*), a vessel that miraculously ushered her to land through the foam, water, and wind. Her deliverance is a metaphor for birth, and the shell a symbol for the vulva. In fact, in some languages the word for "shell" and the "female sex" is the same. The shells of scallops, oysters, and snails are all included in this imagery, and in the past they were often ground into a paste and eaten as a means of invigorating manhood. Other shellfish, such as clams (*vongole*) and mussels (*cozze*), are devoured hungrily in Italy.

MOZZARELLA

Creamy, white, and voluptuous, mozzarella is a delicate milky cheese, said to be hankered after by men nostalgic for their mother's milk. Real *mozzarella di bufala* is made from buffalo's milk—a rare breed of the animal native to the Campania region—which is why it is impossible to find outside of Italy. The cheese must be consumed fresh, which poses an obstacle for exporters. Huge plastic vats of water with mozzarella inside line the streets of small towns in Campania. Locals carve into the cheese with a butter knife and eat it whole. Sometimes a *filo*, or "thread," of olive oil is drizzled on top. Puglia is home to *burrata*, which is like mozzarella only infinitely more decadent: When you pierce the outer skin of the cheese, fresh cream gushes out. *Fior di latte* is a smaller version made from cow's milk.

MUSHROOMS AND TRUFFLES

Mushrooms have many mysterious qualities: Many species are impossible to cultivate; most "good" mushrooms have an identical poisonous twin; and even legally sold mushrooms can spark psychedelic episodes in some people. For these reasons, they are deeply linked to the mystical world. Like most foods with properties that were not fully understood, they were explained as "aphrodisiac."

From Calabria to the Dolomites. the woods and forests of Italy are teeming with mushrooms, and mushroom hunters, after September's first rain. Towns throw elaborate parties to honor their local fungi, which are prominently featured in local dishes. The most decadent of Italy's wild mushrooms are *porcini* (the name means "little pigs," but the Latin name is *boletus pinicola*). They are so rich, one grilled mushroom can replace a meat at a meal. Porcini have a thick white stem and a large, spongy brown cap.

Italy's most expensive and sought-after mushrooms are truffles (either white or black) that grow in Piedmont and Tuscany. Special dogs are trained to find these tasty morsels that thrive underground, near tree roots. Just one shaving of a black truffle is enough to transform a meal, and if you store a truffle in your refrigerator, it takes weeks for the smell to go away (even your eggs will taste like truffle). Truffles can fetch as much as €80 per ounce, and truffle venders loiter at the edges of forests like drug dealers looking for clients.

MYRTLE

This shrub with shiny evergreen leaves and white, scented flowers is sacred to the goddess Aphrodite, because it is one of the species said to have sprung from under her feet when she landed on earth. Its flowers are associated with purity and virginity, and so you'll often see myrtle in the background of Renaissance paintings of the Virgin Mary. Because the plant never goes dormant, brides traditionally wore a crown of myrtle as a symbol of longevity in marriage.

Sardinia is covered in myrtle, and its berries are sometimes paired with meat in local dishes the way we would have cranberries with turkey. The best way to enjoy the fruit, however, is by drinking *mirto*. This syrupy *digestivo* is served in restaurants around the island.

NUTS

Thanks to their hard shell, nuts have long been a symbol of marriage and solid union. Nature took great care to protect this precious delicacy, and this fact did not go unnoticed. For example, chestnuts (from the word "chaste"), or *castagna* in Italian, are protected by both a shell and a spiky casing.

Piedmont is famous for its wine, truffles, and hazelnuts (*nocciole*). Local hazelnuts—specifically the *tonda gentile delle Langhe* species native to the provinces of Alessandra, Asti, Cuneo, Novara, and Vercelli—have an intense, refined flavor. Hazelnuts have made their way into an assortment of pastries, cakes, chocolates, and nougat, or *torrone*. When paired with chocolate, hazelnuts are a gastronomic nirvana. This divine union reportedly occurred by accident at the end of the nineteenth century, when sanctions imposed by the English against Napoleon reduced the supply of New World cacao. Under French occupation, Piedmont's chocolatiers used roasted hazelnuts to extend supplies. The Ferrero brothers then gave the world Nutella—a sweet spread found in every Italian kitchen cupboard today. Rival factory Perugina in turn produced "kisses," or *Baci*: These chocolates with a hazelnut filling have a tiny love message hidden inside their silver wrapper.

OLIVE OIL

The oil pressed from olives has deep symbolic roots. Its golden hues stream from the bottle like a fountain of light, and its natural aroma makes it the perfect companion to most foods. In ancient Rome gladiators rubbed it over their bodies to appear virile and strong before confronting the dangers of the arena. For Christians olive oil represents life. And an olive branch is, of course, a symbol of peace.

Many regions claim to make Italy's best olive oil, but it's really a matter of taste. In Liguria, the oil is lighter in color, more delicate and fruitier on the palate. In Puglia, Calabria, and Sicily, strong sunshine and fertile soils make a meatier and darker oil. Tuscany's oil is considered a good compromise, with the best oil from groves located slightly inland away from the varying temperatures and higher moisturre levels of the coast. In general, trees must be at least fifty years old for a quality crop, and the fruit must be hand-picked to avoid the bruising that causes a bitter taste.

OYSTERS

Among the world's most celebrated aphrodisiacs, oysters have been associated with male virility since antiquity. They are high in minerals and glycerin—fundamental for making muscles contract. The seas of Taranto, in Puglia, are home to a smallish oyster that packs a powerful taste.

 ## PASTA

Bread, pasta, cereal, and anything made with grain are associated with Ceres (or Demeter in Greek mythology), goddess of agriculture and fertility. When Ceres's daughter, Persephone, was returned to her mother after being kidnapped by the underworld god, Hades, Ceres gave the world grain as a gift of thanks. That gift is rich in vitamins, oils, minerals, riboflavin, carotene, and vitamin E—which are all said to strengthen sexual organs. Most Italians eat pasta once a day.

 ## PEARS

Pears have been considered to be yet another incarnation of Venus, goddess of love, thanks to their curving feminine form, wide "hips," and sweet taste.

PIZZA

Believe it or not, a group of researchers in Chicago determined that the smell of pizza triggers sexual impulses. Fragrances derived from melted mozzarella, steaming tomato, and basil stimulates blood flow to the organs. Apparently, we associate pizza with pleasure, and this sends a clear signal to our brain and nervous system.

Of all the foods in *cucina italiana*, pizza is the most emblematic of Italy. It's an internationally recognized symbol, ranking up there with gondolas, the Tower of Pisa, and Latin lovers. But Italians worry that pizza's image abroad has been grossly distorted. According to traditionalists, there are but two kinds of pizza. The first is *pizza marinara*, with tomato, garlic, oregano, and olive oil. It first appeared in Naples in about 1760. King Ferdinando of Naples adored this new culinary delight, but his wife, a Habsburg princess, wouldn't allow pizza in the palace, so he snuck out at night to eat it. The second is *pizza margherita*. It was invented in 1889 (not long after Italy became unified) when a Naples chef was called upon to prepare a meal for Queen Margherita. He made a pizza with tomato, mozzarella, and basil to honor Italy's red, white, and green flag.

Since then, an array of toppings has found their way onto the pies—from *porcini* mushrooms and yellow zucchini flowers, to raw *rughetta* and gorgonzola.

POMEGRANATE

Pomegranates are a symbol of marriage, thanks to the story of the underworld god, Hades, who forced the beautiful Persephone to eat a few kernels, thus making her his wife for three months each year. Their mythological connotations, however, run deeper still. The red juice inside the fruit is said to be the blood of the god Bacchus, and the ancient Greeks made an aphrodisiac wine from what was nicknamed "the apple of love."

The pomegranate's thick rind protects its small chambers stuffed with numerous juicy seeds, and these characteristics leave it open to various interpretations. The seeds represent fertility, and the fact that so many are packed into such a tight space is a symbol of unity, friendship, and mankind.

 ## PRICKLY PEAR

A "botanical monster" is how scientists first described the fruit of cacti. For many years, they were considered poisonous, and the bad rap continued until someone actually tried one. Suddenly, the red fruit was attributed with a slew of noble characteristics: It was used as medicine against fevers, a disinfectant for the kidneys—and a healer of broken hearts.

RABBIT

Thanks to a rabbit's ability to reproduce in quick succession, eating the animal is believed to shift human fertility into high gear. During your travels, be on the lookout for rabbit dishes on local menus, including an intoxicating rabbit stew with chopped vegetables, white wine, sage, and black olives.

 ## RED MEAT

Meat is all about carnal pleasure, according to Italy's most famous butcher, Dario Cecchini, whose shop is in Panzano, in the Chianti region of Tuscany. Cecchini is known as the "Poet

Butcher" because he can recite the entire "Inferno" section of Dante Alighieri's *Divine Comedy* by heart. (In keeping with this theme, the 200-year-old, family-run shop is decorated with devils and angels, and gilded flames protrude from behind the meat counter.) "Tuscans like to celebrate gluttony and lust, and beef is all about those things," he says. The most sinful of his products is the phonebook-sized *fiorentina* T-bone steak, served cold-on-the-inside rare.

SAFFRON

If hot chili peppers are said to be an aphrodisiac for men, saffron is the female stimulant par excellence. The expensive red powder that comes from the dried stigmas of Crocus flowers is said to exert special power on lesbians and women otherwise flirting with the Sapphic side. Depending on the dose, saffron can be a stimulant or even an inebriant; in very high doses, it can be toxic. In the past, women have taken it to strengthen the uterus and treat menstrual pains (curry is said to have similar properties).

SNAILS

The French haven't cornered the market on snails. In the south of Italy, they are believed to enhance male prowess, and are fried in oil, garlic, and parsley until the meat emerges from the shell. A small, white snail that lives in wheat fields is a delicacy of Puglia, and in Palermo, Sicily, *babbaluci* are sold to pedestrians as roadside snacks at the feast of patron saint Rosalia.

SWORDFISH

These marine giants are the Mediterranean's most romantic fish. Each March to July, they come to the south of Italy, near the Straits of Messina, to spawn—or "to make love," as the locals like to say. Swordfish, which can reach up to 120 pounds, always travel in two and demonstrate profound fidelity. The fishermen who navigate these waters genuinely believe they feel affection for one another. If a female is speared, the male will not leave her side and will instead swim frantically as if trying to save her. That gives the fishermen time to harpoon him as well, and the loving pair dies together.

TORTELLINI

This is a food stuffed with love lore. The origins of tortellini are disputed by rival cities Bologna and Modena, as each claims to have invented the shapely pasta. But according to a poem written by Alessandro Tasson in the late 1500s, they first were made somewhere between the two cities, when a tavern owner fell madly in love with a countess who often stayed as his guest. He peeked through a keyhole one night to catch a glimpse of her beauty, but only saw her belly button. Inspired by the vision, he rushed back to the kitchen and shaped dough to resemble her navel.

WINE

To the ancients, Italy was *oenotria*, or "land of wine." Today it ranks among the world's foremost wine producers, both in terms of quality and quantity. From Barolo, Barbaresco, Chianti, Soave, Amarone, Sangiovese, Primitivo, and Nero d'Avola, to sparkling wines and international blends, any wine enthusiast will hold Italy dear to heart. Grapes are a symbol of fertility, and wine is the blood of earth to the pagans, and the blood of Christ to the Christians. But the word *vino* comes from Venus, goddess of love.

The ancient Romans lived in a world awash with wine. Because they did not have purifiers for their water, wine was often the only drinkable liquid available. They produced it in massive quantities and planted grapevines across Europe, introducing them to France as well. But the nectar of these ancient imbibers was just short of drinkable. Their wine carried all the nasty tastes of the terracotta amphorae it was stored in, and the lead, wax, or resin used to seal the containers. Wine that had turned to vinegar was often cut with other substances, such as honey, to make it palatable.

But a funky taste wasn't enough to stop the followers of Bacchus, god of wine and sensory delight, from having a good time. Ancient Rome saw the rise and fall of the orgiastic Bacchanalian rite, one of the world's most hedonistic cults. It was a riotous occasion to meet, consume great quantities of wine, dance by torchlight to the music of flutes, and have sex until a mass of bodies lay on the floor quivering in ecstasy. Followers claimed to be practicing "sexual immortality." Needless to say, all this drunkenness and debauchery did not sit well with Roman society, and the cult was quickly banned. Some 7,000 members were arrested or executed, but those who survived continued to celebrate the Bacchanal underground. The Villa of Mysteries in Pompeii was reportedly one of the cult's secret locations.

To most of us, wine is a seductive inebriant associated with good cheer, and more recently with good health, because it activates the metabolism and stimulates appetite. It contains 500 different substances: seven to fourteen percent ethyl alcohol, fruit acids, sugars, tannins, glycerin, vitamins, minerals, phosphates, and proteins. Experts applaud its medicinal properties—some claim a glass a day helps fight cholesterol, and others say it increases female fertility.

Buon *appetito*, and remember: *Sine Cerere et Baco friget Venus* ("love grows cold without food and wine").

R E C I P E S

ARTICHOKES

CARCIOFI ALLA ROMANA

(makes four servings)

Roman-style artichokes (also part of a Jewish culinary tradition) are a delicious and easy-to-find alternative to the chokeless, spineless artichokes required to make carciofi alla giudia.

2 lemons
4 artichokes (the smallest you can find)
2 or 3 cloves garlic, minced
4 tablespoons freshly chopped mint
¼ cup extra-virgin olive oil (depending on the size of the pot) salt

Remove the tough outer leaves of the artichoke until you reach the tender, yellow ones. You may remove up to half the volume of the flower. Cut the stem 1 or 2 inches from the base, and with a knife remove the tough outer skin on the stem. After you prepare each artichoke, place it into a bowl of water with the juice of one lemon squeezed in it; this will stop the artichokes from turning brown. One by one, gently pry open the petals of the artichoke with your fingers, being careful not to crack them at their base. With a spoon or knife, scoop out the choke (the hairy part inside). Rub a bit of salt on the inside of the cavity left by the choke between the petals. Mix the garlic and mint together, and stuff as much as you can inside the cavity. Prepare all four artichokes. Place a cooking pot over low heat and add the olive oil; the oil should be about a quarter inch deep. Place the artichokes in the oil head down, stems up. Drizzle more olive oil, lemon juice, and salt over the artichokes. Cut half a lemon into wedges and place them in the pot. For extra-tender artichokes, add 2 tablespoons of water as well. Cover the pot and cook for about 30 minutes, or until a fork slides easily into the base.

BASIL

PESTO ALLA GENOVESE

(makes six servings)

2 cups tightly packed fresh basil leaves
    (the younger, the better)
2 cloves garlic
3 tablespoons pine nuts
½ cup freshly grated parmigiano cheese
2 tablespoons freshly grated romano cheese
½ cup extra-virgin olive oil
salt

Lightly mash the garlic and wash and dry the basil leaves. Place the garlic, basil, pine nuts, and salt into a large marble mortar. Using a hardwood pestle, grind all the ingredients against the side of the mortar. When you have a green paste, add the two cheeses and mix them in evenly. Lastly, add the oil in a thin stream.

Pesto can be added as a topping to any kind of pasta. Dilute the pesto with a tablespoon of the hot water that the pasta was cooked in, so that it spreads easily. Pesto should not be heated. In Liguria, pesto is sometimes added to boiled potatoes and string beans.

LEMONS

LIMONCELLO

12 large lemons (the yellower a lemon, the higher its sugar content; select fresh lemons because the longer the fruit is off the tree, the more rubbery and bitter the rind will be)
4 cups alcohol (90° proof for cooking)
4 cups water
1½ pounds sugar

Peel the outer rind off the lemons, taking care not to cut too far into the white (it gives limoncello a bitter taste). Put the peels in the alcohol and let it steep for 12 days, shaking gently from time to time. When 12 days have passed, melt the sugar in the water over low heat and let cool. Remove the lemon peels from the alcohol and put them inside the water and sugar mixture for 1 hour. Remove the peels, filter the water, and add the alcohol. Leave the liquid to rest in a dark place for 1 week. Limoncello should be stored in the freezer until served.

SHELLFISH

Zuppa di Cozze

(makes four servings)

2 pounds mussels, live, in their shells
⅓ cup extra-virgin olive oil
1½ teaspoons garlic, finely chopped
2 tablespoons parsley, chopped
1 cup canned Italian plum tomatoes, drained and diced
⅛ teaspoon hot chili pepper flakes

Soak the mussels in a basin or sink filled with cold water for 5 to 10 minutes. Drain and refill the basin with cold water. Vigorously scrub the mussels one by one with a coarse brush. Pull away the fibers protruding from each mussel—these can be ripped off by hand. Scrub them again, and drain and refill the water basin 2 or 3 times until all the sand and debris has disappeared. Choose a pot that can accommodate all the mussels comfortably, and add the oil and garlic. Sauté the garlic until light gold in color. Add the tomatoes and chili pepper, and simmer over low heat, stirring occasionally, for 20 minutes. Add the parsley 2 or 3 minutes before the end of cooking. Increase the heat to high, add the mussels, and cover the pot. Cook until all the mussels have opened their shells, stirring frequently with a long wooden spoon to bring the bottom mussels to the top and distribute the sauce. Some mussels take longer than others to cook, and any that fail to open should be discarded. To serve, often a piece of toasted garlic bread is placed inside a bowl and the zuppa di cozze is ladled over it.

SAFFRON

Risotto alla Milanese

(makes 6 servings)

5 cups homemade broth, or 1 cup canned beef broth diluted with 4 cups water
2 tablespoons diced beef marrow (can substitute sausage or bacon)
3 tablespoons butter
2 tablespoons olive oil
⅓ cup onion, finely chopped
½ teaspoon powdered saffron
2 cups arborio, or other Italian rice for making risotto
⅓ cup freshly grated parmigiano cheese
salt

In a pot with a thick bottom, add the diced marrow (or sausage, or bacon), 1 tablespoon of butter, oil, and chopped onion and cook over medium heat. When the onions are transparent, add the rice, stirring quickly so that the grains are evenly coated. Add 1/2 cup of the beef broth and keep stirring until the liquid is absorbed. Add another 1/2 cup and repeat, continuing this pattern for 20 minutes. Add the saffron. Continue adding broth and stirring until the rice is tender but firm to the bite, or al dente. Turn off the heat and add the remaining butter and stir until it is melted. Add the grated cheese and salt to taste.

SWORDFISH

Pesce spada alla Griglia

In a bowl, mix a quarter cup olive oil, the juice of two large lemons, two tablespoons finely chopped mint, and salt and pepper to taste. The swordfish steaks should be cut about one-inch thick and brushed with the mixture before being placed on the grill. Keep the fish about four inches from the coals or flame. Continue brushing the steaks generously with the oil mixture until the fish is ready, about 6 to 8 minutes.

❧ INDEX ❧

❧ About the Author ❧

MONICA LARNER is a writer and photographer who has lived in Italy on and off since age ten. She is the Italian editor for Wine Enthusiast Magazine, for which she tastes some 1,500 wines per year. Her previous books include Living, Studying and Working in Italy and Buying a House in Italy. When not in Europe, she can be found with harvest shears in hand on Larner Vineyard in Santa Barbara county, California. For more information about the author, please visit www.monicalarner.com.